JIM CROW GUIDE TO THE U.S.A.

JIM CROW GUIDE TO THE U.S.A.

The Laws, Customs and Etiquette
Governing the Conduct of Nonwhites
and
Other Minorities
as Second-Class Citizens

by
STETSON KENNEDY

The University of Alabama Press
Tuscaloosa, Alabama

The University of Alabama Press
Tuscaloosa, Alabama 35487-0380
All rights reserved
Manufactured in the United States of America

∞

The paper on which this book is printed meets the minimum
requirements of American National Standard for Information
Sciences-Permanence of Paper for Printed Library Materials, ANSI
Z39.48-1984.

Library of Congress Cataloging-in-Publication Data

Kennedy, Stetson.
Jim Crow guide to the U.S.A. : the laws, customs and etiquette
governing the conduct of nonwhites and other minorities as second-
class citizens / Stetson Kennedy.
    p. cm.
Originally published: London : Lawrence & Wishart, 1959.
ISBN 978-0-8173-5671-2 (pbk. : alk. paper) — ISBN 978-0-
8173-8564-4 (electronic) 1. Minorities—United States—Social
conditions. 2. African Americans—Social conditions. 3. African
Americans—Segregation. 4. Race discrimination—United States.
5. United States—Race relations. I. Title.
E184.A1K35 2011
305.800973—dc22

                                        2010038470

CONTENTS

WHY THIS GUIDE

While there are many guides to the U.S.A., this is the only one which faces the fact that despite the affirmation of the American Declaration of Independence that all men are created equal, in America in reality some are more equal than others.

Nearly a third of all Americans have been relegated in some degree to second-class citizenship because of their race, colour, nationality, religion, or politics, and are treated accordingly.

At the same time, the two-thirds who count themselves among the first-class citizenry are more or less expected to conduct themselves in certain fashion in their relations with the less fortunate.

The privileges and immunities of first-class citizenship, and the penalties and restrictions of second-class citizenship, are established by an ensemble of national dispositions, state statutes, municipal ordinances, judicial findings, police practices, private regulations, social pressures, and mob violence.

Generally speaking, first-class citizenship is limited to native-born white Protestant Gentiles. Certain of these regard as second-class citizens America's 17 million Negroes, 6 million Jews, 5 million Puerto Rican emigrants to the mainland, 1 million Mexican-Americans, half million American Indians, 150,000 Japanese, 100,000 Chinese, 50,000 Filipinos, and a few thousand Hindus, Koreans, and others. Besides these, there are Uncle Sam's colonial subjects in Puerto Rico, Hawaii, Panama Canal Zone, Virgin Islands, and a number of Pacific islands.

Ever since Europeans first arrived on the North American continent five centuries ago it has been public policy that this was to be a white man's country. This policy has found expression in a four-fold programme:

1. *Extermination* of the native American Indians, with the tribal remnants confined to desert reservations as wards of the government.

2. *Exclusion* of Asian, African, and other coloured immigrants as unassimilable.

3. *Segregation*, including legal prohibitions against the marriage of Negroes and other non-Caucasians with white persons.

4. *Discrimination*, sometimes of genocidal proportions, against various minorities.

And so you can see that other guides, irresponsibly recommending hotels, restaurants, tours, entertainment, and so on, without taking into account the existing taboos, can actually get you killed.

But this Guide tells you everything you need to know about getting along in America, according to the category in which you find yourself.

CHAPTER I

NO ROOM FOR REDSKINS

IF you're a real American—that is, an American Indian—you're lucky to be alive.

For whether he really believed it or not, the white man has acted on the principle that "The only good Indian is a dead one". This was certainly one of the foundation stones upon which the white European invaders of North America and their descendants established and built the republic of the U.S.A.

When in 1492 Christopher Columbus opened the door to the white conquest of the Americas, there were nearly a million native Indians living in what is now the United States. Far from permitting this number to increase, the white man has vigorously pursued—both as individual enterprise and national policy—a genocidal campaign expressly aimed, until quite recently, at the effective extermination of Indians from the continent.

This campaign—consisting of relentless warfare, massacre, confinement, starvation, and neglect—was so successful that by 1923 less than a quarter of a million Indians remained in the U.S.A. Since then the pressures have been relaxed somewhat, permitting a certain increase in the Indian population, but with intensified efforts being made to exterminate Indian culture. By 1958 their number was still only half what it was upon the white man's arrival.

As has been characteristic of white imperialism, the European settlers and their descendants in America were inclined to look down upon the native Indians as "pesky redskins", "savages", and "heathens". This attitude, coupled with an avowed desire to convey the blessings of Christianity and European civilization on the "benighted barbarians", salved the consciences of those who went about the profitable business of divesting the Indians of life, liberty, and property.

The genocidal programme likewise called for expropriating or liquidating the Indians' culture. Four-sevenths of the agricultural production of the U.S.A. now consists of plants which were originally domesticated by the Indians (the white man has failed to domesticate a single important staple on the continent). Numerous other things, including snow-shoes, toboggans, woodland garments, and even methods of warfare were appropriated from the Indians with scarcely an acknowledgment. On the contrary, American history books and Hollywood movies generally perpetuate the notion that the white man contributed all, the Indian nothing. However, one thing which the white man did introduce—Hollywood and the history books to the contrary notwithstanding—was the practice of scalping one's victims.

Because the Indians were thinly scattered, "it was a case where the existing racial and cultural slate could be wiped relatively clean", the historian Dr. Everett Stonequist has observed.

An early Pilgrim in Massachusetts, thanking God for a pestilence that wiped out an Indian tribe, wrote in his journal: "By this means Christ, whose great and glorious works throughout the earth are for the benefit of his churches and his chosen, not only made room for his people to plant, but also tamed the hearts of the barbarous Indians."

Evidently not content with the rate at which the white man's diseases decimated the Indians, one colonial general ordered his subordinates to wage bacteriological warfare as follows: "You will do well to try to inoculate the Indians by means of blankets in which smallpox patients have slept, as well as by other means that can serve to extirpate this execrable race."

In like vein, a pioneer immigrant to California wrote at the time: "I often argued with Good regarding disposition of the Indians. He believed in killing every man or well-grown boy, but in leaving the women unmolested. It was plain to me that we must also get rid of the women."

In the opening up of Oregon to white settlement, even Methodist clergymen expressed no regret at seeing Indian women being clubbed to death and Indian babies dashed against trees by white settlers. One Oregon settler named Beeson wrote: "It was customary [for the whites] to speak of the Indian man as a buck; of the woman as a squaw; until at length in the general acceptance of the terms, they ceased to recognize the rights of humanity in those to whom they were applied. By a very natural and easy transition, from being spoken of as brutes, they came to be thought of as game to be shot, or as vermin to be destroyed."

In Colorado, an early legislature seriously considered adopting a law providing for cash bounty payments for "the destruction of Indians and Skunks".

At the outset of the white conquest of North America, the competing European imperialist powers of Spain, France, Great Britain, and Holland all followed a policy of dealing with the various American Indian tribes as nation-to-nation. Since the American Indians had traditionally looked upon the land as a communal asset, it was relatively easy for the European powers to defraud them of it by "treaty" or "purchase" for some trivial amount. It was thus to the advantage of these powers to acknowledge that the Indians were the original owners of the land, since in subsequent deals among themselves these powers could then transfer with some semblance of legality the lands they had "acquired" from the Indians.

But as soon as the white settlers had thrown off the yoke of European imperialism, the new republic tended to drop the old diplomatic approach of dealing with the Indians as nation-to-nation, and instead decided to dictate its will by force of arms. As Chief Justice Marshall of the U.S. Supreme Court put it, the Indian tribes were no longer to be regarded as independent nations, but rather as "domestic dependent nations".

To facilitate imposing its will upon the native Americans, the white republic of the U.S.A. in 1824 established an Indian Office as an adjunct of its War Department. The so-called Indian Wars, which continued intermittently until the Battle of Wounded Knee in 1890, were in most instances deliberately provoked by the white settlers and troopers as an excuse for massacring the Indians and depriving them of their land and cattle. Official records of the U.S. Government are replete with instances of treaties and truces being violated by whites, including U.S. military commanders in the field. Many U.S. Army generals felt their country's honour was not at stake when they betrayed flags of truce and other confidences of the Indians. This sentiment found expression as national policy when the U.S. Congress in 1871 forbade the Government to enter into any further treaties with the Indians.

The subjugation of virtually all tribes had been completed by 1880, with the only respite for the redmen coming during the Civil War of 1861-5, when the white Americans were busy killing each other. With the Indians disarmed and reduced to military impotence, the U.S. Government herded the remnants of the tribes on to "reservations" on the principle that it was "cheaper to feed them than to fight them".

The official U.S. policy, according to William Christie MacLeod in his book, *The American Indian Frontier*, became "merely to keep the

Indian at peace pending his gradual dying off from more insidious causes than the sword or bullet".

From time to time, U.S. agents resorted to more direct methods of extermination. For example, a Government agent who in 1866 hanged a recalcitrant Indian, upon being called to report the matter, replied: "Indians sometimes have to be dealt with severely and promptly. I made no mention of the execution in my report of Indians, as I did not know whether others could see the necessity for it that I did, and thought it as well to say nothing about it to the authorities at Washington."

U.S. General Ord, in his report to the War Department in 1869, said he "encouraged the troops to capture and root out the Apaches by every means and to hunt them as they would wild animals".

U.S. Commissioner of Indian Affairs Francis Walker said he would prefer to see the Indians exterminated altogether rather than permit them to intermarry with whites. In his official Report of 1872, Commissioner Walker went on:

"There is no question of national dignity, be it remembered, involved in the treatment of savages by a civilized power. With wild men, as with wild beasts, the question whether in a given situation one shall fight, coax, or run, is a question merely of what is easiest and safest. The Indians should be made as comfortable on, and as uncomfortable off, their reservations as it is in the power of the Government to make them; such of them as behave should be protected and fed, and such as go wrong should be harassed and scourged without intermission. . . .

"It is only necessary that Federal laws, judiciously framed to meet all the facts of the case, and enacted in season, before the Indians begin to scatter, shall place all the members of this race under a strict reformatory control by the agents of the Government. . . . No one certainly will rejoice more heartily than the present Commissioner when the Indians of this country cease to be in a position to dictate, in any form or degree, to the Government; when, in fact, the last hostile tribe becomes reduced to the condition of suppliants for charity."

In practice, the U.S. Army often went beyond this in its handling of the Indians. Carolos B. Embry, in his book, *America's Concentration Camps* (1958), tells of the treatment of a tribe of Cheyennes captured in 1879: "In the midst of the dreadful Winter, with the thermometer at forty degrees below zero, the Cheyennes, including the women and children, were kept five days and nights without food or fuel, and for three days without water."

The establishment of a dictatorship over the Indians was accelerated toward the end of the nineteenth century by an influx of former Army officers into the Indian Bureau. Taking note of this, the Commissioner of Indian Affairs in his *Annual Report for 1892* said: "Appointed at first in the capacity of a commercial agent or consul of the United States in the country of an alien people, the Indian agent . . . has developed into an officer with power to direct the affairs of the Indians and to transact their business in all details and in all relations. This is a very curious chapter in our history. There is a striking contrast between 'ministers plenipotentiary' appointed by the U.S.A. to treat with powerful Indian nations, and an army officer, with troops at his command, installed over a tribe of Indians to maintain among them an absolute military despotism."

It was generally assumed by white America that the Indian was the "vanishing American"—that in a short time he would become altogether extinct. U.S. Senators learnedly cited the works of Spencer and Buckle to "prove" that the Indian was incapable of adapting to the white man's civilization.

"Little can be hoped for them as a distinct people," declared General Sanborn. "The sun of their day is fast sinking in the western sky. It will soon go down in a night of oblivion that shall know no morning."

(In view of this record, it was little wonder that when in 1957 American politicos began to venture critical observations concerning the sanguinary struggle being waged by France against the Algerian independence movement, thousands of Frenchmen felt moved to write the U.S. Embassy in Paris, calling attention to the fact that whereas the white settlers of America had set out to systematically exterminate the native population, French settlers in Algeria had, through the introduction of sanitation, facilitated a ninefold increase in the native population.)

Wards of the Government

American Indians today are organized into some 300 tribes speaking about 250 dialects. The elder members of the tribes speak no English, and the others are but semi-educated, with very few having any technical training. At least two-thirds of the Indians live on reservations in the desert lands of the midwest, while less than 10 per cent have become city-dwellers.

American Indians are in the anomalous position of being at the same time citizens of the U.S.A. and wards of the Government, the net result being far from first-class citizenship. The U.S. Congress has adopted no less than 5,000 laws which apply to American Indians as such, and these, together with more than 2,200 regulations imposed by the Bureau of Indian Affairs, regiment the lives of Indians from the cradle to the grave.

Between the years 1800 and 1858 the U.S. Congress passed a series of laws giving the President and the Commissioner of Indian Affairs the powers of absolute potentates over American Indians as subject peoples. These powers included the right to issue or deny passports to persons wishing to visit Indian territory, and to deport from the reservations anyone "deemed detrimental to the peace and welfare of the Indians".

For a long time Indians were excluded from the protection of the U.S. Constitution and Bill of Rights, even though these documents explicitly apply to "all persons under the jurisdiction of" the U.S.A. This meant, among other things, that the Indians were held as prisoners on the reservations. It was not until 1891, when an Indian named Standing Bear defied the authorities, left his reservation, and was arrested by the U.S. Army at the request of the Secretary of the Interior, that the Supreme Court finally admitted that Indians are persons. But it was not until 1924 that Congress saw fit to bestow limited citizenship upon the Indians, in response to a popular demand that they be rewarded for fighting for the U.S.A. in World War I. However, for a long time afterwards the five states where most Indians live refused to let them vote or sit on juries, the last two states to give way being New Mexico and Arizona in 1948.

Under the treaties whereby the Indians were forcibly removed from their ancestral lands and placed on reservations, the Government of the U.S.A. solemnly promised the tribes that they would be permitted to govern themselves and make and enforce their own tribal laws. As has been noted, however, the U.S.A. soon violated this agreement by establishing a military dictatorship over the reservations.

The constitutions adopted by the tribes and approved by the U.S. Government specifically assure the Indians the right to hold their own elections. But since 1950 the Government has repeatedly interfered, directly and indirectly. For instance, in the Blackfeet election of 1952, reservation superintendent Guy Robertson insisted that the election be conducted by Bureau agents. He mobilized his Bureau police, shut down the voting places set up by the Indians, tried to strike 1,000 names from the voters' lists, and confiscated Indian funds to pay for the mock poll which he conducted. The Bureau in Washington not only upheld his action, but asserted its right to take similar steps at any time in the future.

The U.S. Government has also intervened in tribal elections by flooding the reservations with propaganda for or against certain candidates (according to their subservience to the Government). This happened in the Blackfeet elections of 1950 and 1952, and in the Choctaw election of 1952, among others. When the Association on American Indian Affairs wired the Interior Secretary, asking whether such intervention had his approval, he replied that it had.

The American Bill of Rights guarantees that all citizens shall have equal rights under the law. American Indians, however, have never enjoyed this right, even after they were declared to be citizens. The Social Security laws, for example, provide that the Federal Government shall match whatever sums are provided by the states for benefit payments to the aged, the blind, and dependent children. And yet Arizona and New Mexico have been given these U.S. funds even though they refuse to pay any pensions whatever to their Indian citizens. Indians were also excluded from the U.S. Department of Agriculture's housing and other loan programmes until, in 1950, 24 tribes united in protest.

Another gross discrimination lies in a Federal prohibition against the sale of alcohol to Indians in any form—even in hair tonic or vanilla extract. Any liquor dealer caught selling to minors or Indians must forfeit his licence. (Sometimes this prohibition has been enforced by bar-tenders against persons of Asian extraction, such as Filipinos and Japanese-Americans, in the mistaken belief that they are American Indians.)

Efforts in recent years to persuade Congress to repeal this paternalistic prohibition have been opposed by the Bureau. But at the same time Bureau agents have given the Indians to understand that if they will surrender their tribal courts, the Bureau will endorse their demand for an end to liquor prohibition. The tribes of Montana have protested that repeal of liquor prohibition "should not be made conditional upon acceptance of state taxation, the elimination of tribal law-and-order codes, or any other surrender of Indian rights".

During the 12 years Franklin D. Roosevelt was President of the U.S.A. (1932-1945) and Harold Ickes was Secretary of the Interior, the Indian made substantial progress. But this trend has been reversed ever since 1950, when Dillon Myer was appointed Commissioner of Indian

Affairs. A former U.S. State Department official, Myer achieved notoriety as head of the War Relocation Authority which herded Japanese-Americans into concentration camps during World War II.

Upon being made head of the Indian Bureau, Myer promptly fired its most capable officials and replaced them with men who had carried out his orders in the concentration camp agency. A superintendent who was said to be too "soft" with the Indians and Eskimos of Alaska was replaced by a former F.B.I. agent; a former concentration camp warden was made superintendent of the Montana Blackfeet reservation. As Ickes later commented: "A blundering dictatorial tin-Hitler tossed a monkey-wrench into a mechanism he was not capable of understanding."

As if to further fulfil this characterization, Myer asked Congress to give his Bureau agents the right to carry arms and make arrests and searches without warrants, for violations of Bureau regulations both on and off reservations. Not even F.B.I. agents or U.S. marshals have such arbitrary powers. There is no more reason why Indians should be arrested for violating Indian Bureau regulations than why women and children should be arrested for violating regulations of the Women's Bureau or Children's Bureau.

The way American Indians were robbed of one of the richest continents on earth has few parallels in the annals of Empire. Since the Indian had always looked upon his lands as a communal asset, the full implications of the white man's peculiar concept of land as private property were not immediately apparent to him. In a typical transaction between the white man and the red, the island of Manhattan, on which the bulk of New York City now stands, was purchased for 24 dollars' worth of trinkets. It was customary in negotiating such purchases for the white men to first ply the redmen with alcohol until they became so intoxicated they did not know or care what they were signing. When such devices failed, the whites simply bought the signature of any Indians who might be available, regardless of how little right they might have to dispose of the land in question. Then, armed with such documents (and firearms), they simply drove the Indians from the land. The bulk of the continent, indeed, changed hands through military conquest without even token payment being made.

One reason why the Indians agreed to accept the paltry compensations offered was a formal assurance that they and their descendants would not be taxed by the American Government. Since 1950, however, the Indian Bureau has been urging Congress to start taxing Indians.

The reservations to which the Indians were confined in and around the American desert embraced some of the most worthless land in the country. Under a concept unique in American law, these reservations were regarded as hereditary, but held in trust *for* the tribe *by* the U.S. Government. The Indians were forbidden to sell, rent, or lease the reservation lands, or to sell minerals, timber, oil, fish, cattle, or agricultural products from them without the prior consent of the Government. In other words, Indians were put in the same legal class as congenital idiots deemed incapable of handling their own affairs.

When it was discovered that some portions of the Indian lands contained oil and other valuable resources, something had to be done to enable the white man to lay hands on these riches. So in 1887 Congress passed the General Allotment Act, which was hailed by some as a "Red Man's Emancipation Proclamation". The Commissioner of Indian Affairs, it seems, was complaining bitterly that the Indians still thought in terms of "we" instead of "I" in dealing with land. The new law "gave" the *tribes* title to 138,000,000 acres, and provided that after an interim of 25 years much of it was to be given out in parcels to *individual* Indians. It was assumed, as Senator Dawes put it, that this taste of private property would create in the red men "that spirit of selfishness which was the main motivation of white civilization".

Private interests were so eager to get hold of the best of the Indian lands that Congress in 1891, 1902, and 1907 amended the Act, speeding up distribution of the land to individual Indians—and its equally speedy acquisition by whites.

The U.S. Government itself bought much of the land, paying the Indians $1.25 an acre for it; this was justified by the assertion that the Indians were a vanishing race, and would not long need land. In 1923 the Indians' land holdings had decreased two-thirds in acreage, and four-fifths in value. By 1933 they had been relieved of 86,000,000 of their better acres, retaining only 52,000,000, half of which was desert and semi-desert wasteland. Since 1949 Indian land holdings have again decreased, though the Indian Bureau has not published the figures. But in 1957 the truth leaked out: Indian holdings had gone down to 20,000,000 *hectares*, and three-fourths of America's Indians were altogether landless or owned too little land for self-support.

In numerous instances, Bureau agents have defrauded the Indians by selling themselves Indian land at far less than its market value. In a

1952 case, certain Bureau officials sold themselves a tract of Blackfeet timberland in Oregon worth 400,000 dollars for 135,000 dollars, paying an additional 25,000 dollars "commission" to a third party who served as an intermediary to hide the fact that Bureau agents were the real purchasers. Even though this transaction was exposed in the Press, the guilty officials were kept on their jobs.

In spite of everything, the Indians' tradition of communal ownership of the land still survives the centuries of effort by the white man to eradicate it. The U.S. Government, however, has not given up. In 1952 the Commissioner forbade individual Indians to give land to their tribe or even to sell it *to the tribe* at less than market price.

Besides all the land which has been taken from the Indians, many millions of additional acres have become involved in white man's litigation as to who is the rightful owner. In order that these contested acres might be exploited, Congress has authorized the Indian Bureau to lease them. The Bureau permitted overgrazing on 37,000,000 acres, mostly by absentee sheep-raising corporations. This caused erosion to set in, with a 50 per cent loss in carrying capacity.

On paper, the Indians are supposed to be given priority by the Government when Indian-owned lands are offered for lease; but in practice this priority is a dead letter. For many years the Blackfeet have been trying to get into the sheep-raising business. But only eight small operators of the Blackfeet tribe have been granted grazing leases, for which they were charged $5.22 per sheep for a three-year period. At the same time (1950) the Government, over the protests of the Blackfeet, awarded leases to eleven big commercial sheep-raising companies at $2.65 per sheep.

The courts belatedly ordered the eviction of a sheep-raising corporation which had encroached upon the Pyramid Lake Reservation. But when the reservation superintendent proceeded to carry out the eviction order, he was fired by the Commissioner. The Commissioner acted at the insistence of Senator Pat McCarran (author of America's concentration camp and racist immigration laws), who had been hired as legal counsel for the sheep-raising corporation.

There have been many other instances since 1950 of the Bureau's leasing of Indian lands and resources without the consent of the Indians. To cite but one: in 1951 the Bureau leased to a private concern a valuable building-materials deposit belonging to the Pueblos of San Ildefonso. A tribal representative who appeared at the signing of the contract to protest was bodily thrown out by the Government agent.

There is in America an institution known as the U.S. Court of Claims, wherein the humblest citizen may—theoretically—call the highest Government officials and agencies to account for any damages he may have suffered at their hands. Until 1946, no Indian was allowed to come into this court. In fact, in order to sue the Government an Indian first had to obtain the Government's permission through a special act of Congress! But the Indian Claims Act of 1946 gave Indians a five-year period in which to file claims against the Government for past grievances, after which no such further claims were to be made.

In 1953 ten thousand survivors of the Creek Indians gathered for a pow-wow in a baseball stadium at Atmore, Alabama, to discuss what to do about their 139-year-old claim against the U.S. Government for 29,000,000 dollars. The ancestors of these Creeks were deprived, by military conquest and fraud in the war of 1812, of some 23,267,000 acres of land in what are now the states of Georgia, Alabama, and Mississippi. Their claim represented $1.25 per acre for lands now worth many billions of dollars. Because of racial discrimination, many of the Creeks attending the conference had to seek lodging hundreds of miles from the scene.

The right of Indians to press claims against the Government was restricted after World War II by the refusal of the Indian Bureau to permit them to employ attorneys of their own choosing. Just how retrogressive this development was is brought out by the fact that the right of the Indians to freely appoint representatives was recognized in Law 35 promulgated in 1544 by the Spanish Crown. Within five years after 1950, forty tribes complained of being deprived of this right by the U.S. authorities.

After several centuries, disputes between the red man and the white continue to arise over the land. . . .

In 1958, Elmer Buckman, white, of Fort Hunter, New York, retained an attorney to seek a court order for the ejection of a band of Mohawk Indians who, he said, were camping on his property. Chief Standing Arrow counter-claimed that the land belonged to his people under an ancient treaty, and added that the council of six Indian nations at Syracuse, New York, was backing his claim.

Public as well as private enterprise continues to whittle away at the Indians' holdings. It was also in 1958 that representatives of three nations of Iroquois Indians dressed themselves in war paint, feathers, and porcupine quills and held a pow-wow in Federal courthouse in New York City to protest against the State Power Commission's confiscation of a fifth of their reservation. Wally "Mad Bear" Anderson, of the Tuscarora nation, told newsmen the tribesmen had gone to the courthouse "to let the judge see we are people and will fight for our rights".

Fashionable but Famished

In many of its treaties with the Indians the U.S. Government committed itself to provide school facilities for their children. The treaty with the Navajos, for example, stipulates that one teacher would be provided for each thirty children. Today, however, less than half of the 24,000 Navajo children of school age are actually in school; and the situation is much the same with other tribes. Among adult Navajos, 85 per cent are still illiterate. Nor is this due to any innate inferiority. Administration of the Goodenough intelligence test has produced the following comparative ratings:

Hopi	117
Sioux	114
Zuni	112
Navajos . . .	109
White Americans . .	101

Such efforts as have been made to "educate" the Indians have been characterized by ruthless suppression of tribal culture and crude imposition of the white man's ways. Some of the schools have been so unpopular with the Indians that Indian Bureau agents have literally had to kidnap children to put into them; pitched battles have been fought by parents intent upon rescuing their young ones. The Government has also given a free hand to all sorts of religious denominations to establish "mission" schools among the Indians; many of these, from which escape is well-nigh impossible, are little better than the worst public orphanages. Overwhelmed by the drabness and drudgery of these institutions, the free spirit of the Indian child is soon broken.

It is impossible to say whether it is more difficult for an Indian to earn a living on or off a reservation. A typical reservation, that of 4,500 Blackfeet in Montana, embraces 1,200,000 acres; but the land is so arid, and the U.S. Government does so little to assist with its utilization, that the Indians' *per capita* income each year is only 355 dollars, and 65 per cent of the tribe are forced to accept Government pensions in order to survive.

Reporting on a 1950 field trip, the Association of American Indian

Affairs said: "Housing is a quickly-observable test of general living conditions. The substandard economic life of most Blackfeet Indians is pointed up by Moccasin Flat, a large slum within a stone's throw of the U.S. Government's Blackfeet Indian Agency. Blackfeet housing conditions are characteristic of Indian housing conditions almost anywhere in the country."

Adding to this, Felix Cohen, Counsel of the Association, has said: "I have seen on a number of these reservations conditions of helplessness, misery, starvation, and preventable deaths which could not be duplicated in the worst city slums in America—not even in the slums of Puerto Rico, which I have visited."

It was not until 1924 that the U.S. Government established a Division of Health in the Indian Bureau. Even so, the doctors and nurses sent to work under impossible conditions on Indian reservations are underpaid, and many are not fully qualified. The death-rate among Indians is far higher than that of other Americans. According to Embry in his book *America's Concentration Camps*, the life expectancy of the white American has risen to 70 years, and that of the Negro American to 60 years, but the life expectancy of a Papago Indian child is but 17 years, and not much higher in other tribes. Infant mortality is especially high, and such diseases as tuberculosis, syphilis and trachoma take heavy tolls.

A periodic hazard on most reservations is drought, which brings death to herds and Indians alike. By the time the Bureau or Congress acts, both the herds and tribes are decimated. In a typical drought year, 1951, some 4,000,000 acres belonging to Navajos in Arizona were hard hit, the drought affecting 40 per cent of the tribe's sheep and 3,300 families. When a number of these families grazed their stricken herds in an adjoining reserve controlled by the Grazing Service of the Land Management Bureau of the Department of Interior, Senator Arthur Watkins threatened "there may be bloodshed" unless the Indians went back to their reservation.

It is an old American custom, in passing laws for the relief of the Indians, to attach amendments adroitly calculated to relieve them of their few remaining possessions as well. When Congress in 1949 belatedly passed a relief Bill for the Navajo and Hopi tribes which were dying from starvation, amendments were added to take litigation over Indian lands out of the Federal courts and into state courts, where special interests and racial antipathies have relatively free play. As if this were not enough, still other amendments were added to deprive the Indians of their vital water resources. Though faced with continued starvation, the tribal councils petitioned Congress not to pass the Bill as amended, but Congress passed it anyway.

One of the few enterprises other than stock-raising in which reservation Indians can indulge is to cater to white tourists, either by making handicraft articles, or dressing up in feathers and warpaint to pose for snapshots. Arizona and New Mexico, which spend huge sums advertising their Indians as tourist attractions, have also been most adamant in denying Indians their right to vote, social security pensions, etc.

Indians who venture into the white man's world to look for a job encounter many difficulties. Most of them have to be content with farm labour or common construction work, regardless of what skills they may have. As the Rev. David Owl once said: "An Indian can sometimes get a job—if he is twice as good as a white man."

Far from trying to find employment for Indians through the channels of the U.S. Employment Service without discrimination, the Indian Bureau in 1950 set up a separate Placement Service for Indians which simply lent Government sanction to the relegation of Indians to menial jobs. In the Southwest, those Indians who speak Spanish instead of English find it doubly difficult to find work.

"The areas in which job discrimination against the Indian is most extreme are areas where rich natural resources are being siphoned off by absentee ownership," Cohen told a Congressional Committee on Fair Employment Practices legislation. "Such is the case particularly in Alaska, Arizona, and New Mexico. The local managers of these absentee corporations are likely to accept the local lines of prejudice, particularly in so far as these lines of prejudice help to keep different groups of employees at each other's throats.

"The same attitudes that reflect themselves in these forms of public discrimination are also reflected in private discrimination in employment. The result of all this is not only to blacken the economic lot of the Indian, but also to blacken the international prestige of the United States throughout the world. For we must remember that what we do to Alaskan natives, who were once Russian citizens, may be far removed from the American public, but it does reach within two miles of Russian soil and Russian eyes and Russian loudspeakers. And what we do on the Mexican border to Spanish-speaking Indians reaches through the length and breadth of Latin America."

The attention of the United Nations has been called to the plight of the Pribiloff Indians who live on the islands of St. Paul and St. George off the Alaskan coast. Each year over three million valuable fur seals congregate on these islands to breed. Since 1869 the islands have been held by the U.S.A. as a "Government reservation set aside for the protection of the Alaska fur seal herd". Actually the U.S. Government acts as an agent for the Fouke Fur Company of St. Louis, Missouri, to which the Government has granted an exclusive monopoly for the taking of the islands' seals. This Fur Seal Act of 1944 provides: "Whenever seals are killed and sealskins taken on any of the Pribiloff islands, the Native inhabitants of the islands shall be employed in such killing and in curing the skins taken, and shall receive for their labour fair compensation to be fixed from time to time by the Secretary of the Interior, who shall have authority to prescribe the manner in which such compensation shall be paid to the Natives or expended or otherwise used on their behalf and for their benefit." The Commissioner has ordained that the Indians are to be credited with 1 dollar for each skin they deliver. But instead of paying even this paltry sum in cash, the Indians are issued barely enough provisions to keep them alive. These Indians are subjects of the U.S. Fish and Wildlife Service, which forces them to work for the Fouke Fur Company and makes it impossible for them to escape from the islands.

The Indian Bureau itself has in large measure established the pattern for discrimination. Only a relative handful of Indians are employed by the Indian Bureau, despite the training and qualifications of many. Those few who are given jobs are hired in menial capacities, and are rarely permitted to rise to supervisory or administrative positions. One of the very few reservation superintendents who is himself an Indian has been unceasingly hounded by the Bureau—according to the National Congress of American Indians—with charges that his "first loyalty is to the Indians rather than his Washington superiors".

Commissioner Myer, in his handling of the War Relocation Administration, ruthlessly followed a policy aimed at the dispersion of Japanese-Americans without any regard for their own inclinations. He pursued the same policy with respect to the American Indian.

All this was done in the name of "withdrawal"—that is, in the guise of bringing to an end Government control over Indian life. Withdrawal bills, affecting one state at a time, began to go into the Congressional hopper in 1952. The significant thing about these bills, however, is that to facilitate the withdrawal of the Government from Indian affairs, they would give the Government power to "withdraw" what little remains of the Indians' property.

Testifying against such measures before a Senate committee, a member of the Blackfeet tribe said: "We have had 97 years of experience with program-makers who came out on behalf of the Indian Bureau and sold us on programs to do away with the Bureau. They all resulted actually in making the Bureau fatter and our own holdings leaner. After three 10-year programs, one 25-year program, and one 5-year program, our people are left with less than 2 per cent of the land we owned 97 years ago. During this period Blackfeet *per capita* wealth has declined by at least 67 per cent. So you gentlemen can understand why we are very much worried at the prospect of having the Bureau send out another expert program-maker from Washington to improve us any further."

What Truman's Commissioner Myer began, Eisenhower's Commissioner Glenn Emmons, a New Mexico banker, projected toward its illogical conclusion. Far from shouldering the Government's treaty commitments to permit the Indians to retain their tribal cultures and self-government, Emmons frankly proclaimed his intention to "take the Government out of the Indian business".

"The policy of the Indian Bureau today has three aspects", the U.S. Information Agency shamelessly wrote. "First, to make an end of all responsibilities assumed by the Government regarding Indians in matters relative to the disposition of their properties; second, to put an end to the Bureau of Indian Affairs; and finally to assimilate the Indians with the other citizens of the states where they reside."

That the Indians are by no means happy over the prospect of being swallowed up by the white man's "American Way" was vociferously brought out at a big pow-wow they held at Claremore, Oklahoma, in 1957.

"Unless America's Indians hold on to the land they now own, they are through as Indians", Joseph R. Garry, President of the Congress of American Indians, said.

Perhaps there is hope of a sort in the fact that white America shows but little inclination to open its doors to the Indian, and that 30 per cent of those who do venture to leave the reservation eventually go back to it.

"Although sentimental regard for the Indian is now the fashion in America, we do not think of admitting him as an equal", writes Edwin R. Embree of the American Council on Race Relations. "The great American middle classes are so full of colour prejudice that Indians, no matter how fully they adopt white ways, will not for many years be accepted into the white world."

"It is a pity that so many Americans today think of the Indian as a romantic or comic figure in American history without contemporary significance", comments Cohen in his article "The Erosion of Indian Rights Since 1950" in the *Yale Law Review*. "In fact, the Indian plays much the same role in our American society that the Jews played in Germany. Like the miner's canary, the Indian marks the shifts from fresh air to poison gas in our political atmosphere; and our treatment of Indians, even more than our treatment of other minorities, reflects the rise and fall in our democratic faith."

CHAPTER 2

WHITE MAN'S COUNTRY

"WE must keep this a White Man's country", the first of the *Ideals* of the Ku Klux Klan asserts. "Only by doing this can we be faithful to the foundations laid by our forefathers. This Republic was established by White Men. It was established for White Men. Our forefathers never intended that it should fall into the hands of an inferior race. Every effort to wrest from White Men the management of its affairs in order to transfer it to the control of blacks or any other color, or to permit them to share in its control, is an invasion of our sacred Constitutional prerogatives and a violation of divinely established laws.

"We would not rob the colored population of their rights, but we demand that they respect the rights of the White Race in whose country they are permitted to reside. When it comes to the point that they cannot and will not recognize and respect those rights, they must be reminded that this is a White Man's country!"

Get the idea?

It is one which has come a long way in the U.S.A. Where it will go from here is still unsettled, but in the meantime this Guide has been designed to throw light on the subject. The Klan, you might as well know, is fond of saying of itself: "We have come a long way, and are going farther yet. . . ."

Note that the resolve to make America a white man's country is attributed, not without reason, to our forefathers. We have just seen how the first phase of the threefold process of making the U.S.A. a white man's country has unfolded. The decision to expropriate, decimate and contain the native American Indian was taken as soon as it became evident that he would not submit to slavery. But the demand for slaves persisted, and soon began to find satisfaction through the importation and breeding of African Negroes.

Such equalitarian ideals as the pioneer settlers brought with them— as had indeed impelled them—to the New World were generally reserved for their own kind, and did not interfere overmuch with their decidedly different attitude toward Indians and Negroes. Those who sanctioned the importation of Negroes tried to tell themselves that as chattel slaves the Negroes would have no more social significance than other forms of livestock. Even when numerous babies began to be born of white masters and Negro mothers, these too were indiscriminately herded into the slave flock.

And yet there were voices which spoke out, in American accents, in opposition to Negro slavery. In fact, the original draft of the Declaration of Independence, as penned by Thomas Jefferson, contained the following attack upon British King George:

"He has waged war against human nature itself, violating the most sacred Rights of Life and Liberty in the persons of distant people who never offended him, captivating and carrying them into slavery in another hemisphere, or to incur miserable death in the transportation thither. This piratical warfare, the opprobrium of infidel powers, is the warfare of the Christian King of Great Britain. He has prostituted his negative for suppressing every legislative attempt to prohibit or restrain an execrable commerce, determined to keep open a market where men should be bought and sold."

That conception of America was not to come to birth at once, but only in blood three-quarters of a century later; for the indictment of slavery which Jefferson first wrote into the Declaration of Independence was, at the insistence of certain of the signatories, stricken. Invention of the cotton gin and the rise of large plantations brought on an increase in the slave trade until the supply was deemed adequate.

White America's experiences in dealing with the Indian population now stood her in good stead—she was psychologically well prepared to compromise her political and religious precepts by not applying them to Negroes either.

The U.S. Constitution as adopted in 1789 sanctioned slavery in several ways.

Article I, Section 2, Clause 3 provided that Indians were not to be counted in determining each state's quota of Representatives in Congress, and that each Negro slave was to be counted as three-fifths of a person.

Article IV, Section 2, Clause 3 cast Uncle Sam in the role of slave-herder by providing that: "No person held to service or labor in one State, under the laws thereof, escaping into another shall in consequence of any law or regulation therein, be discharged from such service or labor, but shall be delivered up on claim of the party to whom such service or labor may be due."

It remained for the U.S. Supreme Court, in its decision on the Dred Scott case in 1857, to lay down the law that no one of slave descent, free or not, could ever claim American citizenship, even though born in America.

Again, as upon the founding of the republic, voices were to be heard in accents unmistakably American, refusing to accept slavery, with its denial of the humanity of the Negro, as a lasting American institution. Said Abraham Lincoln of the Supreme Court's ruling in the Dred Scott case:

"If the important decision . . . had been before the Court more than once, and had there been affirmed and reaffirmed through a course of years, it then might be, perhaps would be, factious, nay, even revolutionary, not to acquiesce in it as a precedent. But when, as is true, we find it wanting in all these claims to the public confidence, it is not resistance, it is not factious, it is not even disrespectful, to treat it as not having yet quite established a settled doctrine for the country."

Not only did Uncle Sam in his early years serve as runaway-slave-catcher; he even went so far as to solemnly swear that he would never interfere with the institution of slavery in so far as it existed within his boundaries. A joint resolution for an Amendment to the Constitution was passed by Congress and signed by President James Buchanan in 1861, providing:

"No amendment shall be made to the Constitution which will authorize or give to Congress the power to abolish or interfere, within any state, with the domestic institutions thereof, including that of persons held to labor or service by the laws of said state."

(Outbreak of the Civil War, that same year, precluded ratification of this Amendment by the states.)

While the evolution of the U.S.A. as a white man's country was thus progressing through liquidation of the Indian and enslavement of the Negro, something else was added to round out the picture. Negro slavery, associated with cotton culture, had been confined to the South and Southwest. Elsewhere in the country, the demand for cheap labour had led to encouragement of the immigration of poverty-stricken Europeans, Chinese and Japanese who were put to work building railroads, mining, etc. But so soon as the proprietors of such enterprises felt that the labour supply was adequate, they gave encouragement to such outcroppings of organized bigotry as the Nativist Movement of the 1840s and the Know-Nothing Movement which thrived from 1853 to 1860. These groups not only opposed further immigration and those aliens already in the country, but, as time went on, did so increasingly on the basis of race and colour (see Chapter 3, "America's Great Wall").

The Know-Nothings, members of a secret "Order of the Star Spangled Banner", got their name from the answer they invariably gave when asked the purposes of the Order: "I know nothing." Under the slogans "Americans must rule America!" and "No papacy in the republic!" they opposed at the polls the Irish and German Catholic immigrants who had become a political force in a number of cities. Pitched battles were fought in the streets, and the Know-Nothings succeeded in electing a Know-Nothing Governor, legislature and Senator in Massachusetts and some other states, and threatened also to dominate New York. A national convention of Know-Nothings held in Philadelphia in 1856 formed an American Party, nominating for the Presidency former President Millard Fillmore, who accepted.

Abraham Lincoln, then an Illinois lawyer but already taking a profound interest in national affairs, wrote at the time:

"Our progress in degeneracy appears to me to be pretty rapid. As a nation, we began by declaring 'all men are created equal'. We now practically read it 'all men are created equal, except Negroes'. When the Know-Nothings get control, it will read 'all men are created equal, except Negroes, and foreigners, and Catholics'. When it comes to this I should prefer emigrating to some country where they make no pretence of loving liberty—to Russia, for instance, where despotism can be taken pure, and without the base alloy of hypocrisy."

In the course of the Civil War which came after Lincoln entered the White House, his hand was long stayed from signing the Emancipation Proclamation by the knowledge that some of his troops were willing to fight to preserve the Union, but not to free the Negroes. Indeed, many a Negro was lynched in the bloody anti-conscription riots which shook New York in 1863.

The Ku Klux Klan—the white-robed and hooded terrorist band which originated in the South in 1867 as a means of virtually re-enslaving the Negroes—eventually fell heir to the varied hatreds which had been fostered by the Know-Nothings in other parts of the country.

In becoming a hyper-nationalistic secret order based upon hatred of Jews, Catholics, Asians and all foreign-born as well as Negroes, the Klan by the mid-1920s had expanded into a politically-potent super-government operating behind the scenes throughout the country on the national, state and local levels. Its "Invisible Empire" encompassed all 48 states, and, with more than 8 million members, was in fact something of a government within a government.

America, as the Klan boasted, was "Kluxed".

In fact, this Guide can reveal for the first time that President Warren G. Harding was inducted into the Klan in a robed and masked ceremony conducted in the Green Room of the White House! After taking the oath to obey the edicts of the Imperial Wizard, the President of the United States presented him with a War Department licence plate for his limousine as a token of esteem.

It is with good reason, therefore, that this chapter opened with a quotation from the *Ideals* of the K.K.K., for the role played by the Klan in propagating the concept of America as a white man's country has been a prominent one.

If we turn back the pages of American history to that night in 1915 when, on the windswept slope of Georgia's Stone Mountain beneath the light of a fiery cross, the Klan was revitalized, we can hear Imperial Wizard William Joseph Simmons proclaiming:

"The Anglo-Saxon is the typeman of history. To him must yield the self-centered Hebrew, the cultured Greek, the virile Roman, the mystic Oriental. The Psalmist must have had him in mind by poetic imagination when he struck his sounding harp and sang: 'O Lord: Thou has made him a little lower than the angels, and hast crowned him with glory and honor. Thou madest him to have dominion over the works of Thy hands; thou hast put all things under his feet. . . .' An inevitable conflict between the white race and the colored race is indicated by the present unrest. This conflict will be Armageddon, unless the Anglo-Saxon, in unity with the Latin and Teutonic nations, takes the leadership of the world and shows to all that it has and will hold the world mastery forever!"

Simmons' successor as Wizard, Hiram W. Evans, brought the theme forward when he wrote in 1937:

"The first essential to the success of any nation, and particularly of any democracy, is a national unity of mind. Its citizens must be *one people* . . . they must have common instincts and racial and national purpose. It follows that any class, race, or group of people which is permanently unassimilable to the spirit and purpose of the nation has no place in a democracy. The negro, so far in the future as human vision can pierce, must always remain in a group *unable* to be a part of the American people. His racial inferiority has nothing to do with this fact; the unfitness applies equally to *all alien races* and justifies our attitude toward Chinese, Japanese, and Hindus. No amount of education can ever make a white man out of a man of any other color. It is a law on this earth that races never can exist together in complete peace and friendship and certainly never in a state of equality."

The Klan, of course, has not been alone in cultivating these fields, but it has been by far the most influential of the outspoken groups engaged in spreading the doctrine of white supremacy.

To cite but one other example: William Blanchard of Miami, Florida, leader of the White Front, put it this way in his official organ, *Nation and Race*:

"If one believes in history before effeminate and fallacious ideologies, the recognition of the superiority of the Nordic and the Nordicized world is immediate. A dangerous upsurge of democracy and self-determination throughout the world of color is robbing the Western world of some of its power, but we have not yet lived to see the end of white supremacy."

If you believe such sentiments are confined to the leaders of terrorist groups you are very much mistaken; they often resound through the halls of Congress. . . .

For example, Senator James O. Eastland, now Chairman of the Senate Sub-committee on Internal Security inherited from McCarthy, has said on the floor of the Senate:

"I believe in white supremacy, and as long as I am in the Senate I expect to fight for white supremacy, because I can see that if the amalgamation of whites and Negroes in this country is permitted, there will be a mongrel race, and there will come to pass the identical condition under which Egypt, India, and other civilizations decayed. . . . The cultural debit of the colored peoples to the white race is such as to make the preservation of the white race a chief aim of the colored, if these latter but understood their indebtedness. That the colored race should seek to 'kill the goose that lays the golden egg' is further proof that their inferiority, demonstrated so clearly in cultural attainments, extends to their reasoning processes in general. Asiatic exclusion and Negro repatriation are expressions of the eugenic ideal."

Don't get the idea that views such as these are confined to some lunatic fringe, for they are not. They are representative of an extant majority of white people in the South, and of many millions more outside the South. This is no mere accident, nor an indication of any innate bias, but the result of centuries of indoctrination. The *Kloran* of the K.K.K. for many years superseded the Constitution of the U.S.A. as the governing instrument of the Southern states in matters having to do with race relations and the status of Negroes as citizens and persons. And if you were to take the trouble to put to white persons elsewhere in the United States the question of the Klan: "Do you believe this should be a white man's country?" you would undoubtedly find very many responding in the affirmative, even though they may have never before thought of the question consciously. It has ever been thus, even before the founding of the republic.

This is a fact of interest not alone to the historian, but to everyone living in or passing through the U.S.A. The doctrine of white supremacy, transplanted to American soil by European colonists in a pristine state while European empire was yet young, has been kept alive in its original unsophisticated form, just like certain archaic Anglicisms which have long since passed out of existence in the British Isles, but which you can still find in the Appalachian Mountains of America. Ostensibly holding title to relatively limited colonial possessions of her own, America has not been compelled by the pressure of independence movements to refine the doctrine of white supremacy after the manner of European colony-holders.

You may or may not be one of them, but in the latter case you ought to know that there are those in the world who feel that the call of the Klansmen for "American participation in white control and regulation of the world of color" has by no means fallen upon deaf ears. In witness whereof, they point to certain evidence.

As a classic case in point, they cite the atomic bombing of open Japanese cities by America in World War II. No atomic bombs were dropped upon the white Germans, but in the bombing of Hiroshima alone 224,000 men, women, and children were wiped out. A decade later, the bombing was still claiming its weekly quota of casualties from among the ranks of 30,000 remaining injured survivors.

Harry S. Truman, who as President of the U.S.A. and Commander-in-Chief of its armed forces authorized the bombings, said on a television programme in 1958 that he had experienced "no qualms" in giving the order. When the city council of Hiroshima protested against this remark, Truman replied that the bombing would not have been necessary "had we not been shot in the back by Japan at Pearl Harbor". Whereupon the Hiroshima council asked why, if that were the case, a military target had not been chosen for retaliation, and added, "You committed the crime of the largest-scale massacre in man's history as revenge, and you are still trying to justify it. Such a reply reflects the mean, colonial-type sentiment of a conqueror against the conquered."

During World War II, and in the Korean conflict afterwards, U.S. fighting men manifested a tendency to refer contemptuously and indiscriminately to all Asians—whether allies or enemies—as "gooks". In time this word became such a liability in psychological warfare that the Pentagon was obliged to frown upon its use.

More than a word was involved, however. It was in 1951 that the Stars-and-Bars of the Confederate States of America—the banner of race slavery—appeared beside the flags of the U.S.A. and United Nations in Korea. According to International News Service, Marine Sergeant Howard Arndt explained: "I stuck that flag in there the moment I got here, and she's going to stay there until we take her down and put her up again in Seoul. The only reason the Yankee boys go along with that Confederate flag is that we've converted them to The Cause."

That Sergeant Arndt's viewpoint also existed in higher quarters was made evident by the recommendation of American military leaders in the Pacific theatre to pit "Asians against Asians".

Then came the speech of General Douglas MacArthur to the Veterans of Foreign Wars. Denying that "if we defend Formosa we alienate continental Asia", MacArthur added:

"Those who speak thus do not understand the Orient. They do not grant that it is the pattern of Oriental psychology to respect and follow aggressive, resolute, and dynamic leadership."

In calling for MacArthur's dismissal, Labour Member of the British Parliament Woodrow Wyatt said in the Commons that the General had said in effect:

"Kick the Orientals in the face; they like it."

The cease-fire in Korea did not put an end to demonstrations of white "superiority". For instance, in 1957, Sergeant William S. Girard, an American soldier stationed in Japan, shot and killed Mrs. Naka Sakai, mother of several children, while she was salvaging empty shell casings on a firing range. Girard baited her by tossing empty casings toward her, called out in Japanese for her to come get them, and then raised his rifle and shot her in the back. When Japanese courts claimed jurisdiction, many U.S. newspapers portrayed Girard as a "hero" and "martyr" and Congress sent a Committee to Japan to investigate.

c

"It was a childish smart-aleck trick and he should pay a penalty commensurate, but I do think it should be done by our own officials," concluded Chairman Omar Burlson of Texas.

The Japanese court set Girard free.

In the same spirit, in 1958 U.S. Captain Marvin Kemp, Major Thomas James, and Robert Weidensaul beat a small Korean boy for pilfering, nailed him in a box, and shipped him by helicopter to the demarcation line between South and North Korea. Under Army regulations the men might have been confined for three and a half years; actually they drew light fines and reprimands.

With that thumbnail sketch of how the ideology of white supremacy took root in the U.S.A. and grew, we can proceed to look into the various areas in which this doctrine has flourished.

First, however, a word of caution: Don't let yourself be lulled into a false sense of security by all the Press notices hailing recent court decisions against race segregation as ushering in the millennium in race relations. The American republic has often committed herself to the ideal of equality—and almost as often backslid to the theory and practice of inequality. This is not said to throw a wet blanket on any hopes and plans you may have, but simply to prepare you to cope with reality as you think best.

As you will see as you go along, this Guide does not presume to guide. It is intended as a flare to light up the scene, with highlights on the barbed-wire entanglements and Jim Crow segregation signs to be encountered along the way of life in the U.S.A.

In passing, perhaps you are wondering about the origin of the appellation "Jim Crow". It seems that it found currency toward the end of the last century, after a black-face (burnt cork) minstrel popularized a stage dance ditty which went something like this:

> I look about and jump about,
>   and do just so;
> But every time I turn about,
>   I jump Jim Crow!

Jim Crow, whose middle names are Segregation and Discrimination, is far from being dead yet. By reading this biography you can know just what to expect wherever you come across him.

This Guide appears at a time when those who believe in white supremacy—aided and abetted by those who champion it purely for mercenary reasons—are busy day and night stringing wire and tacking up new signs, trying to mend the fences cut through by court mandates. Not only are the legalistic fences being mended and heightened (several hundred new race laws being enacted in the Southern states during the first several years following the Supreme Court's 1954 decision); even greater efforts are being made to strengthen the terroristic and psychological barriers.

A vast new programme is well under way to indoctrinate Southern schoolchildren, and the nation at large, with the dogma of white supremacy. In the South, official and quasi-official propaganda seeks on the one hand to convince white children that they are superior, and, on the other hand (as in the Union of South Africa), to convince Negro children that they are inferior.

Censorship of advocacy of racial equality was indeed a common phenomenon in the South long before the courts were finally prevailed upon to rule against segregation. The Klan called upon its members to have their children report the names of teachers who spoke out against the Klan or "for the Negro and Jew".

Florida, while the political witch-hunt was at its peak, saw fit to insert into the state's non-communist "loyalty" oath (required of all public employees, including teachers) the questions: "Do you support the race segregation laws of this state? If not, why not?" Even Negro teachers have to reply affirmatively, or lose their jobs.

Mississippi, Georgia, Louisiana, and South Carolina adopted in recent years laws forbidding members of the National Association for the Advancement of Coloured People to teach in the public schools.

South Carolina has banned from public schools and libraries all books and magazines deemed "antagonistic to the traditions of South Carolina". Mississippi and Louisiana, in similar measures, have specifically banned as "anti-South" such conservative magazines as *Time* and *Life*. The book *Southern Exposure*, by Stetson Kennedy, containing a chapter entitled "Total Equality, and How to Get It", has been banned by the school authorities of Georgia and other Southern states.

The Armstrong Foundation, founded by a Texas oil multi-millionaire, has been doling out large financial subsidies to military colleges, universities, and other institutions of higher learning, on the condition that they pledge to teach the doctrine of white supremacy in perpetuity. Some institutions, like Jackson Military College in Mississippi, have refused this offer, while others, like Emory University of Georgia, have accepted.

Mississippi, ever supreme among white supremacists, has established a State Sovereignty Commission to combat "all elements antagonistic to the state's way of life", earmarking a portion of a quarter-million-dollar appropriation to propagandize The Mississippi Way throughout the U.S.A.

Not content with all this, the White Citizens' Council of Mississippi has launched an intensive drive of its own to assure that white supremacy will be expressly taught in the public schools. Mrs. Sara McCorkle, inaugurating the campaign with a television programme in 1958, complained that certain magazines, television programmes, and religious periodicals have been giving school children false notions about racial equality. To counteract this, the Citizens' Council has offered a prize for the best school essay on "Racial Integrity". With the collaboration of school officials, Mrs. McCorkle said she was making an average of twelve lectures on white supremacy in school auditoriums each week. In addition, the Council was busily stocking Mississippi schools with such volumes as *The Cult of Equality*, by Stewart Landry, which says in part:

"Negroes are lazy. It is difficult to tell when they are lying and when they are telling the truth. They will steal chickens, food, small sums of money. Negroes do not face difficulties or adversity with courage or determination. There is also a resemblance between a great ape and a pure-blooded Negro."

CHAPTER 3

AMERICA'S GREAT WALL

ACCORDING to legend, the United States of America is a "melting-pot" of the peoples of the world.

The fact is, however, that the ingredients which have gone into the pot have been carefully screened for whiteness.

The Statue of Liberty, a gift of the French people, stands in New York Harbour and "lifts her lamp beside the golden door", but her inscribed invitation to the world to "send your tempest-tossed to me" has been amended by American immigration laws to be mostly valid for whites.

The roots of U.S. immigration policy reach back to colonial days and beyond. To an appreciable extent, the American policy is a lineal descendant of the original doctrine of white supremacy fabricated by the European powers when they first took up the "white man's burden".

When the British finally won out over their French and Spanish competitors for the privilege of exploiting North America, it was but natural that the settlers they dispatched to do the job were preconditioned to look with disdain upon the American Indian and coloured peoples generally.

As we have seen, when the red man refused to work for the white man, the latter imported the black man, thinking he could pen him up as an item of livestock. Then came the Civil War, releasing the Negro from the corral, whereupon the white man promptly penned him up again behind the barbed wire of segregation. Still, the country was young and there was much dirty work to be done. But far from thinking in terms of inviting Africans to enter America as free men, prodigious official and private efforts were made to ship the Negro freedmen in America back to Africa.

The slavery question having cost America so much blood and suffering, there was much sentiment in the land against any further influx of coloured persons. At the same time, employer interests were in the market for the cheapest possible labour. White foreign labour of certain nationalities was cheap enough, but coloured labour was even cheaper. In this conflict between popular and employer sentiment, the employers had their way until they felt they had enough.

A vast railroad-building boom, coupled with the California "Gold Rush" of 1849, gave impetus to the importation of Chinese "coolie" labour even before the Civil War made an end of Negro slavery in 1865. Abolition of Negro slavery by Great Britain in 1833 and the West Indies in 1838 had set this so-called "pig traffic" in motion. Although there were tremendous economic pressures inside China, 80 per cent of the migrants had to be kidnapped or decoyed into the barracoons to be transported to distant shores, where contracts for their labour were sold in much the same manner as Negro slaves had been sold earlier.

For a time many white Southern planters gave serious consideration to replacing Negro slave labour with Chinese coolie labour. A convention of planters met at Memphis in 1869 and sent delegations to China to investigate this possibility.

In California, meanwhile, trends were developing which were destined to shape the course of the entire nation. As the supply of white labour in the state increased, and the mining and railroad booms subsided, sentiment developed for the exclusion of any further immigration from Asia and the Pacific. For 16 years, beginning in 1860, California sought to accomplish this by a series of so-called "Hottentot Laws" (which Federal courts eventually declared unconstitutional).

Approximately a third of California's pioneer settlers had been white Southern planters, who had brought their Negro slaves and racial prejudices with them. Indians, Mexicans, Hawaiians, Chileans, Chinese, and Japanese—all were successively utilized and discriminated against by these planters. In no time, California succeeded in selling the rest of America the notion that "Chinks" were all "moon-faced lepers" who constituted a grave "Yellow Peril".

And so, when Congress adopted the Naturalization Act of 1870 as a corollary of the Thirteenth Amendment abolishing Negro slavery, it not only made possible the naturalization (in negligible numbers) of "aliens of African nativity and persons of African descent", but at the same time, at the insistence of California, limited other groups eligible for naturalization to "free white persons".

Interestingly, many Congressmen who voted for Negro suffrage also voted for Oriental exclusion, despite the fact that the arguments advanced by California for the latter were identical with those employed by white Southern opponents of Negro enfranchisement.

This proved to be the first of seven major Congressional Acts aimed at the exclusion of Asian peoples, introduced by California on the eve of national elections (in which both parties were anxious to secure Pacific Coast support), and supported by a West-South coalition that assured passage.

In 1882—again at California's instance—the Chinese Exclusion Act was adopted, forbidding all further Chinese immigration for ten years, and expressly declaring all Chinese, in and out of the U.S.A., to be "ineligible" to U.S. citizenship. Adoption of the Act precipitated rioting against Chinese in California, Washington, and Oregon.

Protesting at the time, Senator Hawley of Connecticut said: "Make the conditions what you please for immigration and for attaining citizenship, but make them such that a man may overcome them; do not base them on the accidents of humanity."

"The clamor of a single state [California] was sufficient to change the policy of a nation and to commit the United States to a race discrimination at variance with our professed theories of government, and this so irrevocably that it has become an established tradition", Mary Roberts Coolidge records in her book, *Chinese Immigration*.

Shortly after the U.S.A. adopted the Chinese Exclusion Act, Canada, Mexico, Guatemala, El Salvador, Nicaragua, Colombia, Ecuador, and Peru followed suit, thus erecting a "Great Wall" against Chinese immigration along the entire Pacific Coast of the Western Hemisphere.

Australia and New Zealand also soon followed Uncle Sam's example. Wherever the British or American flag flew, Chinese were *verboten*.

During the preceding few years, the first contingents of Japanese immigrants had begun to arrive in the U.S.A. It was in 1884 that the Japanese Government dropped its traditional death penalty for any Japanese who emigrated to another country. This action was taken at the behest of the Hawaiian Sugar Planters' Association, a trust formed by American sugar magnates, who were anxious to import Japanese labourers to Hawaii, having already exhausted the Chinese and other groups on the islands. By 1890 there were 2,039 Japanese in continental U.S.A., most of them in California. And on May 7, 1900, the first anti-Japanese mass meeting was held in San Francisco.

In 1905 the San Francisco Board of Education prohibited all Oriental children from attending white schools. The measure was sponsored by Mayor Eugene Schmitz, who said he would lay down his life if necessary battling the Japanese. (Japan had just contributed 100,000 dollars for the relief of victims of the San Francisco earthquake and fire.)

In 1907 President Theodore Roosevelt halted all further immigration of Japanese from Hawaii, Canada, and Mexico. He also negotiated a "Gentleman's Agreement" with Japan, permitting the immigration of so-called "picture brides".

In 1908 W. L. Mackenzie King (later Prime Minister of Canada) charged that the Hawaiian Sugar Planters' Association had subsidized the potent "Asiatic Exclusion League of North America" in an effort to halt the departure of labourers from Hawaii to the American mainland.

In 1909 seven anti-Japanese bills were introduced in the California leglislature. One legislator referred to the Japanese as "a bandy-legged set of bugaboos—miserable craven Simians—degenerate rotten little devils". Other common epithets were "skulking, servile, immoral, treacherous, sneaking, insidious".

In 1910 California suppressed the report of her Labour Commissioner which said: "Japanese or some form of labor of a similar character, capable of independent subsistence, quick mobilization, submissive of instant dismissal, and entailing no responsibility upon the employer for continuous employment, is absolutely necessary in the California orchard, vineyard, and field, if these vast industries are to be perpetuated and developed."

In 1913 California adopted an Alien Land Act, of which its author said: "The fundamental basis of all legislation upon this subject has been, and is, race undesirability." The Act itself was expressly aimed at races which were "ineligible to citizenship", and it was upheld by the courts.

In 1914, Kaiser Wilhelm of Germany launched a propaganda campaign about the "Yellow Peril" in an effort to break the alliance between the U.S.A. and Japan.

At the Versailles Peace Conference terminating World War I, China and Japan sought a declaration upholding racial equality, but eight powers—including the U.S.A., Great Britain, and the British Dominions—defeated the proposal.

As early as 1917 the U.S. Congress had extended the immigration ban by lumping all of continental and south-eastern Asia into what it called a "Barred Zone".

By 1921, newspapers on the Pacific coast of the U.S.A. were saying:

"The Japanese problem in California will make the black problem in the South look white." The *San Francisco Bulletin*, urging a strong hand in dealing with Asians, said: "We have learned a lesson from the experience of the Southern states. Our race problem is in the future. We can prevent it from developing further if we act firmly and sanely now and put aside the counsels of doctrinaires and academicians."

It was in 1924 that the Johnson Immigration Act was adopted, firmly establishing whiteness as the yardstick for measuring the eligibility of would-be immigrants. Claiming credit for the adoption of this law, which has been the basis of U.S. immigration policy ever since, the K.K.K., in its booklet *The Klan Today*, boasts that it raised a one million dollar lobbying fund for the purpose.

The Johnson Act fixed annual immigration quotas on the basis of a certain percentage of the various nationality groups which made up the population of America, as indicated by the 1920 Census. In arriving at these quotas, however, the presence of American Negroes, American Indians, and certain other nonwhites was totally ignored. The Act declared that the peoples of twelve great political and geographic entities in Asia and the Pacific, as well as the colonial subjects of European powers, were "ineligible to citizenship" and hence were barred from entering the U.S.A. Under the quota system which this law established, immigration was cut from 1,500,000 per year to 150,000.

The Johnson Act reiterated Chinese exclusion, and went on to forbid even those Chinese men in the U.S.A. who had already become American citizens to bring in Chinese wives. Coupled with various state laws forbidding persons of Chinese descent to marry whites, this condemned thousands of Chinese men in America to live out their lives in celibacy.

China and India, along with certain other Asian countries, were extended annual quotas of 100 each—but Chinese and Indians could not enter the U.S.A. under these quotas, which were reserved for whites and others of "eligible race" who happened to have been born in those countries.

In interpreting the Act, U.S. courts ruled that Burmese, Afghans, Parsees, and Polynesians were to be excluded from the U.S.A. On the other hand, people from western Asia, such as Armenians, Persians, and Syrians, were held by the courts to be white, and hence eligible to enter. As for Arabs generally, there have been conflicting court opinions as to whether they are white or not.

In adopting the Philippine Independence Act in 1934, Congress decided that thenceforth Filipinos were to be considered as aliens who would be admitted to the U.S.A. at the rate of 50 per year during the interim Commonwealth period, but after achieving independence all Filipinos would be regarded as being of ineligible race, and hence inadmissible.

The Nationality Act of 1940 made it possible for persons of Chinese, Indian, and Filipino descent who were already in the U.S.A. to become *citizens*, but did not relax the bars against *immigration* by these groups.

That the sentiment for excluding Asians from U.S. citizenship carried over to similar sentiments toward native-born American Negroes was indicated by the fact that in 1942 the California Joint Immigration Committee (sponsored by the Native Sons and Daughters of the Golden West, the American Legion, California State Federation of Labour, and the California Grange) informed the Tolan Congressional Committee that the U.S.A. "made a grave mistake in granting citizenship to the Negroes after the Civil War".

In 1943, after a long Congressional debate as to its necessity for ideological warfare against Japan, the President of the U.S.A. was authorized to extend an annual immigration quota for Chinese, which was set at 105.

Again, when in 1945 Congress adopted a law to expedite the bringing in of alien wives by U.S. servicemen, the law was limited to "eligible" races only.

It was not until 1946 that Congress adopted Public Law 483, making Indians and Filipinos eligible for citizenship and extending quotas of 100 per year to each. Unlike the Chinese, who were given a quota of 105 for persons of Chinese ancestry in addition to the quota of 100 non-Chinese eligibles born in China, India had to share her 100 quota with persons of non-Indian stock born in India.

This Act of 1946 applies to:

"1. White persons, persons of African nativity or descent, and persons who are descendants of races indigenous to the continents of North or South America or adjacent islands, and Filipino persons or persons of Filipino descent;

"2. Persons who possess, either singly or in combination, a preponderance of blood of one or more of the classes specified in Clause 1;

"3. Chinese persons or persons of Chinese descent, and persons of races indigenous to India; and

"4. Persons who possess, either singly or in combination, a preponderance of blood of one or more of the classes specified in Clause 3, or either singly or in combination, as much as one-half of those classes and some additional blood of one of the classes specified in Clause 1."

The 1946 Act further specifies that "The term 'Filipino person or person of Filipino descent' as used in this Act shall mean persons of a race indigenous to the Philippine Islands, and shall not include persons who are as much as one-half of a race ineligible to citizenship." This was aimed against persons of Chinese and Japanese ancestry who live in the Philippines.

A total of 41 Asian, African, and colonial areas were lumped together into the "minimum quota" category, each being permitted to send a maximum of 100 persons to the U.S.A. each year. There were still, however, a considerable number of Asian and Pacific peoples who were totally taboo. The following partial list will serve to indicate the range of discrimination:

Great Britain	65,721
Greece	307
China	105
India	100
Philippines	100
Pakistan	100
Fiji Islands	100
Afghanistan	100
Non-Asian Colonies . .	100

Totally Taboo

Korea	Nauru
Japan	Siam
Indonesia	New Guinea
Burma	Eastern Samoa
Ceylon	Nepal
Butan	Pacific Trust Territory

In addition to blacklisting as congenitally unfit to become American citizens natives of the Asian lands listed above as taboo, the U.S.A. holds to the theory, "once a Chinese or Indian, always a Chinese or Indian".

This means that if a person is of British ancestry, but was born in

France, the U.S.A. will regard him as a Frenchman and permit him to enter under the quota of that country; but if a person is of Chinese or Indian ancestry, the U.S.A. will regard him as Chinese or Indian, no matter what country he or his antecedents were born in—and so he can only hope to enter under the very limited quotas of his ancestral land.

In 1951 two new immigration bills were introduced in Congress. One, drafted by Congressman Franklin D. Roosevelt, Jr., was quite liberal. The other, sponsored by Senator Pat McCarran, not only embodied the existing racial criteria, but also added a host of new discriminations, both racial and political.

McCarran welcomed the support of all sorts of nationalistic elements for his bill, even going so far as to insert in the *Congressional Record* an endorsement signed by 23 "patriotic organizations". Among the signers were such notorious figures as Allen Zoll, whose "American Patriots, Inc." is listed by the U.S. Attorney-General as fascist. Other signatory organizations were the "Wheel of Progress" and "Ladies of the Grand Army of the Republic". Signing for these were Dr. Maude S. DeLand and Mrs. Margaret Hopkins Worrell, both members of the so-called "American Justice for Tyler Kent" Committee (Kent, a de-coding clerk in the U.S. Embassy in London, was sentenced to five years by the British for selling Hitler 1,500 secret communications between Churchill and Roosevelt).

Labour leaders vigorously opposed adoption of the McCarran Act, pointing out that "an Administration hostile to labor could easily use these vastly expanded powers to punish or intimidate union members and union leaders of foreign birth". The Ku Klux Klan, just as vigorously, lobbied for adoption of the measure.

"If the bill passes in anything like its present form, we might as well send the Statue of Liberty back to France", observed columnist Drew Pearson.

The bill was passed by Congress in 1952 by a vote of 203 to 53, and encountered only token opposition in the Senate. It went into effect on December 24—the eve of the birthday of the Nazarene, who, had He been alive today, would have been branded an "undesirable" by the Act and barred from entering America.

An official Commission appointed by the previous Democratic Administration to study the McCarran Act concluded that "it is an arrogant, brazen instrument of discrimination based on race, creed, color and national origin".

There were powerful interests, however, behind the Act. The *New York Herald-Tribune* (Republican), in commenting on the above report, declared: "The Commission has made out a strong case against the national origins quotas, but the fact remains that quotas thus established are definite and automatically resist the pressures of special groups."

Because it extended token quotas of 100 per year to those Asian and Pacific peoples who were still taboo, the law was hailed by the press (American) as "ending discrimination". In reality, it perpetuates the ancient injustices and finds new ways to tag nonwhites as "undesirables". By clinging to the 1920 Census as the basis for arriving at quotas, instead of using the 1950 Census for computing the origins of the U.S.A.'s present population, the law avoids giving larger quotas to southern and eastern Europeans.

Efforts to repeal the requirement of specification of race and ethnic classification on requests for entry permits, and the clauses aimed against Asian spouses and adopted children, were rebuffed by the Senate Judiciary Committee in 1957. Congress voted to keep the door closed on racial "undesirables", but opened it to let in persons claiming to be fugitives from communism in East Europe and from Arab nationalism in Egypt and elsewhere in the Middle East.

Section 212 of the McCarran Act, under 31 general headings in seven closely-printed pages, lists the classes of aliens which are barred from admittance. The list includes psychopaths, drug addicts, alcoholics, lepers, paupers, beggars, polygamists, prostitutes, those coming to the U.S. to engage in "any immoral sexual act", anarchists, communists, and "advocates of the economic, international and governmental doctrines of world communism, or the establishment in the United States of a totalitarian dictatorship".

It should be noted that while communists are barred as such, including those who are only ideological communists without party connections, fascists of all kinds are admissible unless they advocate a "totalitarian dictatorship" *for the U.S.A.* Previous postwar immigration laws which banned "totalitarians" had proven highly embarrassing to the hosts of German Nazis, Italian Fascists, Spanish Falangists, and Argentine Peronistas who had entered the U.S.A. with the blessings, and often in the employ of, the U.S. Government. By making this distinction, the McCarran Act saved the Attorney-General the trouble of having to make special exceptions so these assorted fascists could enter and remain in the U.S.A.

The Act adds over twenty new grounds for the deportation of aliens and naturalized citizens (including refusal to answer questions put by Congressional committees). At the same time it gives the U.S. Attorney-General arbitrary powers to deport practically any such person whom he might decide "holds a purpose" to engage in activity "prejudicial to the public interest".

An international scandal was created in 1958 when U.S. immigration bureau agents kidnapped William Heikkila, 52, on the streets of San Francisco and bundled him aboard a plane bound for his native Finland. Heikkila, who had been brought to the U.S.A. as an infant, had been fighting deportation in the courts ever since 1948. He admitted having joined the Communist Party for two years during the Depression of the early 1930s, but insisted that he had not been affiliated with the party since then. The kidnapping by Government agents was carried out in defiance of a restraining order issued by Federal District Judge George Harris. Said the judge of the event after the event: "It smacks of the Gestapo . . . the thumb and screw . . . things I don't approve of. We are a government of laws, not of men, and we want to keep it that way." Immigration Commissioner Joseph M. Swing said he considered the kidnapping perfectly legal, but acceded to the court's request to bring Heikkila back, swearing to deport him once more "if it takes another 11 years".

Senator Thomas Hennings, chairman of the Senate Constitutional Rights subcommittee, said in calling for remedial legislation: "Insensitive and less-than-human practices such as this by a subdivision of the Department of Justice only serve to discredit traditional American concepts of fair play."

CHAPTER 4

WHO IS COLOURED WHERE

AFTER that briefing on the blood-letting, brain-washing, and fence-building intended to make the U.S.A. a "white man's country", the next thing you need to know is: Who is coloured where.

Coloured persons are variously defined by the U.S. Government and the 29 states which have statutory definitions of race.

Are you sure you're white? Or Negro? Or some other colour?

Perhaps you can legally change your race by changing states.

In fact, you will find there are intrastate as well as interstate variations in the legal definitions of what constitutes a coloured person, and conversely who may qualify as white. Hence a person rated as white in one state may be labelled coloured in another state, and be segregated accordingly.

Then there are some states where a person who passes the racial prescription for attendance at white schools and who enjoys all other benefits of whiteness under the segregation laws may nevertheless be defined as coloured by anti-miscegenation laws, and thus forbidden to marry a white person.

Most of the American laws defining race are not to be compared with those once enforced by Nazi Germany, the latter being relatively more liberal. In the view of the Nazis, persons having less than one-fourth Jewish blood could qualify as Aryans, whereas many of the American laws specify that persons having one-eighth, one-sixteenth, or "any ascertainable" Negro blood are Negroes in the eyes of the law and subject to all restrictions governing the conduct of Negroes.

The Nazi Nürnberg Code made a distinction between half-Jews and quarter-Jews, who were classified respectively as *Mischlings* (mongrels) of the first and second degrees, and both were forbidden to marry Aryans. The American laws permit no such gradations: you are either white or nonwhite.

The U.S. Census Bureau, in its *Enumerator's Reference Manual*, instructs census-takers to "Report 'Negro' for Negroes and for persons of mixed white and Negro parentage". This represents a change from the 1930 Census, in which only those persons having one-half or more

Negro blood were listed as Negroes, while those having less were recorded as mulattoes.

The Bureau goes on to say: "A person of mixed Indian and Negro blood should be returned as a Negro, unless the Indian blood definitely predominates."

On the other hand, if you are of mixed white and American Indian blood you can qualify as white under the Census if you are not more than one-fourth Indian.

The Census Bureau further instructs its enumerators to "Report race of nonwhite parent for persons of mixed and nonwhite races. Mixture of nonwhite races should be reported according to the race of the father."

This means that if your father is white and your mother is Negro, you are recorded as a Negro. On the other hand, if your father happens to be Chinese and your mother a Negro, you are recorded as Chinese.

Under U.S. Census regulations, you are neither asked nor informed how your race is to be recorded: "The race question is answered by the enumerator from observation."

Moreover, U.S. Census-takers are told to "Assume that the race of related persons living in the household is the same as the race of your respondent".

The constitutional and/or statutory definitions of race which exist in 29 of America's 48 states are of comparatively modern origin, and have been tightened several times since the Civil War.

These definitions are so at variance that anyone living or visiting in the U.S.A. should study carefully the following tabulation, which gives the formulas for nonwhites by states. Where the races are not legally defined, the courts decide.

Alabama

"The term 'negro' includes 'mulatto'. The term 'mulatto' or 'person of color' is a person of mixed blood, descended on the part of the father or mother from negro ancestors, without reference to or limit of time or number of generations."

Arizona

Anyone having any Negro blood whatever.
American Indians.
Mongolians.
Hindus.
Malays.

Arkansas

"Persons in whom there is a visible and distinct admixture of African blood shall be deemed to belong to the African race; all others shall be deemed to belong to the white race."—Anti-miscegenation law.

"The words 'persons of negro race' shall be held to apply to and include any person who has in his or her veins any negro blood whatever."—Anti-concubinage law.

Colorado

Negroes.
Mulattoes.

Delaware

Negroes.
Mulattoes.

Florida

Anyone having Negro blood "to the fourth generation" (1/16th Negro blood—as much as one Negro great-great-grandparent).— State constitution.

Anyone having 1/8th or more Negro blood (one Negro great grandparent or more).—Anti-miscegenation law.

Georgia

"The term 'white person' shall include only persons of the white or Caucasian race, who have no ascertainable trace of either Negro, African, West Indian, Asiatic Indian, Mongolian, Japanese, or Chinese blood in their veins.

"No person, any of whose ancestors has been duly registered with the State Bureau of Vital Statistics as a colored person or person of color, shall be deemed a white person."

Author's Note: The term "West Indian" may include anyone with a West Indies background, regardless of whether his antecedents were British, French or Spanish Caucasians, Negroes, or American Indians.

Idaho

Negroes.
Mulattoes.
Mongolians.

D

Indiana

Anyone having 1/8th or more Negro blood.

Kentucky

Anyone having 1/4th or more Negro blood.—Early anti-miscegenation court ruling.

Anyone having an "appreciable" amount of Negro blood.—Court decision (1911) imposing school segregation on a person having 1/16th Negro blood.

Louisiana

All "persons of color". Defined by courts to include anyone having 1/16th or more Negro blood. Louisiana courts have taken judicial cognizance of the following categories of colour.

Negro	.	.	. 3/4th or more Negro blood
Griffe	.	.	. 1/2 Negro, 1/2 mulatto
Mulatto	.	.	. 1/2 Negro, 1/2 white
Quadroon	.	.	. 1/4 Negro, 3/4 white
Octoroon	.	.	. 1/8 Negro, 7/8 white

Maryland

Anyone having Negro blood to "third generation inclusive" (1/8th or more Negro blood).

Malays.

Mississippi

Anyone having 1/8th or more Negro blood.—Anti-miscegenation law.

Anyone having any "appreciable" Negro blood.—Court ruling on school segregation.

Anyone having 1/8th or more Mongolian blood.

Evidence of Whiteness

Among the evidence of whiteness declared to be admissible by the courts is testimony to the effect that a person:

1. Is reputed to be white.
2. Associates with whites.
3. Enjoys high social status.
4. Exercises the rights of whites (attends white theatres, votes, etc.).

Evidence of Colour

Although in all ordinary cases the rules of evidence will permit only experts (as in ballistics, fingerprinting, handwriting) to voice their *opinions* from the witness stand, the courts in race cases will allow any witness to give his opinion as to the race of the defendant or party in question. No American court has ever called an anthropologist to appraise a person's race.

Any person whose race is being judicially appraised, as well as relatives both direct and collateral, may be required to appear in court and submit to a physical examination by judge and jury.

Physical appearance is regarded as among the best evidence of race. Photographs and hearsay are also admissible. Among the characteristics commonly held by courts to be evidence of Negro blood are dark complexion, curly hair, full lips, and broad nostrils. It has been ruled that for a person to prove he is of Sicilian or other Mediterranean stock does not necessarily prove he is white.

In conducting courtroom examinations into a person's race, one court required the witness to remove his shoes, it having been asserted that persons of colour have a peculiar configuration of foot.

Another court required a woman to bare her breasts to the jury, following testimony that the nipples of coloured women lack a pinkish pigmentation said to be found in white women only.

Appearance is Important

In many parts of the U.S.A., your race may be judged by the clothes you wear, the way you cut your hair, or the language or accent in which you speak.

If you are a white man and wish to avoid the many disabilities and hazards incumbent upon being nonwhite, you should avoid wearing anything suggestive of the so-called zoot-suit, whose distinguishing characteristics are a drape coat and peg trousers. The white community has come to look upon the zoot-suit as a badge of rebellion against its style dictates, and consequently not even a white person may wear one with impunity.

In 1943 in Los Angeles, California, a number of people were killed, hundreds were injured and thousands were arrested for no other ostensible reason than that they were wearing zoot-suits. In fact, the affair is known as the "Zoot-suit Riot". Most of the victims were of Mexican ancestry, although some were of Negro and Japanese antecedents. To cope with the situation, the Los Angeles City Council adopted a law forbidding the wearing of zoot-suits. Thousands of youths were caught in police dragnets (after being assaulted by gangs of U.S. servicemen), fingerprinted, photographed, their zoot-suits cut off, and their "Argentine ducktail" haircuts shaved.

Passing is Prohibited

In the 29 states having laws governing certain relations between whites and nonwhites, it is of course illegal for the latter to "pass" as the former, or vice versa, when such passing entails violation of the segregation or anti-miscegenation laws.

Nevertheless, an estimated five to eight million persons having some ascertainable amount of Negro blood have passed over into the white community, in order to enjoy the special privileges and immunities everywhere enjoyed by whites in the U.S.A. This explains what happened to the half-million persons who were registered as mulattoes in the Census of 1910, but as whites in 1920. Every year an estimated 50,000 Americans make this changeover. To facilitate such passing, a giant multi-million-dollar industry for skin bleaching, hair-straightening, and plastic surgery has developed.

When Jay Jones, a Creole native of New Orleans, applied at the Bureau of Vital Statistics for a copy of his birth certificate, the clerk discovered that on the original form the space for designating Jones' race had somehow been left blank.

"What is your race?" she asked Jones.

"What do you mean?" Jones countered. "I don't know—does it matter?"

"Why yes, we must put down either white or Negro."

"I don't think I'm either one."

"But you must put down something," the clerk insisted.

"Well, which one offers the most advantages?" Jones asked.

At that, the clerk handed him his birth certificate—the space for indicating race still blank.

For such "raceless" individuals to be at large in the segregated territory is said to create quite a problem for the law enforcement authorities; and it is to liquidate this legal problem that the laws are so stringently drawn for the specification of every individual's race according to fixed formulas. Every effort is made to eliminate the factor of "reasonable doubt" in the determination of race.

The advantages of passing are psychological, social, economic, political, and biological. In the matter of health and longevity, the advantages of living a white life are manifest. Because of their colour, whites enjoy better living conditions, sanitation, public health services, and medical facilities. The results are interesting.

For instance, if you live the life of a white the chances are that you will-live ten years longer than if you lived the life of a Negro.

As a white, there are only 43 chances out of 1,000 that your children will die at birth, as compared to 72 chances if you were a Negro. Moreover, the odds of your dying while giving birth are only 3 out of 1,000 if white, 8 if Negro.

Negroes are five times as likely as whites to contract tuberculosis, eight times as apt to get syphilis.

It Pays to Be Un-American, Sometimes

Interestingly, you will find that foreign-born nonwhites are sometimes extended all the privileges enjoyed by white Americans, while native-born nonwhites are relegated to second-class citizenship.

Thus, if you are an American nonwhite you may be able to achieve emancipation merely by affecting some foreign dress, accent, and a superior air.

The Rev. Jesse W. Routte of Jamaica, New York, found that by donning a turban and affecting a "slight Swedish accent" he could travel freely as a white man throughout the segregated territory, where he was treated as a "visiting dignitary". In conversing with whites he was careful not to forget his affected accent, lest he be "late getting home".

The affectation of a foreign accent has also proven effective in gaining admission to restaurants, hotels, and theatres which cater to whites only, in the nation's capital as elsewhere. If you are nonwhite, you may want to acquire some knowledge of a foreign language, such as Spanish, to this end.

A further example of the way it pays to look un-American took place when a group of 29 students from the University of Ohio—including natives of India, Brazil, Argentina, China, Norway, and Turkey— arranged through the Young Men's Christian Association to visit the nation's capital. When, upon their arrival, it was discovered that several of the Americans were Negroes, Y.M.C.A. officials insisted that they be quartered in the Negro branch of the organization.

The classic example of this sort of thing occurred during World War II, when captured Nazi German prisoners of war were welcomed to eat in a Southern restaurant, while American Negro soldiers were obliged to pass hungry through the town because there was no restaurant for Negroes.

That it pays to be un-American if you are nonwhite is further attested by the policy of the Congress of the U.S.A., which permits foreign-born nonwhites to dine in the House and Senate cafeterias at the invitation of a member, but not native-born nonwhite Americans.

According to a report of the Committee on Civil Rights in the Nation's Capital, a noted American Negro educator, having taken advantage of an invitation to dine in the House cafeteria, was approached by a Congressman who asked:

"Sir, are you a coloured man?"

"Yes."

"Are you an *American* coloured man?"

"Yes."

"Then you can't eat here!"

Needless to say, if you are a dark-skinned native of some foreign country, it will pay you to cling to your own national dress and accent while visiting in the U.S.A.

Race-changing

A number of American states have adopted laws requiring the registration of the race of each individual in the population. The Virginia Act of 1930, entitled *Preservation of Racial Integrity*, is typical of these. Even in some states which lack such laws the Bureau of Vital Statistics often takes an exceptional interest in the matter of race, as witness the following news item from the Miami, Florida, *Herald*:

BABY'S RACE "CHANGED"
BY CERTIFICATE SWITCH

An interchange of birth certificates made Friday in state records officially switched a Miami baby's race from Caucasian to negro.

The unusual quirk diverting the course of the 20-month-old girl's life was disclosed when the state registrar at Jacksonville directed the Miami office to substitute an adoption birth certificate listing the names of negro foster parents for the original birth certificate which recorded the natural parents as of white lineage.

On the face of the official records it appeared that a negro couple was adopting a white child.

The child was born to a 20-year-old white mother in Jackson

Memorial Hospital and kept for a year in a white family before its negroid characteristics became evident. The mother, months earlier, had been sent to a mental hospital.

The experience and precedents accumulated in the United States of America have provided the prototype for much of the Union of South Africa's *apartheid* segregation system. The U. of S.A.'s *Population Registration Act* of 1950, for example, has much in common with Virginia's *Preservation of Racial Integrity Act* of 1930. The former requires everyone in South Africa to carry an identity card complete with photo and labelling the bearer as "European" (white), "Coloured" (mixed white and nonwhite), "Asian", or "Bantu" (native African Negro).

Like an echo of the Miami, Florida, story of a decade earlier came the following United Press dispatch from Capetown, South Africa, in 1958:

"WHITE" MAN IN S. AFRICA
NOW OFFICIALLY COLORED

A young South African with two children who has lived all his life as a white man was informed today that in the future he would be considered colored under the dominion's Apartheid policy.

The decision was typical of hundreds made in the last four years but now being stepped up by a newly opened Regional Population Registration Office here.

The man until today held a responsible position in a white factory. He and his family lived in a European suburb.

In the future they will have to carry an identity card labelling them as non-white. The man will have to quit his job and his residential district. His children will have to go to colored schools.

The first indication that the family was suspect came a few weeks ago when the man and his wife were summoned to the Registration Office.

Tactfully the officials took notes of the color and texture of their hair, eyes, skin and bone structure of the face.

Then they were submitted to a searching inquiry on their ancestry, social habits, and friends. The classified details were sent to the administrative capital, Pretoria, and assessed by officials who had never seen the man or his wife.

No figures of how many South Africans are forced to change their "official" race status were immediately available.

In judicially appraising the race of registrants the South African magistrates have also generally made use of the precepts embodied in American court procedures and findings. Mass protest meetings took place in 1955 in Johannesburg, when hundreds of people who had been living as "Coloureds" were officially classified as "Bantu". A Labour Party member of the South African Parliament, Leo Lovell, pointed out that for a 25-year-old bricklayer who had been living as a "Coloured" to be reclassified as a "Bantu" represented, among other things, the imposing of a 40,000-dollar fine payable in monthly instalments—racial wage differentials being what they are.

In 1958, the United Press had this to say further about events in the U. of S.A.:

WHITE OR NONWHITE—
DOUBT IN SOUTH AFRICA

Thousands of people in the Cape Province are today on the thin edge of an awful doubt—are they white or nonwhite in the eyes of the law? And their doubt mounts daily into a nagging horror as they realize that the thud of a rubber stamp on an identity card may place them in another social world. For that official stamp could mean that they are no longer white. It could mean that they are colored—persons of another racial group—with all the humiliations and indignities that follow in the wake of racial reclassification.

For these people, living as they are today in the turmoil of uncertainty, will have to give up the social contacts they have enjoyed for years. They will have to live in a colored area. Their children will be taken from white schools and transplanted to institutions that cater to nonwhites.

And capping the misgivings is the knowledge that once they are reclassified the "Whites Only" notices in public places will apply to them.

Today, officials of the Interior Department are going ahead with their examination of some of those cases who they say are on the borderline between different racial groups.

The Population Registration Act is linked solidly with the Group Areas Act, which specifies certain areas for the various racial groups, and with the Mixed Marriages Act, which forbids marriage between persons of different racial groups.

It states that persons are classified as white if they are obviously white in appearance or by general repute and acceptance.

But if by general repute persons are colored they would not be considered white even if they are white in appearance. Anyone who has sunk culturally or socially into the lower group is considered to belong to that group. So the officials who sit in judgment decide to what racial group they belong by way of life as well as by appearances.

Reports based on the physical tests are conflicting. Interior Minister Dr. T. E. Donges himself admitted recently that the definitions of the Act on the different races are unsatisfactory.

Of course the U. of S.A. has only been seeking to administer such laws for a single decade. Those states of the U.S.A. which have pioneered in this field have long since ceased to experience any real practical difficulty in determining who is white and who is not. Indeed, the white community has constituted itself a Committee of the Whole (approximately) which maintains such a pervasive surveillance over the nonwhite community that passing, even in the larger cities, has been made surprisingly difficult. White Southerners quite generally fancy themselves "expert" in the detection of any admixture of Negro blood. Even they are under some constraint to proceed with caution, however. When a lower court in South Carolina ruled that a white person whom someone called a Negro could not sue for damages unless he could show specifically that he had been damaged thereby, the state's supreme court in 1957 overruled the lower court and reaffirmed that to call a white person a Negro is libellous *per se*.

CHAPTER 5

WHO MAY MARRY WHOM

"As to mixed marriages, the most delicate question of all, it is to be noted that 29 states—all those of the South and many in the Southwest—forbid it. In the North, such marriages are frowned upon, and represent an almost insignificant percentage."—*The American Negroes*, special bulletin published by the U.S. Information Agency, an adjunct of the State Department, 1957.

ON the basis of this peculiarly-phrased statement, one might conclude that the U.S. Government itself frowns upon "mixed marriages", or at least is noncommittal.

In any case, the fact remains that in 29 states of the U.S.A. it is against the law for persons of different race to make love, marry, or have children.

Should you enter into a forbidden interracial marriage in any of these states, your marriage would automatically be void; your children by any previous legal marriage might be taken from you by the state; your children by the interracial marriage would be branded illegitimate and might also be denied their rights of inheritance; and you and your spouse would be charged with lewd and lascivious conduct, a misdemeanour, a felony, or an infamous crime (depending upon the state), and fined and/or imprisoned for as long as ten years in some states. A number of states say that parties to such marriages *must* be sent to jail.

The Constitution of the U.S.A. says that "full faith and credit shall be given in each state to the public acts, records, and judicial proceedings of every other state". However, a Federal court has ruled that this "full faith and credit" clause does not require any state to recognize marriages which are contrary to the local idea of morality—such as an interracial marriage in one of the states which forbid such marriages.

If you are a *bona fide* resident of one of the 19 states which do permit interracial marriage, and you are a party to such a marriage, only two of the 29 prohibiting states—North Carolina and Louisiana—have indicated that they might recognize it as legal.

If you become party to an interracial marriage in some foreign country, it will not be recognized as legal in these 27 American states, even if you are a diplomatic representative not subject to certain other U.S. laws.

If you are a resident of North Carolina, Delaware, Maryland, Mississippi, Montana, Tennessee, Texas, or Virginia and go to some other state and enter into an interracial marriage where it is legal to do so, and then return to your home state, your marriage will be void therein and you may be prosecuted.

If your home is in Mississippi, Oklahoma, Tennessee, Texas, or Virginia, you will also be banished from ever again living within the boundaries of your home state, either with or without your illegal spouse. For example, in 1945 Ted Sesney, a white farmer, and his Negro wife, Josie Douglas, were banished from Oklahoma. Sesney served a year in prison for the offence.

Most of the 29 states which prohibit interracial marriage also prohibit sexual intercourse, cohabitation, and concubinage between the races.

Even in other states where there are ordinary laws against unmarried sexual intercourse, cohabitation, or concubinage, these laws are more strictly enforced when the partners are not of the same race.

If you are contemplating interracial matrimony, but are a resident of a state which does not permit it, steer clear of Massachusetts and Vermont in choosing a state in which to get married. Although permitting such marriages, these two states may void your marriage if it is shown that your intention was to evade the law of your home state and then return to it.

Some People Are 'Verboten'

Twenty-nine states declare marriages between whites and Negroes (variously defined) to be automatically void and non-existent.

Fourteen of these same states also prohibit marriages between whites and Mongolians.

Nine of them forbid marriages between whites and Malays.

Six bar matrimony between whites and American Indians, with two of these also ruling out marriages between whites and *mestizos*, and another banning marriage between whites and "halfbreeds".

Three also forbid Negroes and American Indians to intermarry.

Two prohibit marriage between whites and "Asiatic Indians" and another outlaws marriages between whites and "Hindus" (a religious group encompassing various ethnic groups).

One state outlaws marriage between whites and "West Indians" (a geographic designation actually including both whites and non-whites).

And one state will not permit the marriage of a Negro to a Malay.

If you are party to any one of these illegal combinations, the laws provide that *both* you and your spouse must either be convicted or acquitted (except in West Virginia, where the law punishes the *white* partner only). The only way to win an exception to this rule of mutual guilt is to plead ignorance of your partner's race.

In the matter of prohibited sexual intercourse, you may be prosecuted even though there are no third-party eyewitnesses, the courts having ruled that sexual intercourse may be inferred from circumstantial evidence. In some states, if you are white and male you may not be convicted on the unsupported testimony of your alleged partner. However, the courts have ruled that, "If two persons are seen nude, in bed together and in each other's arms, that is sufficient proof of the *corpus delicti* to admit in evidence a confession made by one of the defendants".

In Indiana or Mississippi it is against the law to so much as advocate social equality or intermarriage. The Mississippi law reads:

"Any person, firm, or corporation who shall be guilty of printing, publishing, or circulating printed, typewritten or written matter urging or presenting for public acceptance or general information, arguments or suggestions in favor of social equality or of intermarriage between whites and negroes, shall be guilty of a misdemeanor and subject to a fine not exceeding $500 or six months' imprisonment or both."

Efforts to censor educational materials which espouse democracy in human relations are constantly being made. Something new in this field arose with the advent of television, which caused great concern among white supremacists because it introduced animated, vocal, and oft-times amorous scenes involving white women into the *parlours* of those Negroes who could afford to buy television sets. Herman Talmadge, while Governor of Georgia (he is now a U.S. Senator), threatened to ban the television show headed by Arthur Godfrey, on the grounds that it included "The Mariners", a vocal quartet consisting of two white and two Negro veterans of World War II, on the same stage with "scantily clad white women".

Two Georgia legislators also announced that they were going to draft a law forbidding movies, plays, and musicals having "an underlying philosophy inspired by Moscow". This action was prompted by a showing in Atlanta of the musical stage show *South Pacific*, which the legislators felt condones interracial marriage.

"To us that is very offensive," Representative David C. Jones declared. "Intermarriage produces half breeds, and half breeds are not conducive to the higher type of society. We in the South are a proud and progressive people. Half breeds cannot be proud. In the South we have pure blood lines and we intend to keep it that way."

It was in 1953 that Georgia's newly created Obscene Literature Commission held its first session, under the chairmanship of the Rev. James Wesberry, who announced that even the nude art work of the great masters is offensive to him. "We are trying to be sane and do a good job," he added. It was proposed that the book *Southern Exposure*, by Stetson Kennedy, an *exposé* of the Ku Klux Klan and other antidemocratic elements, be banned on the grounds that it is "filled with filth". The only citation from the book offered in justification of this action was the statement by a Southern official that, "The only way we're willing to give the niggers equality is by f—ing them white".

Paradoxically, a Negro minister who had from his pulpit deplored sexual relations between white men and Negro women was soon visited by a deputation of white businessmen who warned him to stop voicing such sentiments.

If you believe that any two people have an inherent and inalienable right to fall in love, marry, and have children, regardless of race, it is only fair to warn you that the Constitutionality of laws forbidding interracial marriage has been upheld by the U.S. Supreme Court.

For the most part these laws were adopted after the Civil War, and have been successively strengthened. They are very much alive today, as witness the following cases:

Davis Knight, 23, who had served in the U.S. Navy as a white man, was sentenced (1940) to five years in the Mississippi penitentiary for marrying Junie Scradney, a white girl, after it was testified that his great-grandmother had been a Negro. Knight argued in vain that his great-grandmother was not a full-blooded Negro, and therefore that he himself was not a Negro according to the 1/8th-Negro blood definition established by law in Mississippi.

Clark Hamilton, 20-year-old Negro Navy veteran, was sentenced (1949) to serve three years in the Virginia penitentiary for marrying Florence Hammond, white. The couple had moved to Maryland, and his sentence was suspended after he pleaded guilty. But while awaiting trial he served 82 days in a Virginia jail, and his marriage was declared void.

An interesting case arose in Buffalo, New York, when (1949) New York State Supreme Court Justice Alger A. Williams ruled that Mr. and Mrs. Emerson Marshall of that city would have to surrender their 5-year-old daughter Mary to her maternal grandmother. Mrs. Marshall is white, while Mr. Marshall is of mixed Irish, American Indian, and Negro ancestry.

"This case poses a certain complicated and intricate social problem because of the peculiar facts involved," Judge Williams said. "It is a question of whether this girl is to be raised as white or colored."

In justification of his ruling taking the child away from its parents, he observed that Mr. Marshall was obviously "Negroid" and lived in a "colored neighborhood," that "the child has a dark skin, but her appearance does not necessarily denote colored blood", and that the grandparents (who were given custody of the child) "are white and live in a white neighborhood".

Judge Williams also took judicial note of the fact that the child's father earned only 200 dollars per month as a butcher, while the grandfather made 500 dollars per month as a railroad engineer. The judge ignored the report of the probation officer who had investigated the Marshall home at his order, and found it fit in every respect.

In a similar decision (1953), Judge Wakefield Taylor of Oakland, California, took away the two children—aged 10 and 3—of Mrs. Barbara Smith Taylor, after she divorced her husband and married a Negro. The father, Walter G. Smith, was awarded custody of the children when he contended that his former wife's marriage to a Negro was "detrimental to the children". He had the same to say of his ex-wife's progressive "political leanings". Judge Taylor took the children away from their mother despite pleas by the older daughter, Amanda, that she be allowed to stay with her mother. The testimony of social workers that the children had a happy home was also brushed aside.

There are cases on record where children have been taken from their mothers because they taught their children not to make racial discriminations. For example, an Oklahoma court decreed (1953) that

Jean Field was to be deprived of her two daughters, Jay, age 15, and Mary, age 13. In letters to her daughters while they were visiting their paternal grandparents, the mother had counselled them against racial prejudice and expressed opposition to the war in Korea. The children were ordered and placed in the custody of their father, despite the fact that he had deserted the family for ten years, admitted in court that he had been an alcoholic, and was guilty of such crimes as perjury, forgery, and incest.

So that's how things are. Before choosing a lover or spouse you may want to consult the following tabulation in order to acquaint yourself with the laws governing such matters in various states of the U.S.A.:

Love Limited by 29 States

Alabama

"The legislature shall never pass any law to legalize any marriage between any white person and a negro, or a descendant of a negro."—State Constitution. *Penalty*: "If any white person and any negro, or the descendant of any negro intermarry, or live in adultery and fornication with each other, each of them must, on conviction, be imprisoned in the penitentiary for not less than two nor more than seven years."

Anyone issuing a licence for an interracial marriage may also be punished.

Ministers or officials performing an interracial marriage may be fined from 100 to 1,000 dollars, and/or sentenced to six months in jail.

Court rulings: A single act of sexual intercourse, or cohabitation for a single day, is sufficient to convict, if it can be shown that the parties intend to continue the relationship.

The fact that the penalty for *interracial* sexual intercourse is greater than for cohabitation or adultery between two people of the *same* race does not make the former law unconstitutional under the Fourteenth Amendment guarantee of equal protection of the laws, because *both* parties to the offence must be punished equally.

In one Alabama case, a mulatto who applied for a licence to marry a "Creole" was arrested, and the judge left it to the jury to decide whether a Creole is white or coloured.

Arizona

Prohibits marriage between whites and anyone having any Negro blood whatever, or between whites and Hindus.

Arkansas

Under the contradictory laws of Arkansas, a person having any Negro blood may not engage in concubinage with a white, but may marry a white *provided* the Negro blood is not "visible and distinct".

"Concubinage between a person of the Caucasian or white race and between a person of the negro or black race is hereby made a felony."

Penalty: One month to one year "at hard labor" for each offence.

Court rulings: "Living together or cohabitation, whether open or secret", is contrary to law. However, "occasional intercourse" does not constitute concubinage or cohabitation. "No person shall be convicted of the crime of concubinage upon the testimony of the female, unless the same is corroborated by other evidence."

Childbearing: "Any woman who shall have been delivered of a mulatto child, the same shall be *prima facie* evidence of guilt without further proof and shall justify a conviction of the woman." It is the duty of magistrates to issue warrants in such cases in the name of the state, and to prosecute. No *Negro* mother of a mulatto child has ever been prosecuted under this law.

Registration: Clerks issuing marriage licences are required to register the race of both applicants, under penalty of a 25-dollar fine.

Divorce: Attorneys and chancery clerks are required to register the race of divorcing parties, "if other than Caucasian", under penalty of a 25-dollar fine.

Colorado

Forbids marriage between whites and Negroes, mulattoes. No definitions.

Penalties are provided for parties to and persons performing such marriages.

Delaware

Same. *Penalties* are provided for parties to such a marriage and for any person licensing it or performing or assisting at the ceremony.

Florida

Forbids marriage between whites and anyone having 1/16th or more Negro blood.

Forbids cohabitation between whites and anyone having 1/8th or more Negro blood. (Hence a white person and a person having 1/16th Negro blood, although they may not marry, may cohabit without violating the race law.)

"All persons of different race and opposite sex who habitually occupy the same room at night" shall be deemed guilty of concubinage, and punished. Offenders may be prosecuted at any time within two years following commission of the offence.

Whites and persons having 1/8th or more Negro blood who cohabit for even a single day are guilty of a criminal offence and are subject to punishment.

Any white woman who has sexual relations with a Negro man shall be fined 1,000 dollars. (No penalty provided for white men who have sexual relations with Negro women.)

Georgia

Forbids marriage between whites and: anyone having any "ascertainable trace of either Negro, African, West Indian, Asiatic Indian, Mongolian, Japanese, or Chinese blood in their veins".—State Constitution.

"It shall be unlawful for a white person to marry anyone except a white person."—Acts of 1927.

Applications for marriage licences must state the race of both applicants and their parents. False statements may be punished by imprisonment from two to five years. Anyone issuing a forbidden interracial marriage licence shall be fined 500 dollars or sentenced to 10 years. Parties to an interracial marriage are subject to imprisonment from one to two years. Ministers or officials knowingly performing such ceremonies are likewise subject to punishment.

Special prohibition: "Ordained colored ministers of the Gospel may celebrate marriages between persons of African descent only."

Registration: A state statute adopted in 1927 requires all persons in Georgia to register their race.

Childbearing: "When any birth certificate, showing the birth of a legitimate child to parents one of whom is white and one of whom is colored, shall be forwarded to the Bureau of Vital Statistics, it shall be the duty of the State Board of Health to report the same to the Attorney General of the State. Thereupon it shall be the duty of the Attorney General to institute criminal proceedings against the parents of such child."

Sexual Intercourse: "Any charge or intimation against a white female

B

of having sexual intercourse with a person of color is slanderous without proof of special damage."

Idaho

Forbids marriage between whites and: Negroes, mulattoes, Mongolians. No definitions.

Indiana

A marriage is void in any of the following circumstances:

1. When either party has a wife or husband living at the time of such marriage.

2. When either party is insane or idiotic at the time of such marriage.

3. When one of the parties is a white person and the other is possessed of 1/8th or more Negro blood.

Penalties: In the event of a forbidden interracial marriage, punishment is provided for:

1. Parties to the marriage.
2. Persons issuing the marriage licence.
3. Persons performing the marriage ceremony.
4. Anyone assisting at the ceremony.
5. Anyone who advised the marriage.

Kentucky

Prohibits marriage between whites and: Negroes, mulattoes.

Louisiana

Prohibits sexual intercourse, cohabitation, concubinage, and marriage between whites and all "persons of color". Persons of colour are defined by courts to include anyone having 1/16th or more Negro blood. The state also prohibits such relationships between American Indians and Negroes.

The right of the City of New Orleans to segregate white and non-white prostitutes has been upheld by the courts.

Maryland

Prohibits marriage between whites and: anyone having 1/8th or more Negro blood; Malays. Also prohibits marriage between Negroes and Malays.

"All marriages between a white person and a negro, or between a white person and a person of negro descent, to the third generation inclusive, are forever prohibited, and shall be void; and any person violating this section shall be deemed guilty of an infamous crime, and punished by imprisonment in the penitentiary not less than 10 months nor more than 10 years."

Childbearing: "Any white woman who shall suffer or permit herself to be got with child by a negro or mulatto" shall be sentenced to not less than 18 months nor more than 5 years.

A special law requires a white woman (but not a nonwhite woman) to divulge the name of the father of any illegitimate child she may bear, regardless of the race of the child. State courts have upheld this law as constitutional and not violating the equal protection guarantee of the Fourteenth Amendment.

Mississippi

Prohibits marriage between whites and anyone having 1/8th or more Negro or Mongolian blood. Cohabitation also prohibited between whites and anyone having 1/8th or more Negro blood. (Cohabitation between whites and Mongolians is not specifically banned.) This law does not apply to "occasional" sexual intercourse.

Inheritance laws give white descendants, regardless of whether legitimate or not, and no matter how remote, precedence over all descendants of mixed blood.

Divorce bills must include an affidavit as to both parties' race. Fee, 35 cents.

Missouri

Prohibits marriage between whites and: anyone having 1/8th or more Negro blood; Mongolians.

Montana

Prohibits marriage between whites and: anyone having any Negro blood whatever; Mongolians.

Penalties are provided for parties to the marriage, also for person performing the ceremony.

Nebraska

Prohibits marriage between whites and anyone having 1/8th or more Negro or Mongolian blood.

Nevada

Prohibits fornication, adultery, or marriage between whites and: Negroes, Mongolians, Malays, American Indians. No definitions.

Penalties are provided for parties to the marriage and persons performing and assisting at the ceremony.

North Carolina

Prohibits marriage between whites and anyone having 1/8th or more Negro or American Indian blood.

Penalties: Minimum of 4 months, maximum of 10 years imprisonment for parties to marriage, who may also be fined. Issuer of licence may be fined 500 dollars and imprisoned 10 years. Performer of ceremony may also be punished.

Special prohibition: Indians of Robeson County expressly forbidden to marry anyone having 1/8th or more Negro blood.

North Dakota

Prohibits fornication, cohabitation, adultery, and marriage between whites and anyone having 1/8th or more Negro or Mongolian blood.

Penalties are provided for parties to the marriage, and persons issuing the licence, performing the ceremony, or concealing the record.

Oklahoma

Prohibits marriage between anyone of "African descent" and: whites, American Indians.

Penalties are provided for parties to the marriage, for persons issuing the licence and officiating at the ceremony, and for anyone concealing the record.

Oregon

Prohibits marriage between whites and anyone having

> 1/4th or more Negro blood.
> 1/4th or more Chinese blood.
> 1/4th or more Kanaka (Malay) blood.
> 1/2 or more American Indian blood.

Penalties are provided for parties to the marriage and for persons issuing the licence and performing the ceremony.

South Carolina

"It shall be unlawful for any white man to intermarry with any woman of either Indian or negro races, or any mulatto, *mestizo*, or half-breed, or for any white woman to intermarry with any person, other than a white man, or for any mulatto, half-breed, Indian, negro or *mestizo* to intermarry with a white woman."—State Constitution.

Note: This law prohibits white women from marrying Mongolians or Malays, but leaves white men free to do so.

Court rulings: The South Carolina courts have defined a coloured person as anyone having 1/8th or more Negro blood.

Penalties: Parties to marriage and person performing ceremony are subject to a minimum fine of 500 dollars and/or a minimum jail sentence of 12 months.

Adoption: The adoption of a white child by a negro is expressly prohibited.

South Dakota

Prohibits sexual intercourse and marriage between whites and: Negroes, Mongolians, Malays. No definitions.

Tennessee

"The intermarriage of white persons with negroes, mulattoes, or persons of mixed blood descended from a negro, to the third generation inclusive, or their living together as man and wife in this state, is prohibited." Sexual intercourse and adultery between whites and Negroes are also expressly forbidden.

Texas

"If any white person and negro shall knowingly intermarry with each other in this state, or having so intermarried in or out of the state shall continue to live together as man and wife within this state, they shall be confined in the penitentiary not less than two nor more than five years."

Note. Due to a discrepancy in definitions as to what constitutes a Negro in Texas, all interracial marriages involving any Negro blood whatever are *void* in Texas, but the parties may not be *punished* unless the admixture of Negro blood is 1/8th or more.

Adoption: "No white child can be adopted by a negro person, nor can a negro child be adopted by a white person."

Special prohibitions: Sexual intercourse between whites and Negroes within the city limits of Fort Worth is prohibited by municipal ordinance.

Utah

Prohibits marriage between whites and: Negroes, Mongolians. No definitions.

Virginia

Prohibits marriage between whites and:

1. Anyone having any ascertainable Negro blood.
2. Anyone having more than 1/16th American Indian blood.
3. Mongolians.
4. Asiatic Indians.
5. Malays.

"It shall hereafter be unlawful for any white persons in this state to marry any save a white person, or a person with no other admixture of blood than white and American Indian. For the purpose of this Act, the term 'white person' shall apply only to the person who has no trace whatsoever of any blood other than Caucasian; but persons who have 1/16th or less of the blood of the American Indian and have no other non-Caucasian blood shall be deemed to be white persons.

"No marriage license shall be granted until the clerk or the deputy clerk has reasonable assurance that the statements as to color of both man and woman are correct. If there is reasonable cause to disbelieve that applicants are of pure white race, when that fact is stated, the clerk or deputy clerk shall withhold the granting of the license until satisfactory proof is produced that both applicants are 'white persons' as provided for in this Act.

"The clerk or deputy clerk shall use the same care to assure himself that both applicants are colored, when that fact is stated."

Penalties: Due to discrepancies in definitions, all forbidden interracial marriages are *void* whenever any ascertainable Negro blood is involved, but the parties may not be *punished* unless the admixture of Negro blood is 1/4th or more. The penalty is a minimum of 1 year and a maximum of 5 years in jail. The parties to the marriage may also be prosecuted for "lewd and lascivious cohabitation". The penalty for performing an interracial marriage is a 200-dollar fine, 100 dollars of which is set aside as a reward for the informer. Penalty for issuing the licence: 500 dollars and 10 years.

Registration: Act of 1930 entitled *Preservation of Racial Integrity*: "The state registrar of vital statistics may, as soon as practicable after the taking effect of this Act, prepare a form whereon the racial composition of any individual is shown as a Caucasian, Negro, Mongolian, American Indian, Malay, or any mixture thereof, or any other non-Caucasic strains, and if there be any mixture, then the racial composition of the parents and other ancestors, in so far as ascertainable, so as to show in what generation such mixture occurred."

Registration fee, 25 cents. Penalty for false registration: 1 year in jail.

West Virginia

Prohibits sexual intercourse and marriage between whites and Negroes. No definitions.

Penalties are provided for persons issuing the marriage licence and performing the ceremony and for *white* parties to such a marriage. (Texas once had a similar law punishing the white party only, which was upheld by the U.S. Supreme Court as a reasonable discrimination on the ground that Negroes had *no proper sense of moral responsibility.*)

Wyoming

Prohibits marriage between whites and: Negroes, mulattoes, Mongolians, Malays. No definitions.

CHAPTER 6

WHO MAY LIVE WHERE

ONCE you have found yourself a legal spouse of matching colour, your next problem will presumably be: Where to make a home?

If you are a Caucasian and a Christian, you are more or less free to live anywhere you can afford in the U.S.A.

But if you lack one or both of these qualifications you will find yourself barred by one or more such factors as laws, contracts, conspiracies, and terrorism from buying, leasing, renting, inheriting or otherwise acquiring or occupying a residence in many neighbourhoods, both desirable and undesirable.

It is true that Congress passed a law in 1866 which said: "All citizens of the United States shall have the same right, in every state and territory, as is enjoyed by white citizens thereof to inherit, purchase, lease, sell, hold, and convey, real and personal property."

But that law was repealed in 1894.

The Fourteenth Amendment to the Constitution—which was supposed to take the place of this law—does not assert any right to acquire property, but only forbids the states (*not individuals*) from depriving anyone of property without due process of law.

You can invoke Federal law against such discrimination only if your property was acquired in accordance with some Federal provision, as in the case of public lands made available for homesteading by the U.S. Government.

Needless to say, the restrictions against racial and religious minorities make housing more expensive for everybody.

If you *are* a Christian Caucasian, you have to pay extra for living in a neighbourhood restricted to your own race and creed.

If you *are not* a Christian Caucasian, you will generally have to pay more than your Christian Caucasian neighbours in order to live in a mixed neighbourhood. For instance, in a U.S. Supreme Court case it was shown that Negroes living in a mixed neighbourhood in Washington, D.C., are being charged 30 per cent more rent than their white neighbours.

Even if you make your abode in some non-Christian or non-Caucasian neighbourhood, you will probably be charged premium prices because of the housing shortage created by the restrictions on other sections.

Zoning by Law

For generations, residential zoning on a racial basis was widely accomplished in the U.S.A. by municipal laws, some of which were backed up by state statutes.

These laws set aside certain sections of the city for the exclusive habitation of whites, and consigned all nonwhites to other (undesirable) sections. The Virginia statute, adopted in 1912, was typical:

"The map so prepared and certified and corrected shall be *prima facie* evidence of the boundaries and racial designation of such districts. . . . Nothing contained herein shall preclude persons of either race employed as servants by person of the other race from residing upon the premises of which said employer is the owner or occupier."

Such laws were widely adopted in 1910 and in the years that followed. The courts of Virginia, Georgia, and Kentucky, among others, upheld these laws as a valid exercise of a state's powers "to promote the general welfare". North Carolina, on the other hand, ruled that such laws were contrary to public policy (the state at that time—1914—was trying to discourage its Negro citizens from moving to the North).

All racial zoning laws were ruled out in 1915 when the U.S. Supreme Court decided that they interfered with *the rights of owners to dispose of their property* to whomever they please. Proponents of the laws had argued that they helped to enforce anti-intermarriage laws and promoted more peaceful relations between the races.

Various states have since tried various ways to perpetuate racial zoning, with much success.

Some states adopted laws forbidding anyone to move into a block occupied *exclusively* by members of another race. Virginia tried a law forbidding anyone to move into a block *principally* inhabited by persons of another race with whom intermarriage is prohibited by law. But the U.S. Supreme Court ruled these out, too.

In Texas, large groups of private citizens drew up signed agreements as to racial boundaries within their communities, and these communities then passed laws to enforce these agreements. But the state courts ruled this out.

In Louisiana, the city of New Orleans passed a law requiring a prospective home-purchaser to get the consent of a majority of the racial group which predominated in the subdivision. But a test case was brought, and the Supreme Court said no to this.

In Oklahoma, Governor "Alfalfa Bill" Murray in 1935 declared martial law to enable Oklahoma City to pass a law setting up racial boundaries and prescribing punishment for each day anyone resided out of bounds, including those whose homes were already established. But the Supreme Court, when called upon, ruled against this also.

An untested law in Louisiana says you cannot occupy space in an apartment building in which members of another race also live, even if there are partitions between the races and separate entrances for each (exception is made where persons of one race are employed as servants of the other).

In Alabama, the courts ruled in 1926 that there is an *unwritten covenant* embracing all white people in the state not to rent an apartment to Negroes in the same building with whites. In a case where this unwritten covenant was violated, the court ruled that the aggrieved white occupants could sue the owner for (in effect) evicting them, and also claim damages for mental anguish suffered from having to share toilet facilities with nonwhites.

Despite the rulings obtained from the U.S. Supreme Court against racial zoning laws, many such laws remain on the books, and are enforced by social pressure and terrorism just as effectively as they formerly were by court action.

In fact, the City of Birmingham, Alabama, in 1949 proceeded to re-enact and enforce an ordinance forbidding Negroes to move into white neighbourhoods and vice versa, until again stopped by the courts.

The plain truth is that, whether you are white or nonwhite, any attempt on your part to live under the same roof with anyone of the other race in the South—unless he is your employer or employee—will be met with instantaneous police action. The customary charge in such cases is "disorderly conduct". This taboo extends also to whites visiting Negroes in their homes, and vice versa.

You will also find racial zoning now being enforced by municipal zoning commissions, many of which refuse to issue building permits to non-Christians and non-Caucasians in Christian Caucasian neighbourhoods.

The Miami, Florida, zoning commission denied a permit for the construction of a housing project for Negroes, following protests by the Press, Ku Klux Klan, and Businessmen's Association that the proposed site was in a section set aside for whites only.

Similarly, building inspector Carl Horns of Milton, Massachusetts, ordered a halt in the construction of a Jewish Centre (where religious as well as recreational activities were to be conducted), even though zoning regulations for the neighbourhood specifically permitted the building of "houses of worship".

Still another means of perpetuating and extending racial zoning is through real estate boards and commissions. Many of these organizations of realtors—licensed by the states—have a written or unwritten policy of refusing to rent or sell to non-Christians in Christian neighbourhoods or to non-Caucasians in Caucasian neighbourhoods.

For instance, the Code of Ethics adopted by the Real Estate Board of Washington, D.C. (1948) provides: "No property in a white section should ever be sold, rented, advertised, or offered to colored people." This Board takes the position that a neighbourhood is white if 50 per cent or more of its residents are whites.

The Georgia Real Estate Commission has revoked the licences of Atlanta firms accused by Ku Klux Klansmen of selling white property to Negroes.

If a white purchases a dwelling on the assurance of the owner or realtor that it is in a white neighbourhood, and it turns out to be in a Negro neighbourhood, the purchaser can charge fraud and sue for damages.

Zoning by Covenant

If you are a non-Caucasian—and in many instances if you are non-Christian—you cannot acquire a home in some 40 million dwelling units in the U.S.A., due to restrictive covenants entered into by their previous and present owners.

Such covenants cover about 90 per cent of all housing erected in the U.S.A. since World War II, leaving 10 per cent from which you may choose freely.

Most of these covenants are "perpetual", with each successive owner pledging never to dispose of the property in any manner to a non-Caucasian, non-Christian, or whatever other minority is forbidden.

Among the groups frequently barred—besides Negroes and Jews—

are "Orientals, Mongolians, Syrians, and American Indians". The result has been a substantial ghettoization of American life.

In some covenants the language is so vague as to give rise to much confusion. For instance, a West Virginia covenant barring "Ethiopians" has been held by a court to exclude all Negroes; while in a midwestern case the white Native Sons of the Golden West (a Klan-like group) asked the courts to rule that a covenant barring "Orientals" excluded American Indians as well as Asians.

Over a period of years restrictive covenants were upheld by the courts of many states. In virtually every other state, covenants were adhered to without being tested in the courts.

California—which has a law prohibiting any limitation of the right of property-owners to dispose of their holdings—ruled out covenants against *selling* and *renting* to certain minority groups, but upheld covenants barring *occupancy*. As a result, certain minorities were free to purchase such property, but could not occupy it. Michigan, Ohio, and West Virginia took this same position.

Illinois approved bans against both purchase and occupancy in 1937, and New York did likewise the same year. In the New York case, the court enforced a covenant barring the purchase of a certain lot by "Negroes". The couple who wished to make the purchase consisted of a man who was 3/4ths Negro and 1/4th white, and his wife who was 1/8th Negro and 7/8ths white. (Had the court considered the couple as an entity, its composition would have been 9 parts white and 7 parts Negro.)

Some states have held such covenants to be binding even though the covenanted property in time became surrounded by Negroes. For instance, the District of Columbia once refused to let a white man sell his covenanted property to Negroes, ruling that its having been surrounded by Negroes did not necessarily render it unfit for occupancy by whites.

Conversely, Illinois, California, Kansas, and Missouri ruled that when the racial composition of a neighbourhood changed, restrictive covenants were no longer binding.

In 1948 a ruling was won from the U.S. Supreme Court that no *court* may be called upon to *enforce* a restrictive covenant.

This decision did not invalidate the covenants which then covered 40 million dwellings, nor did it put a stop to the making of such covenants. As the *Atlanta Constitution* said, the Supreme Court "backed into a decision that segregation of races in housing may be accomplished by voluntary agreement and such agreements may not be set aside by law".

A nation-wide survey conducted by the United Press in 1949 found no breakdown in existing covenants. and no decrease in the number of covenants being entered into. In addition, the U.P. found covenants were being enforced effectively by banks and loan companies, most of which refuse to finance the purchase or repair of a home that is "out of bounds".

Besides this, it appears to be possible for a neighbour to sue you for damages if you violate a covenant, by charging that you have caused a depreciation in the value of his adjacent property.

In fact, if you so much as advertise property in a Christian Caucasian neighbourhood as being available to Negroes and Jews, you may be sued by persons living in the neighbourhood.

On the other hand, even if you are a Negro you have a right to acquire a home *close* to a white residence in some sections of the U.S.A., some courts having ruled that a Negro dwelling is not a nuisance *per se*.

But if you deliberately deceive anyone as to your race or religion in order to rent or buy a home, he can go into court and have the lease or sale declared void. This is likewise true if you employ some agent, of acceptable race or faith, to make the transaction for you.

However, if you are prohibited by covenant from purchasing a desired property, you might find it practical to incorporate your family and make the purchase in the name of the corporation. A Virginia court has ruled that a corporation has no race; and it would also seem to have no religious faith.

Of course, even in the absence of a restrictive covenant, if you are a member of some minority group you will find that many Christian Caucasians will simply *refuse* to rent or sell to you.

Negroes were not permitted to rent apartments in the Metropolitan Life Insurance Company's Stuyvesant Town project in New York City, long after a majority of the occupants petitioned the Company not to discriminate.

If you happen to be one of the nearly 100,000 persons of Chinese ancestry in the U.S.A., you will know that 80 per cent of your kind are forced by various pressures to live in the congested "Chinatown" slums of the following cities:

San Francisco	Philadelphia
Los Angeles	Washington, D.C.
New York	Detroit
Chicago	Baltimore
Portland	St. Louis
Seattle	Pittsburgh
Boston	

The "Yellow Ghetto" of the City of San Francisco is the most populous of these, containing 40 per cent of all the Chinese in California and 22 per cent of all the Chinese in the U.S.A. According to the San Francisco Housing Authority, 81·9 per cent of the Chinese-occupied dwellings in that city are sub-standard, as compared to 19·7 per cent sub-standard dwellings in the rest of the community. Similar conditions obtain in the other Chinatowns across the country.

"The heart of Chinatown is frustrated, perplexed, discontented, restless", reports the *Christian Science Monitor*. "The patience of the Chinese is legendary. In the United States for ninety-two years they have endured hardship, racial persecution, social degradation, without complaint outwardly, without uprising, without inefficiency. But things are different in Chinatown today. Both the old and the new generation have become highly skeptical, not only of the value of acquiring an education, but of American political ideals."

A classic example of racial "zoning" carried out by the U.S. Government was the forcible uprooting and evacuation of 110,000 Americans of Japanese ancestry from the Pacific coast of the U.S. following the Japanese attack upon Pearl Harbor. (No such action was taken against Americans of German or Italian descent following the outbreak of hostilities with those countries.)

These Japanese-Americans were confined to barbed-wire concentration camps in the American desert for the duration of the war. After the war, the U.S. Court of Appeals declared that the camps were "unnecessarily cruel and inhuman" and "in major respects as degrading as a penitentiary". To this the Supreme Court eventually added that the Government had had no Constitutional right to take such "discriminatory action against these people wholly on account of their ancestry". Many of the persons thus held became so embittered they renounced their American citizenship. An incidental effect of their persecution by the Government was to create such a wave of anti-Japanese feeling that some Chinese-Americans (soon after Pearl

Harbor) felt obliged to wear placards identifying themselves as such, to avoid being mobbed.

While the war was still in progress, California sought to make permanent the grip which white persons had gained on the extensive holdings formerly held by these Japanese residents; a law forbidding persons of Japanese ancestry to acquire property in the state was adopted, but was overthrown by the courts. At the war's end, terrorism was invoked to the same end.

In a typical case, Army Privates Alvin and Elmer Johnson and bartender James Watson were acquitted at Auburn, California, of attempting to burn and dynamite the home of Sumio Doi, a native-born American of Japanese ancestry whose brothers served in the American Army. The defence attorney made no effort to refute the charges, but instead cited Japanese war crimes. The judge also permitted him to conclude his appeal to the jury with these words: "This is a white man's country—let us keep it so!"

The U.S. Government has almost invariably followed a policy of racial segregation in its housing activities.

In fact, a Federal Housing Administration *Manual* has declared: "Protective covenants are essential to the sound development of harmonious neighborhoods."

With a few exceptions outside the South, all of the public housing projects built by the U.S. Government are either for whites only or for Negroes only. This is likewise true of U.S. Government housing in the Panama Canal Zone.

Local custom is *not* the determining factor in all this. For instance, when the Federal Government built a wartime housing project at Willow Run, Michigan, Negroes were excluded, even though there was no tradition of racial segregation in the community.

"The Federal Housing Administration has never insured a loan to build a housing project of mixed occupancy", F.H.A. Assistant Commissioner W. J. Lockwood pointed out in 1949.

In considering applications for loans to build both individual and project housing, the F.H.A. official said that racial, religious, and national characteristics "are given the same consideration as all other characteristics".

"If infiltration will be unacceptable to the local real estate market and desirability of properties will be reduced in the market's mind, the F.H.A. must recognize these conditions", the F.H.A. said.

In 1950, the F.H.A. announced that thenceforth it would not insure any loans for dwellings covered by restrictive covenants. This created a furore, and many municipalities rejected Federal housing loans which had already been approved. To cope with this situation, the F.H.A. issued a supplementary announcement explaining that its ban only had to do with *written* covenants, thus making it clear that loans could be had for construction of dwellings that would be segregated by other means.

Three years later, United Press reported: "Republicans and Southern Democrats of the House of Representatives combined today to reject the first civil rights legislation of the new Congress—an attempt to ban Government-insured loans unless property-owners bar racial or other discrimination." The vote was 49 to 16.

That the problem is a continuing one is indicated by the fact that in 1958 the National Association for the Advancement of Coloured People called upon the Federal Government to hold upan 18,000,000-dollar slum clearance programme launched by Atlanta, Georgia, charging that Negro slums were being ignored and that the new construction for whites was designed to accentuate the pattern of residential segregation in the city.

Zoning by Terror

If you are of the Negro race or Jewish faith, you will find yourself barred by terrorism from establishing residence in many American communities. A number of all-white Southern towns display signs at their city limits such as this:

> Nigger, If You Can Read
> You'd Better Run;
> If You Can't Read
> You'd Better Run Anyway!

Similarly, the Ku Klux Klan burned a fiery cross in Mattituck, New York, leaving a placard reading:

> The Jews Are Invading Mattituck!
> No Jews Wanted Here!
> K K K

That such threats are not idle was shown by an incident at Palmer, Tennessee. According to the Associated Press, Dr. Oscar Clements, white, being unable to find any bricklayers in Grundy County, employed four Negro bricklayers from Chattanooga. But the Negroes were driven away by a band of white men who told them, "We won't even allow Negroes to come into Grundy County, much less work here."

However, if you care to run the risk of incurring mob action such as that, you do have, nominally, a Federally-guaranteed right to establish residence in any community in the U.S.A. But not since 1903 has the Federal law against conspiracy been used against a community for excluding Negro residents, though such communities continue numerous.

Since the breakdown of legalistic devices for maintaining race segregation in housing has been going on for some time, terrorism, as the ultimate weapon, is currently being applied in this sphere more than in any other.

Rather much of this activity is of an organized nature, the most prominent groups being so-called Home-owners' Protective Associations.

"Race segregation here is a natural state, and certain groups which agitate against it are unscrupulous and un-American", the president of the Federation of Citizens' Associations of Washington, D.C., has said.

Local officers of these groups are often more outspoken.

"It's too bad you can't take a nice healthy club or crowbar and lay the niggers in the gutter where they belong!" said a speaker before the Dahlgreen Terrace Citizens' Association in Washington, D.C.

Some of these associations are fronts for the Ku Klux Klan.

One such is the West End Co-operative Corporation of Atlanta, Georgia, presided over by Joseph M. Wallace, a leading member of Klan Klavern No. 297. This Corporation's slogan is "Not strife, but psychology". Wallace claims to have 1,500 "watchdogs" scattered through Atlanta, who telephone him the moment they see a Negro moving into a white section. A mob is quickly mobilized by telephone, and Wallace assures the Negro of his right to move in—but warns that there will probably be violence if he does.

This procedure represents a refinement over the technique of the K.K.K.'s housing Kommittee, which simply pays nocturnal visits to Negroes living in white neighbourhoods and tells them to move out in ten days "or else". In most cases the Negroes move, leaving signs reading:

For Sale

To White People Only

F

The Klan has long served as an unofficial police force for maintaining racial zoning.

When a housing project for Negroes was proposed at Miami, Florida, robed and hooded Klansmen touched off fiery crosses on the four boundaries of the site, burned several Negro homes in the vicinity, and announced from a sound-truck: "When the law fails you, call on us!"

Another typical bit of Ku Kluxery came when Mrs. J. W. Sweat, a Negro schoolteacher who had moved into a white neighbourhood in Richmond, Virginia, received a letter containing a bullet and a note from the K.K.K. reading: *You are not smart.*

An offshoot of the Klan—sometimes referred to as the "juvenile delinquents of the K.K.K."—was the Columbians, Inc., a brown-shirted storm-trooper movement which cropped up in Atlanta in 1946. The special function assumed by the Columbians was the turning back of what it called the "nigger invasion" of white neighbourhoods. Zoning placards were posted, and were backed up by Columbian patrols armed with blackjacks, knuckle-dusters, pistols, and dynamite. A number of Negro homes were dynamited, and one Negro youth, Clifford Hines, was held at gunpoint and blackjacked into unconsciousness for "walking down the wrong side of the street"—even though he had lived on that side of the street for four years.

One of the most common forms of intimidation employed against persons who establish residence in the "wrong" neighbourhood is a barrage of threatening telephone calls and letters.

When William Lowe of East Orange, New Jersey, advertised his home for sale to either white or Negroes, he received numerous threats, including one which read: *Sell to Negroes and Suffer.*

Should you persist in living in the "wrong" neighbourhood, your house may be picketed, stoned, bombed, or burned during the night. For example, in Chicago 167 homes established by Negroes in white neighbourhoods were bombed during the two years immediately following the end of the Second World War, killing four persons, permanently crippling eight, and injuring scores of others. During the following decade, hundreds of Negro homes have been bombed in Atlanta, Birmingham, Miami, and other cities across the country. The pattern has been much the same. . . .

When Negro postal clerk Roscoe Johnson purchased a home in a white Chicago neighbourhood, a mob of 2,000 whites surrounded it and hurled stones and firebrands through the windows. Johnson and his wife were obliged to lie upon the floor all night to avoid being struck. Two hundred policemen assigned to patrol the spot made no effort to disperse the mob.

At Cicero, Illinois, police at first prevented Mr. and Mrs. Harvey Clark from moving into an apartment building occupied by whites. When a Federal court intervened, a white mob formed and reduced the interior of the building to a shambles. Of the 120 mobsters arrested, two were convicted and fined 10 dollars each. A grand jury proceeded to indict the owner of the building, the rental agent, and the attorney of the victim. A year later, Cicero's Chief of Police and two policemen were fined from 250 to 2,000 dollars, but the fines were rescinded another year later by the U.S. Court of Appeals. Eventually, the owner of the building, Mrs. Camille Derose, sued the Clarks and eleven other Negroes for 1,000,000 dollars, charging that they had conspired to defraud her and send her to prison and a mental institution (she was admitted to the latter).

Similar violence may be encountered even in connection with housing facilities over which the U.S. Government has jurisdiction. Such was the case when a number of Negroes were stoned upon trying to move into the Sojourner Truth Housing Project, which the Federal Government originally built for them in Detroit. Named after a Negro ex-slave woman who helped slaves escape from Southern plantations to the North, the housing project was diverted for occupancy exclusively by whites at the time of its completion.

In 1951, Miami was rocked by a series of blockbuster dynamite bombings, which did hundreds of thousands of dollars' damage to apartment buildings which had been built privately for occupancy by Negroes.

When Mr. and Mrs. Carl Braden, white, of Louisville, Kentucky, went to the aid of a Negro whose newly-acquired home in a white neighbourhood was under siege by a mob, they were both arrested and placed under heavy bond on a charge of "criminal sedition".

In 1957, when William Myers, his wife Daisy, and their three children moved into a new home in Levittown, Pennsylvania (population 60,000, previously all white), they had to personally carry in their furnishings through a hail of missiles, some of which struck a state policeman and a photographer.

That same year, Willie Mays, Negro centre-fielder of the San Francisco Giants baseball team, was refused the right to purchase a home on Miraloma Drive. Edward Howden, director of the San

Francisco Council for Civic Unity, said: "The shocking rejection of Mr. and Mrs. Willie Mays as neighbors by a handful of Miraloma Drive residents is nothing less than a civic disgrace. Regrettably, it is typical of practices in a large portion of the private housing market today."

It was also in A.D. 1957 that the "American Resettlement Foundation" (a brainchild of Roy Harris, high priest of the Talmadge political machine in Georgia) announced that it had taken an option on a 75,000-dollar six-bedroom, three-bath house in the fashionable Wesley Heights section of Washington, D.C., "a few doors from the home of one of the leading exponents of integration", and that a Georgia Negro family "with ten or fifteen kids" would be moved into it. The neighbour in question was Vice-President Richard Nixon. The Foundation said it would undertake such "resettlement" on a massive scale.

Shortly afterwards, the American Resettlement Foundation (chartered by the State of Georgia) sent five of its officials, headed by Georgia legislator Alpha Fowler, on a cross-country "reconnoitering" expedition which ranged from Kansas City to Seattle. Besides "threatening" to install Negroes in the neighbourhood of Vice-President Nixon, they likewise turned their attention to the neighbourhood of Democratic Senator Hubert Humphrey. Said the committee to the Press: "What we're going to resettle is the blue-gum, stinking scum of the earth, the niggers with common-law wives and passels of little black bastards!"

Unique in American history was a reception given in 1958 by William Atkins, white, of Norwalk, Connecticut, to welcome Mr. and Mrs. Robert J. Randall, Negroes, to the neighbourhood. The party was attended by some thirty white neighbours, and the Randalls said they were made to feel "more than welcome".

The U.S. Information Agency, in its bulletin, *The American Negroes*, makes no mention of the widespread violence which seeks to perpetuate segregation in housing, asserting instead that, "The rapport between the races, where residence is mixed, is very satisfactorily resolved after a period of becoming accustomed".

From Here to Eternity . . . ?

The U.S. Information Agency, in this same bulletin, poses magniloquently the question: "There being no segregation after death, why segregation, then, in life?"

Perhaps the authors were not aware that the notion that nonwhites are not fit to occupy the same ground with whites is enforced in death even as in life in a great many places in the U.S.A.

Not only are Negro corpses commonly barred from burial in white cemeteries; in the nation's capital a cemetery for pets refuses to inter the remains of pets that were owned by Negroes.

For many years, Japanese residents of the Los Angeles area who have sought to bury their dead in the "public" paupers' field have been turned away by the authorities with the explanation that the "Japanese sector" of the burial ground has been filled. The problem of finding a burial ground for these Japanese-Americans has long been a major project of the Los Angeles Japanese Chamber of Commerce.

Not even the original Americans, who once possessed the whole continent, can be sure of finding in death an escape from the colour bars erected by the white man. The body of an American Indian who fell in the Korean War was denied burial in the cemetery of his home town in the midwest, and had to be transhipped elsewhere for interment.

Segregation is not the only hazard. If you are of the Hebrew faith you may find no peace beyond the grave in the U.S.A., where anti-Semitic vandals vie with their ideological cousins in West Germany in desecrating Jewish cemeteries. To cite but one clipping from the thick scrapbook:

Albany, New York, May 12, 1958—UP—Vandals roamed through three Jewish cemeteries on the outskirts of Albany last night, heavily damaging three chapels, and ripping up 40 burial stones. The Hebrew Tailors' Cemetery estimated damage to its chapel alone at between 15,000 and 20,000 dollars.

CHAPTER 7

WHO MAY STUDY WHERE

NOT only your class, but your race, religion and ancestry may largely affect for better or worse your opportunities for education in the U.S.A.

The system of separate schools for white and Negro children, imposed by law for nearly three-quarters of a century in seventeen states and the nation's capital, has been most conducive to inequality of opportunity. Although the U.S. Supreme Court was at length prevailed upon in 1954 to rule against compulsory race segregation in the public schools, the decision has been slow in taking effect, and powerful forces are at work to subvert it altogether; so it might not be amiss to look into the history and provisions of these laws.

Most of these laws require segregation at all levels of public education, and some, like that of Kansas, apply to private schools as well.

Florida, Oklahoma, Kansas, Tennessee, and other states have made it a criminal offence to permit children of different race to attend the same school, the latter state stipulating a fine of 50 dollars and imprisonment from one to six months.

Georgia law is content to say: "No teacher receiving or teaching white and colored pupils in the same school shall be allowed any compensation at all out of the common school funds." The state also denies tax-exempt status to any private school which might admit students of both races.

Various states have gone to various extremes in their determination to keep education of the races as separate as possible.

Texas law, in requiring school officials to keep a census of all children living in their district, stipulates that the names of white and Negro children be kept on *separate lists*.

Mississippi law (Act of 1940) requires that the free textbooks provided by the state for white and Negro students be kept in *separate warehouses*. Furthermore, white and Negro applicants for teaching licences are required by law to take their examinations in *separate rooms*.

South Carolina law contains a proviso: "Persons having less than 1/8th Negro blood shall be entitled to full rights of full-blooded whites, provided however that full-blooded whites do not object to their attending a common school; if there is objection, the state is obligated to provide a separate school for the mixed-bloods, neither white nor colored."

American Indian children are likewise commonly barred from attending white schools. Mississippi law provides: "In a county where there are Indian children, or children of any race not otherwise provided for by law with educational advantages, the county board may locate one or more schools exclusively for Indians, or children of such other race."

Persons of Mexican descent are also very often assigned to separate schools, despite a 1946 ruling against the practice (handed down by Federal Judge Paul J. McCormick in Los Angeles).

In the nation's capital, separation of schools according to race was based upon a Congressional Act of 1878. The U.S. District Court of Appeals in Washington ruled that all children having 1/16th or more Negro blood were precluded by law from attending white schools in the capital. This was reconfirmed in 1947, when a U.S. District Judge in Washington threw out the petition of Marguerite Daisy Carr, Negro, 13, who had asked that she be permitted to attend a white school because the Negro school, due to overcrowding, offered only a half day of study.

In addition to the seventeen states which have laws requiring separate schools, Arizona requires segregation in elementary schools and makes it permissive in high schools; and New Mexico, Maryland, and Wyoming have state laws expressly permitting local school authorities to segregate—the latter state restricting this privilege to cities of more than 15,000 population.

Certain other states, including Ohio, Pennsylvania, Illinois, and New York, have condoned a considerable amount of segregation in schools in certain sections, achieved by one or more of the following extra-legal means:

1. The gerrymandering of school districts to conform with already-segregated residential areas.
2. Edicts of school boards.
3. Discriminatory action by school principals.
4. The issuance of "permits" to Negro students, forcing them to travel outside the district in which they live to some other district which has a Negro school.

5. Social pressures against Negroes enrolling in white schools.

So effective have such methods been that the N.A.A.C.P., in a survey of 37 Pennsylvania communities in 1948, was obliged to conclude that at least a third of them were formally compelling white and Negro students to go to separate schools.

Most of the state school segregation laws make use of the phrase "separate but equal", though the North Carolina law speaks merely of "equal opportunities".

In reality, of course, the facilities provided have been far from equal. In fact, the burden of maintaining a dual system has resulted, in the relatively poor South, in lowering the standards of white education to such an extent that Army intelligence tests during World War I revealed higher ratings by Northern Negroes than Southern whites.

Official U.S. Government figures have shown, throughout the decades, the gross discrepancies between white and Negro educational facilities in the states segregated by law.

The value of school property accessible to you, if Negro, is less than one-fourth what it would be if you were white.

The annual *per capita* expenditure by the state on your schooling, if Negro, is but one-half what it would be if you were white.

Your chances of getting a ride to school on a free school bus are but one-third those of a white student.

Your classrooms, overcrowded in any case, will contain on the average an additional dozen students if you are attending a Negro school.

Functional illiteracy (five years of schooling or less) is three times more prevalent among young Southern Negroes than among young Southern whites.

Even so, the racial differential in the quality of instruction offered in the South is so great that you might not learn as much in six years as a white child learns in three.

Should you succeed in getting more than six years of schooling, if Negro you will be offered only such vocational courses as bricklaying, carpentry, and sewing, whereas if you were white you would be given a chance to study such things as aviation, printing, and cosmetology.

Only about 10 per cent of the Negroes in America have been able to complete ten years of school, whereas 30 per cent of the native-born whites get that far.

Although a fourth of the South's school children are Negroes, almost no Negroes have ever been permitted to sit on state or local school boards in this region.

The Lowdown on Higher Education

So you want to go to college!

Perhaps you've heard that in America even a poor boy can work his way through . . .

But, rich or poor, before you start there are some other things you ought to hear about, if you are not white and Christian.

Only about 7 per cent of native-born white Americans have finished as much as four years of college, 3 per cent of foreign-born whites, and 2 per cent of Negroes.

Negroes have been barred not only from the state-supported white colleges throughout the region where race segregation has been the law, but also from a great many of the private universities throughout the land. Consequently you will find, if Negro, that 85 per cent of your kind are perforce enrolled in Negro colleges.

The discrepancy which is so marked between white and Negro primary and secondary schools in the segregated states rises to even higher levels in the realm of higher education. In this segregated region, the ratio of public and private expenditures for white colleges as compared to Negro ranges from 42 to 1 in Kentucky to 3 to 1 in Washington, D.C.

Outside this territory the practices of private universities vary, from a minimum of discrimination against Negroes at such institutions as Harvard, Columbia, and the University of Chicago to the lily-white policy of Princeton and the "token Negro" formula of many minor colleges.

Such state-supported facilities as are available to Negroes in the seventeen states which have segregation laws are extremely limited in certain spheres of advanced study. No such Negro institution in this region offers degrees in medicine, dentistry, pharmacy, or philosophy. Only one offers a degree in social work, and one in library science. A bare half-dozen include some sort of law school.

One result of this is that, of the approximately 4,000 Ph.D. degrees issued in the U.S.A. in a recent year, only 8 went to Negroes.

Despite the dire need of the Negro population for more physicians, it is extremely difficult for Negroes to obtain training in this field. Of the 77 medical colleges in the U.S.A., 20 are located in the South and will accept no Negroes. Of the remaining 57, only 19 will admit Negroes. Out of the total of approximately 600 Negro medical students enrolled in a recent year, less than 100 were in white medical colleges. Howard, a private Negro university near Washington, is able to take in 75 medical students per year; its yearly applications average well over a thousand. The same is true of Howard's dental school.

If you are a Negro and want to be a nurse, this is to advise you that 1,214 of the 1,280 nursing schools in the U.S.A. are open to whites only.

Getting a college education in the U.S.A. often depends on still other factors than the colour of your skin.

A survey by the New York State Commission on the Need for a State University has examined the application forms of 125 colleges located in that state. Of these, 67 per cent required a photograph of the applicant, 63 per cent asked the mother's maiden name, 53 per cent inquired about the parents' birthplace, 32 per cent wanted to know the applicant's religion, and 16 per cent asked about race or colour. The Commission came to the "inescapable conclusion" that the institutions were "extremely anxious to ascertain the racial origins, religion, and color of the various applicants for a purpose other than judging their qualifications for admission".

The situation is much the same everywhere in the U.S.A.

For instance, the University of Southern California—should you apply there—will want to know whether you are "Anglo-Saxon, French, Germanic, Italian, Negro, Oriental, Scandinavian, Slavonic, or Spanish".

The University of Virginia—perhaps less particular—will ask you to specify whether you are "English, French, Hebrew, or Italian".

Should you come across an application blank which does not ask such questions, you shouldn't think that this necessarily means the doors of that institution are wide open. As pointed out by the Connecticut Interracial Commission: "No institution of higher learning is operating in a vacuum with respect to racial, religious, or national origin criteria merely because it has removed a specific question on race, religion, or national origin from its application form."

Some colleges may bar you solely on the basis of your name as indicating that you belong to some religious or national minority. Or, your address may be sufficiently revealing, especially as to race. Beyond this, some colleges will ask you for a personal interview—or a letter of recommendation from your clergyman.

The greatest handicap in getting a college education in the U.S.A. is to be of the Negro race, and the next greatest is to be of the Jewish faith.

Some colleges exclude Jews altogether. For instance, a Jewish parent who inquired about enrolling her daughter at Harcum Junior College in Bryn Mawr, Pennsylvania, was told by the president: "I assume that you are Jewish and, since we have no girls of the Hebrew faith at Harcum this year, and have none enrolled for next year, I sincerely believe that your daughter would be happier at another junior college."

A nation-wide survey, made possible by a grant from the Anti-Defamation League of B'nai B'rith and the Vocational Service Bureau, has been conducted for the American Council on Education by the Elmo Roper research organization.

From a sampling of 10,000 high school seniors, it was found that about one-third intended to go to college. However, of those who applied for admission, 77 per cent of all Protestant *applications* were accepted, as compared to 67 per cent of the Catholic and 56 per cent of the Jewish.

This means that if you are Jewish you may have to apply to a number of colleges before you will be accepted, if at all. Application fees range from 5 to 10 dollars, and are generally not refunded.

To gain admission to a college in a northeastern state, you will have to make one-third more applications if you are Jewish than if you are Christian.

There is a further penalty if you are both Jewish and bright. A separate sampling of male students in the north-east who were in the upper fifth of their class scholastically revealed that such Jews had only a 53 per cent chance of acceptance, as compared to 71 per cent for the Catholics and 74 per cent for the Protestants.

The nationwide B'nai B'rith survey also brought out the extent to which your chances of entering professional colleges have been declining in recent years, if you happen to be Jewish.

In the case of law schools, Jewish enrolment was reduced from 25·8 per cent in 1935 to 11·1 per cent in 1946. In private engineering schools, Jewish enrolment was pushed down from 6·5 per cent to 5·6 per cent; in architecture, from 8·5 per cent to 4·4 per cent; in dentistry, from 28·5 per cent to 19·7 per cent; in social work from 13·6 per cent to 11·1 per cent; in commerce, from 16·7 per cent to 10·7 per cent; in fine arts, from 15·5 per cent to 8·4 per cent.

In the medical profession, too, there has been a concerted effort to squeeze Jews out. If you are Jewish, your chances of getting into a medical college are not even half as good today as they were 20 years ago. Only one out of every 13 Jewish applicants is admitted, as compared to three out of every four Christian applicants.

Here are some typical figures on the drop in enrolment of Jewish medical students at the following universities: Columbia, from 46·92 per cent in 1920 to 6·4 per cent in 1940; Long Island University, from 42·24 per cent in 1932 to 14·14 in 1940; Syracuse, from 19·44 in 1936 to 6·0 in 1942; Cornell, from 40 per cent in 1920 to 5·0 in 1945.

The rationale of the "quota system" which has brought about this sort of thing has been expressed by Dean Willard C. Rappleye of Columbia's College of Physicians and Surgeons as follows: "There is a general belief that the representation of the various social, religious, and racial groups in medicine ought to be kept fairly parallel with the population makeup."

This point of view has in effect been endorsed by Dr. Morris Fishbein, editor of the *Journal* of the American Medical Association.

If you are Jewish and are in search of medical training, you will find the following colleges employ the quota system against persons of your faith:

Yale	Duke
Johns Hopkins	Bowman Gray, N.C.
Harvard	University of Virginia
Dartmouth	Northwestern
Columbia	Syracuse
Cornell	Baylor
University of Rochester	

Also discriminating, but somewhat less grossly, are:

University of Chicago
University of Maryland
Boston University
Wayne University
Washington University (St. Louis)
University of Cincinnati
University of California
Jefferson (Philadelphia)
Temple University
University of Pennsylvania

The first break-throughs in the court battles against segregated schools were scored in higher education. During the two decades from 1927 to 1948, all of the seventeen states having school segregation laws adopted additional laws, providing for payment of out-of-state stipendiums to individual Negro students who insisted upon pursuing some line of study which the state offered to white students but not to Negroes. In short these states shipped such Negro students off to Negro colleges or to such white colleges outside the South as would admit them.

But in 1935 the Supreme Court agreed with a Negro plaintiff seeking entrance to the University of Maryland that he was entitled to equal educational opportunity *within his native state*. Again, in 1938 in a case involving the University of Missouri, the Court reasserted this principle. (Interestingly, the plaintiff in this case, Lloyd Gaines, disappeared soon after the Court decision, and is still a "missing person".)

Nearly a decade later, in 1946, when the courts ordered the State of Texas to admit Heman Marion Sweatt, a Negro, to the University of Texas law school, a three-room law school was hastily erected instead at the Texas college for Negroes.

A year later, in 1947, Federal Judge J. Waites Waring ordered South Carolina to fulfil the Constitutional right of Negro war veteran John H. Wrighten by:

(*a*) Admitting him to the University of South Carolina law school, or

(*b*) Establishing a law school for Negroes equal in every respect to the white school, or

(*c*) Closing the white law school.

Whereupon a one-room law school was established at the state college for Negroes.

That same year, the U.S. Supreme Court ordered Oklahoma to provide equal opportunity for the study of law by Ada Lois Sipuel "and all others similarly situated"; but in this case too a one-room law school was set up at the Negro college.

In all of these cases, the Negro plaintiffs refused to accept the make-shift schools as equal, and appealed again to the courts, to no avail.

In 1948 the University of Oklahoma did admit its first Negro student, Professor G. W. McLaurin, 54, following a Federal court order that he be provided equal opportunity to secure a doctorate degree in education. However, a separate booth for Professor McLaurin was built inside the classroom, and subsequently a Federal court ruled that the university was within its rights in thus segregating him.

Meanwhile, the governors of nine Southern states got together and devised a plan for pooling appropriations from their states to establish regional colleges in certain specialized fields of study, some for whites and some for Negroes. In this way they hoped to satisfy the insistence of the courts that they provide equal opportunities, and yet save money. Congress approved this plan in 1948 by a vote of 236 to 45, but the Senate rejected it by a vote of 38 to 37 after almost every Negro organization in the country had protested against it.

Despite this, 14 Southern governors went ahead and established a Regional Education Board, which began by building a regional veterinary college for white students in Georgia; but the plan bogged down as court decisions spurning it piled up.

A case of more than passing interest was that of Julius Caesar Hill, who in 1949 posted an application blank to the University of Oklahoma, enclosing dormitory fee of 10 dollars, and specifying under the heading "Race" that he was "American". Hill's fee was accepted and his name duly inscribed, but when upon arriving at the university it was seen that he was a Negro American, separate living quarters were hastily erected for him. The university's board of regents instructed the president to enforce segregation of Hill "to the greatest extent".

Similarly, when a group of Negroes were admitted to the University of Kentucky after a court battle in 1949, a sign was placed on a cafeteria table reading "Reserved for Negroes".

And so the years and decades passed, and a few token Negroes were admitted to a few white universities in the states fringing the South, but in a half-dozen Deep South states the doors to white state universities remained as tightly barred to Negroes as ever. In 1951 Congress actually passed a law providing Federal financial aid for the state school system with a proviso that no such aid would be given to any Southern school which was not segregated; only with difficulty was President Truman prevailed upon to shelve the measure.

Here's an added fact, presented at face value, whose significance you can judge for yourself, along whatever lines you choose: a chief support of separate Negro colleges has long been America's big business enterprises. Through an organization called the United Negro College Fund, some of the country's leading industrial magnates contribute an average of 30 million dollars to thirty-two Negro colleges each year. In 1953 the Fund conducted a fast-flying two-day excursion, escorting a party of twenty-five of its biggest supporters on a tour of Negro college campuses so they could "see where their money goes". The party included John D. Rockefeller III; the chairman of the Chase National Bank, Winthrop W. Aldridge (sometime Ambassador to Great Britain); the chairman of the Firestone Rubber Company, Harvey S. Firestone, Jr.; Robert E. Wilson, chairman of the Standard Oil Company of Indiana; Richard K. Mellon of the Mellon banking interests; and Devereux C. Josephs of the New York Life Insurance Company. Rockefeller launched the year's campaign with a contribution of 5 million dollars.

You may regard this as pure charity—or as an effort to reduce the pressure for opening the doors of white colleges to Negroes—or as an attempt to assure that Negro professionals will embrace the philosophy of big business.

(Should you be inclined to the latter view, you may be interested to note in passing that the interest of the business community in higher education is by no means limited to Negro education. The American Council on Education has estimated that five and a half billion dollars will be needed merely to house increased university enrolment by 1970. "Where is that sort of money coming from?" *Time* magazine has asked. "With the announcement of a two million dollar per year gift program by General Motors, one thing had become clear: U.S. industry is well started on a program to give help to U.S. colleges and universities—and thereby to help itself." You may recall the remark of Charles E. Wilson, longtime General Motors head, who as Secretary of Defence declared: "What's good for G.M. is good for the U.S." Other big subsidizers of higher education in America are U.S. Steel, Standard Oil, Bethlehem Steel, and DuPont chemicals.)

Golden Rule Days?

Meanwhile, the American Negro's unremitting courtroom battle to have segregation ruled out of the public school system moved toward its climax. At the same time, many white Southern politicos busied themselves issuing threats intended to influence the Supreme Court's decision on this question.

In South Carolina, Governor James F. Byrnes (former U.S. Secretary of State) threatened that his state would abolish public education rather than comply with any court order against separate schools. In Georgia,

Governor Herman Talmadge said his state would do the same thing, and added that "blood would flow in the streets" if such a court order were forthcoming. A Georgia state convention of the Democratic Party called upon every public official in the state to "fight with all the resources of the state" to maintain separate schools for the races, depite any and all court rulings to the contrary.

"We will go to jail before we will let white and colored students go to school together!" shouted convention floor leader Roy Harris.

Inspired by such statements from official circles, the K.K.K. proceeded to organize a sort of S.S.-group under the name "American Confederate Army for White Christians". Launched at a secret meeting held in Orlando, Florida, in 1952, this K.K.K.-S.S. sent an announcement through the U.S. mails:

"If necessary this organization will bear arms to uphold our Constitutional rights. If the Supreme Court ever outlaws racial segregation in the public schools, all members will take this as an invasion of our Constitutional rights."

In preparation for a *Der Tag* of that sort, Klan Dragon Bill Hendrix said the new group was compiling lists of the members of the N.A.A.C.P. and Anti-Defamation League of the Jewish B'nai B'rith fraternity. He warned: "If law and order [by which he means segregation] ever break down, we will hold them responsible!"

During December of 1952 the Supreme Court listened to the arguments of Negro complainants against segregation in South Carolina, Delaware, Virginia, Kansas, and Washington, D.C. All these cases made a frontal attack upon the Constitutionality of segregation in public schools, and were bitterly contested by the attorneys-general of the states involved. After six months of deliberation, the Court took the unusual action of admitting that it had been unable to come to any decision, and asked the attorneys to again come before the Court to argue both sides of the question.

Re-argument began in December of 1953. Heading the contingent of lawyers who defended the South's segregation laws was the Wall Street corporation counsel, John W. Davis, whose firm represents such clients as Standard Oil, American Telephone and Telegraph, International Paper Company, Guaranty Trust, and the banking House of Morgan. A former assistant U.S. attorney-general, Member of Congress, and Ambassador to Great Britain, Davis in previous appearances before the Supreme Court had succeeded in winning a number of dismissals of anti-trust prosecutions.

"I always go for the jugular vein!" Davis said of his courtroom technique. He refused to accept any fee for defending the segregation laws. "The differences between the races are as undeniable as the differences between the sexes, and this fact is the key to an understanding of history."

On May 17, 1954, however, the Supreme Court by a vote of 5 to 4 took a different view, and did what it had stubbornly refused to do ever since 1896 when it took the opposite view—it declared public school segregation unconstitutional.

"Today, education is perhaps the most important function of state and local governments," said the Court. "In the field of public education the doctrine of 'separate but equal' has no place. Separate educational facilities are inherently unequal."

No deadline was set by the Court for an opening of school doors without discrimination. On the contrary, it called upon local school boards to adopt plans for "gradual desegregation", and left it to the U.S. district courts to decide whether or not these plans were "adequate".

You can imagine—if you have not been an eyewitness—what a stir the Court's ruling caused everywhere that segregation holds sway.

Virtually all the Southern Congressmen and Senators in Washington, quite without regard to their oath of office to uphold the Constitution, affixed their signatures to a "Manifesto" pledging to oppose the Court's ruling "by all legal means". Typical of their public pronouncements was that of Senator James O. Eastland of Mississippi, chairman of the Senate Subcommittee on Internal Security, who said on a television programme that the Supreme Court's ruling against segregation was due to some members of the Court having been subjected to "Left-wing brainwashing".

The governors and attorneys-general of the Deep Southern states pledged "eternal" opposition to the Court order, and called their legislatures into special session. South Carolina, Georgia, Virginia, and others made good their earlier threats to adopt laws abolishing their public school systems if and when the Court order were enforced. In addition, hundreds of new laws intended to "keep the Negro in his place" were feverishly enacted.

"The real purpose of the Supreme Court's decision against school segregation is to open the bedroom doors of our white women to Negro men!" state Senator Walter Givhan of Mississippi charged at a mass meeting. "The Negroes want to see to it that the nation gets a

G

Negro Vice-President, so they can then assassinate the President and thus get a Negro President!"

Some Southern jurists were scarcely more reserved. In Texas, Judge William H. Atwell threw out of his court the appeal of 19 Negro children that they had a right to enrol in a white school. Said the judge: "That would be a civil wrong, not a civil right."

In Florida, the state supreme court, in a 4 to 1 decision, dared to hold that the U.S. Supreme Court had made a "great mistake" which would "retard rather than accelerate the removal of inequalities".

"Whether or not the doctrine of separate-but-equal has a place in the field of public education is a question of policy determinable by the legislature," Florida's Chief Justice Glenn Terrell opined. "It is not a judicial question, as I understand the canons of interpretation. Likewise the question of segregation is for the same reason a legislative rather than a judicial question.

"It is inconceivable that the Supreme Court will undertake to settle the question of segregation in Florida, Georgia, Mississippi, and other states, each of which has its peculiar problems with reference to the matter. It is further inconceivable that the Supreme Court would impose conditions on those states that neither the Congress nor any of the state legislatures have designed to impose on them, that none of them has asked for or want, that they are violently opposed to and have deep and decided convictions against."

All over the South, self-styled "White Citizens' Councils" sprang up. Officered mainly by bankers and businessmen, these Councils are a sort of plain-clothed Ku Klux Klan. While threatening a "Century of Litigation" in opposition to court orders against segregation, they specialize in the economic lynching of Negroes and whites who work for desegregation, and are not above indulging in old-fashioned lynchings, ambuscades, dynamitings, etc. The Southern states and Washington, D.C., obligingly issued corporate charters to these councils as tax-exempt "educational societies". In Georgia, for instance, one such charter was awarded to Dr. Marvin Head, Klan leader of Griffin, and another to Klan leader Jack Dempsey of Augusta.

The announced purpose of these Councils is to "stop desegregation before it begins". Alston Keith, chairman of the Dallas County, Mississippi, group, said they were going to "make it difficult, if not impossible, for any Negro who advocates desegregation to find and hold a job, get credit, or renew a mortgage".

Immediately it became apparent that these were not idle threats.

At Columbus, Mississippi, the Bank of Commerce informed Dr. Emmett Stringer, a Negro dentist and former president of the local N.A.A.C.P., that it would no longer loan him any money. In addition, Dr. Stringer's mother began receiving anonymous nocturnal telephone calls saying: "Dr. Stringer is dead!"

At Belyoni, Mississippi, the Citizens' Council warned Negro mortician T. B. Johnson that he could never again obtain even one cent of credit in Belyoni—and added that he might be run out of town.

At Indianola, Mississippi, a sort of secondary boycott was organized by the Citizens' Council, which not only deprived Negro Dr. Clinton Battle of credit, but warned his patients that they would lose their jobs unless they stopped patronizing him.

Elsewhere in the South it is much the same, and in some instances Negro community leaders, their homes dynamited, have had to flee to the North. In an effort to counteract the economic sanctions imposed by the Citizens' Councils, groups of Negroes and whites have been formed in other parts of the country to render financial assistance to those victimized by the Councils.

Most spectacular during the first year following the Court's decision was the "National Association for the Advancement of White People, Inc.", headed by Bryant Bowles, with headquarters in Washington, D.C. Bowles, a former U.S. soldier, utilized low-flying aeroplanes equipped with loudspeakers to mobilize mobs of from 5,000 to 10,000 whites in Delaware to attend harangues he staged in sports stadia. Bowles called upon white parents not to let their children attend any school to which a Negro had been admitted; so effective was the boycott that Delaware officials gave in and sent all such Negroes back to Negro schools.

A favourite Bowles technique was to hold his own three-year-old daughter on high and shout:

"This little girl will never attend school with a nigger so long as gunpowder will burn!"

Among the featured speakers at rallies staged by Bowles was none other than Sheriff Willis McCall of Florida—he who in 1951 had defeated the Supreme Court by emptying his pistol into two of the "Groveland Four" Negroes for whom the Court had ordered a new trial. Sheriff McCall and other speakers spoke frequently of impending "blood baths". Bowles claimed to have the support not only of such men as Talmadge of Georgia and Byrnes of South Carolina, but also the Texas oil millionaire, W. C. Hunt.

Maybe you think all this has to do with no more than a lunatic fringe of fanatics. But what do you think of the fact that the Gallup Poll, conducting a nation-wide survey of public opinion shortly after the Supreme Court decision against school segregation was handed down, found only 54 per cent supporting it?

Another straw in the wind was the election of 1954 of Strom Thurmond as Governor of South Carolina. Campaigning on a promise to keep the state's white schools lily-white, Thurmond won overwhelmingly, even though his name did not appear on the printed ballots, but had to be written in. (This is the same Thurmond who in 1948 campaigned for the Presidency of the U.S.A. as the nominee of the white supremacist "Dixiecrats".)

The year 1956 saw a further intensification of the struggle pro and con segregation. On January 27 a huge rally sponsored by the Citizens' Council of South Carolina was addressed by Senators Eastland, Thurmond, and Johnston, and Congressman Fred Vinson of Georgia, chairman of the House Preparedness Committee. Former Secretary of State James F. Byrnes was also present to hear Eastland charge that the anti-segregation drive was "backed by the communists", and Vinson call for a Constitutional Amendment enabling the states to segregate.

Congress itself appointed a sub-committee, chaired by Congressman James C. Davis of Stone Mountain, Georgia (whose district is a Klan stronghold), to probe de-segregation as it was getting under way in the schools of the national capital. Davis proceeded to use his Congressional committee as a sounding-board for the most rabid pro-segregation propaganda.

The Supreme Court, on the other hand, struck another powerful blow at the foundations of segregation by ruling in 1955 that financial contributions to educational institutions which barred anyone because of race could no longer be tax-exempt.

A year later the state of Georgia affirmed an opposite public policy by announcing that any educational institution within its boundaries which admitted both whites and Negroes would be subjected to state taxation.

This was also the year of Clinton, Tennessee, where the professional rabble-rouser John Kasper appeared and provoked such a riot that Governor Frank Clement had to send in two battalions of state guardsmen, equipped with tanks, to break it up. In the course of Kasper's trial on a charge of inciting to riot, his defence attorney, Ross

Barnett, told the jury that Senator Eastland had advised him to "tell the jury what's happened to Washington". The Senator's news: "In the nation's capital 874 schoolchildren have loathsome and contagious diseases, and 97 per cent of these children are Negroes." A Kasper supporter, Joseph Diehl, disrupted the proceedings by distributing through the courtroom a large sheet containing photographs of 50 Jewish community leaders and an inflammatory text headed "Asiatic Marxists". Kasper, significantly, was convicted by an all-white jury.

By the beginning of 1957, the Gallup Poll found nation-wide public support, for an end to school segregation had risen from 54 to 63 per cent. . . .

If you don't already know what happened as a result of nine Negro students enrolling in 1957 in the formerly all-white Central High School in Little Rock, Arkansas, U.S.A., you are really out of this world. There is no need to go into any great detail here, for if you have a special interest you can find literally tons of reading matter on the subject, in newspapers, magazines, and books, in many languages. But here are just a few of the highlights:

There seemed to be every prospect for peaceful adjustment to the new situation by the student body, until Governor Orval Faubus, on the eve of the 1957-8 school year, went on television to conjure up visions of violence and bloodshed. To avoid this, he said, he was obliged to order the Arkansas state militia to stand guard over the opening of the school. The militia men were under orders not to prevent white mobsters from preventing the Negro children from exercising the right which the Supreme Court had said the Constitution gives them to enter the school, but to openly defy the Court by forcibly depriving the Negro children of that right. As was only to be expected under such circumstances, a white mob did surround the school, violently attacked Negro journalists and tried to terrorize the Negro students by spitting in their faces and threatening them with lynching —while the state militia smiled approval.

Day after day such scenes were repeated, until at length the international scandal moved President Eisenhower to send in Federal troops, with orders to uphold the right of the Negro children to enter. There had already been advance indications that Governor Faubus had acted not entirely on his own initiative, but rather as a volunteer to find out on behalf of the entire Southern officialdom just how far the Federal Government would go to enforce the Court ruling against segregation. Having succeeded beyond their fondest dreams in provoking Washington to send in troops and draw the blood of Southern whites with bayonet pricks, the outrage of the politicos who owe their tenure in office to white supremacy knew no bounds.

"Eisenhower has lit the fires of hate!" orated Senator James Eastland of Mississippi, chairman of the Senate Subcommittee on Internal Security.

"I wish I could cast one vote for impeachment right now!" said Senator Herman Talmadge of Georgia.

"If I were Governor Faubus I'd proclaim a state of insurrection down there, and call out the state militia, and then I'd find out who's going to run things in my state!" said Senator Olin Johnston of South Carolina, in a veritable call for civil war.

Such sentiments resounded in the halls of Congress, without sounding at all inhibited by the oaths of office taken by the speakers to uphold the Constitution. Nor did Congress at any time go so far as to even remind any of these Southern gentlemen of their oath.

On somewhat lower levels, Southern political and business circles were no less outspoken than their representatives in Congress.

"This is the darkest day in Southern history since the Reconstruction period!" said a speaker at the businessmen's Kiwanis Club of Marshall, Texas; after which the Kiwanians refrained from reciting their customary pledge of allegiance to the American flag.

In Alabama, where a gubernatorial election campaign was in progress, the four contenders vied with one another as follows:

Candidate 1: Wired Faubus congratulations.

Candidate 2: Promised to back Faubus "at all costs".

Candidate 3: Offered to go to jail to maintain segregation.

Candidate 4: Said he stood ready to die for segregation.

The incumbent Governor of Alabama, "Kissing Jim" Folsom, swore to disband his state's militia if Washington ever made any move toward inducting it into the Federal army with a view to using it to uphold the Court's decision.

In Florida, a veteran of the U.S. Air Force sent his four Air Medals and six battle stars back to Eisenhower as a protest against the sending of U.S. troops into Little Rock.

At Albany, Georgia, someone put the torch to the Albany State College for Negroes; the fire did 300,000 dollars' worth of damage.

At Ozark, Arkansas, a Negro boy was struck with a book and a Negro girl with a coat-hanger, after which a white motorist tried to run them down with his car as they emerged from a formerly all-white school.

At Nashville, Tennessee, rabble-rouser John Kasper took his stand on the steps of the War Memorial Building, which is inscribed with these words of America's World War I President, Woodrow Wilson: "America is privileged to spend her blood and her might for the principles that gave her birth and happiness and the peace which she has treasured."

Against this backdrop, John Kasper said to the mob which harkened to his call:

"The Constitution gives you the right to carry arms. If one of these niggers pulls a razor or a gun on us, we'll give it to 'em! When they fool with the white race they're fooling with the strongest race in the world, the most bloodthirsty race in the world!"

That night a blast of dynamite demolished Nashville's Hattie Cotton School, where a Negro girl had that day enrolled.

Elsewhere across the South, the inciters and dynamiters made themselves heard. The spirit thus stirred up in certain sectors of the white population was summed up in the song improvised by a mob intent upon keeping Negroes out of a Louisville, Kentucky, school:

> Stand firmly by your cannon,
>   Let ball and grapeshot fly;
> Trust in God and Faubus,
>   And keep your powder dry!

Most of the states in the Deep South lost no time passing laws which would close down their public schools in the event that U.S. troops were sent in to enforce the Supreme Court's order.

The august Senate of the United States took an interest in the proceedings through its Sub-committee on Internal Security, whose chairman Eastland went personally to Little Rock to cross-examine a white woman who had protected a Negro girl from the mob. Later, a packet of dynamite was found in the woman's garage.

The White House, having unwittingly stirred up the whole hornet's nest, refused to place the blame for the mob violence on the gubernatorial and Senatorial levels where it primarily belonged, preferring to inveigh instead against the mobsters themselves. At the same time, a special U.S. emissary was sent to the 82-nation Social and Humanitarian Committee of the United Nations to say that the events triggered by Little Rock were "only an episode in a great advance toward the elimination of racial discrimination". The American people and Government, the spokesman added, "have an open and active national policy against race discrimination".

The American people by and large were more open and active than the Government. A public opinion poll found 74 per cent of the people in˙the Northern and Western states supported the use of Federal troops in support of the Supreme Court. In the South, the evidence was mixed. The *Arkansas Gazette*, which called in moderate tones for respect for the courts, lost only 10 per cent of its readers. Voting in 1957, the (white) voters of Little Rock elected seven city councilmen, six of whom were reputedly willing to abide by Supreme Court rulings. On the other hand, a baker lost his clients because his daughter fraternized with Negro students; and Faubus was re-elected Governor in 1958 with nearly 70 per cent of the total vote cast.

That same year, Senator Gore of Tennessee was re-elected on a platform of respecting the Federal courts, winning out over opponents who advocated defiance.

Another straw borne on the same wind was a resolution adopted, 33 to 1, by Southern university delegates to the National Student Congress, as follows:

"Though we are proud of the Southern community's way of life [racial separation—Author], we do not feel that a [school] system that denies equal opportunity to some Southern citizens is either necessary or desirable as a part of that way of life."

And yet something other than straws, borne by something other than the wind, brought the total number of blasted schools and synagogues to 47 during the fifteen-month period ending in May, 1958.

After three school years had come and gone after the Supreme Court's 1954 decision, its effect was being variously measured. The manner in which the courts were interpreting, and the Justice Department enforcing, the 1955 mandate of the high court that desegregation proceed "with all deliberate speed", was hardly worth advertising.

Sources intent upon presenting the situation in a favourable light were able to do so by juggling the figures just a bit. Their progress report, covering the first three years, has it that, of the 9,004 school districts in the 17 states long segregated by law, 740 districts had admitted some Negroes to some white schools, leaving "only" 2,263 districts where whites and Negroes live but do not attend school together. The residents of the remaining 6,001 districts, these reports blandly explain, are either all white or all Negro; "and hence the question of segregated schools does not arise".

The boundaries of these latter districts, needless to say, were not fixed by any colour-blind god, but by highly colour-conscious white officials. Having thus achieved racial segregation on the primary level of residence, it is argued that all-white schools in all-white districts, and all-Negro schools in all-Negro districts, is a natural phenomenon. Official circles in Washington, with a stake in showing that the problem is fast being solved, have been inclined to accept such gerrymandering of school districts without question, thus giving aid and comfort to those who would preserve segregation by this means.

There are 2,800,000 Negro grammar and high school students in the 17 Southern states and the national capital (constituting 24 per cent of the total school population in the area). Of these, only 122,000, or 4 per cent, found themselves in mixed schools by the beginning of the 1958-9 school year. Washington, D.C., boasted of being integrated, but actually a fifth of its Negro students were still in all-Negro schools.

Such de-segregation as had taken place had occurred mostly in the states bordering the South; in the Deep South states, the doors of white schools were as tightly closed to Negroes as before, except that $1 \cdot 5$ per cent of the Negro students of Texas, and $0 \cdot 003$ per cent of those of North Carolina, had been admitted to white schools.

In the realm of higher education, in which the Court ruled against segregation in 1935, the picture was not much brighter. According to the U.S. Information Service, "Practically, Negro students are today admitted to certain faculties of universities of the majority of Southern states and the District of Columbia, and practically all the universities of the rest of the country." Actually, by the end of the 1957 term, only 109 of the 202 state-supported white institutions of higher learning in the Southern states had let in any Negroes.

This will give you an idea what you might expect, if you are a Negro resident of a Deep South state, and decide to take the Supreme Court at its 1935 word, even two decades thereafter:

In 1956, Autherine Lucy, a 26-year-old library science student, won a three-year court battle for admission to the University of Alabama. Mobbed by a portion of the student body, *she* was suspended from school; and though the courts eventually reaffirmed her right to enrol, by that time she had chosen marriage instead.

In 1957, two Negroes seeking to enrol in Texarkana College were blocked by a mob of 400 whites, and the police refused to give the Negroes any protection. "The results of integration are sure to be degeneration of the schools," the president of the college proclaimed publicly. In 1958, when the Rev. Clennon King, Negro, sought to enrol at the University of Mississippi, he was taken into custody by the police, held incommunicado, examined by two physicians before Chancellor Stokes Robinson, Jr., and committed to the state lunatic asylum. In the course of the sanity hearing, Chancellor Coleman ejected the Rev. King's attorney, Sidney Tharp, with the allegation that Tharp was "under the influence of alcohol or goof-balls". Governor J. P. Coleman seized upon the occasion to hold a Press conference, at which he voiced defiance of the Supreme Court. A bit later, steps were taken to evict Rev. King from his home, whereupon he placed an advertisement in the Biloxi-Gulfport *Daily Herald* offering all his household goods for sale, and announcing that he was giving up his post as professor at Alcorn Agricultural and Mechanical College and "going back to Africa in search of the freedom our African-American people lost 339 years ago".

As the 1958-9 school year approached, some dilatory voices spoke out from the Federal bench, giving enormous encouragement to the forces intent upon perpetuating segregation. Whatever their intent, the effect of these court rulings was to say "Mobism does pay", and "Perhaps the segregationists are correct".

First to speak in this vein was U.S. District Judge Harry J. Lemley, who on June 20 gave the Little Rock school board permission to throw the nine Negro students out of Central High, and keep them out for two and a half years.

Apparently taking his cue from Judge Lemley, U.S. District Judge Sterling Hutcheson on August 4 gave the Prince Edward County school board of Virginia permission to wait seven and a half years before making a move to comply with the Supreme Court's order to open the doors of its white schools to a few Negroes.

Judge Lemley's ruling was appealed to the U.S. Circuit Court of Appeals at New Orleans. There the attorney for the Little Rock school board, A. F. House, said frankly that much of the prolonged violence in Little Rock had been due to the fact that, at the outset of it, Governor Faubus and U.S. Attorney-General William P. Rogers had publicly proclaimed that no one would be prosecuted for resorting to violence in opposition to the Supreme Court's ruling.

"You can imagine what that did in a place where the storm was already raging," House said.

Thurgood Marshall, chief counsel for the N.A.A.C.P. and victor in many a courtroom battle against segregation, summed up the situation thus: "The Governor can do what he wants to. The school board can ignore its duties. But a Federal court cannot deny an individual his Constitutional rights because of threats of violence."

On August 18 the Court of Appeals agreed with Marshall, reversed Judge Lemley, and ordered Little Rock to let the Negro students go back to Central High. Then the court gave the school board time to appeal to the Supreme Court.

On August 27 the Arkansas legislature, summoned to a special session by Faubus, voted 94 to 1 (representative Ray Smith dissenting), and the state senate ratified, 33 to 0, a law requiring the closing of any and all mixed schools.

That same day, the U.S. Air Force Base at Little Rock announced that the base school operated with Federal funds for its personnel would be segregated.

Like fuel upon the fire came the words of President Eisenhower the following day. After first refusing to express his personal opinion about the Supreme Court's decision against school segregation, the President went on to say that he "could disagree very violently with a decision", and that this would make his duty to enforce the decision "much more difficult to carry out". A bit later he denied the report of a national news magazine that he had told intimates he regretted the Court decision; but he admitted that he "might have said" enforcement should slow down.

Thus caught between the fire of Little Rock and the White House, the Supreme Court was itself called upon to define precisely the meaning of its mandate of 1955 that school de-segregation proceed "with all deliberate speed".

It decided, to the eternal credit of the country, that there was no legitimate ground for postponement of the integration orders.

Segregationist Senators, Governors and lesser politicos screamed defiance.

"The South will not accept this outrage which a communist dominated Government is trying to lay on us!" declared Rev. Wesley Prudent, president of the Arkansas White Citizens' Council, in a typical statement. "We will carry on the fight for our freedom to govern ourselves for a thousand years if necessary. And posterity will say of us, 'This was our finest hour!'"

Both Arkansas and Virginia went ahead with their plans to close all schools affected by integration orders; in the latter state 13,000 students were left without instruction by the closure of nine schools. Movements to reopen the schools on a segregated basis under the aegis of "private" corporations were nipped in the bud by the Supreme Court which, without waiting for a test case to be brought, declared forthrightly that the rights of Negro students "can neither be nullified openly and directly by state legislators or state executives or judicial officers, or nullified indirectly by them through evasive schemes for segregation, whether attempted ingeniously or ingenuously".

Undaunted, segregationists sought to give instruction to locked-out white students by providing lessons through television, and conducting classes under church auspices. Such efforts were highly unsatisfactory, and opposition to this form of "massive resistance" began to make itself felt. Even so, the moderate segregationist Congressman Brooks Hays of Arkansas, a veteran of eight terms in the House, was defeated by the militant segregationist Dr. Dale Alford, who had the backing of Faubus. In Virginia, the all-powerful political machine of Senator Harry Byrd captured 70 per cent of the votes with an endorsement of massive resistance to integration, but Dr. Louise O. Wensel, mother of five and advocate of compliance with the court orders, did receive 113,000 votes.

CHAPTER 8

WHO MAY WORK WHERE

"No Segregation in the Economy" is the title of an article in *The American Negroes*, published by the U.S. Information Agency.

Don't be surprised, however, if you take the trouble to read that article and fail to find any facts or figures in substantiation of its title. For the truth is that the facts and figures (which the Information Agency does not publish) reveal a vast amount of segregation and discrimination in the economic life of the nation.

Here they are.

If you are a native-born white Gentile you are not likely to be denied a job or promotion because of your race, religion, or national origin. But if you lack one or more of these qualifications you will find many jobs and professions closed to you, and in a much larger number will encounter discrimination and special hardships. No matter where you look, you will find such discrimination throughout the U.S.A., varying only in intensity, comprehensiveness and the sorts of people victimized.

No need to look to the U.S. Constitution for relief, for there is nothing in it to assure equality of opportunity regardless of race, creed or national origin. The assertion contained in the Declaration of Independence that "all men are created equal, that they are endowed by their Creator with certain unalienable rights, that among these are Life, Liberty, and the pursuit of Happiness" does not say anything about pursuit of a job. Even if it did it wouldn't mean a thing, since the Declaration is but the statement of an ideal, and has no legal status whatever.

During World War II President Franklin D. Roosevelt established a Fair Employment Practices Commission (F.E.P.C.), but Congress killed it in 1945, and has refused ever since to re-establish anything of the sort. A fourth of the states, and a score of cities, have enacted such laws; but enforcement is lax, and most of the peoples victimized are not even aware that the laws exist.

In short, The American Way of free enterprise is notoriously inoperative in so far as competition between whites and nonwhites is concerned.

Wanted: White Gentiles

If you belong to some racial minority—and particularly if you are a Negro—you are far more likely to be hit by job discrimination (and hit harder) than if you are white but belong to some religious minority.

As evidence of this, 80 per cent of the complaints made to the short-lived F.E.P.C. maintained by President Roosevelt were registered by Negroes. Only 8 per cent of the total complaints charged religious discrimination, and of these 80 per cent were registered by persons of the Jewish faith.

After World War II, discrimination increased.

A survey made by the National Community Relations Advisory Council in 1946, covering 134 private employment agencies in the ten non-Southern cities of Boston, Chicago, Cincinnati, Cleveland, Detroit, Kansas City, Milwaukee, Philadelphia, St. Louis, and San Francisco revealed that 89 per cent of these agencies required job-seekers to state their religion. A companion survey of Help Wanted advertisements in eight major cities showed a 195 per cent increase in discriminatory ads. in 1946 as compared to 1945.

The manner in which nonwhites were squeezed out of certain jobs after World War II was brought out in testimony by members of the United Electrical Workers Union before the Senate Subcommittee on Labour in 1952:

"This Committee and Congress will be shocked to know that the economic position of nonwhite families has deteriorated since 1944", it was reported. "This startling fact is a complete refutation of those who argue that 'time' alone has brought a lessening of economic and other forms of discrimination against the Negro people and other minority groups. It was not 'time' but the pressures of World War II, a Federal F.E.P.C. and other democratic efforts which brought about the temporary improvement in the conditions of Negroes and minority groups in World War II. The proportion of male jobs held by Negro men increased from 8·6 in 1940 to 9·8 per cent in 1944, then fell to 8·3 per cent in 1950. Negro men held 2·8 per cent of all professional and semi-professional men's jobs in 1940; by 1944 this percentage had risen to 3·3 per cent, but by 1950 it had fallen to 2·6, which was a lower percentage than in 1940."

One large private employment agency in Chicago reported that 83 per cent of all the calls it received for workers included discriminatory specifications as to race or religion. Sixty per cent of its calls for executives, 41 per cent of male clerical jobs, and 24 per cent of female clerical jobs were not open to Jews.

An investigator who applied for 100 jobs in New York City as stenographer, secretary, accountant, and auditor was told in 91 cases that Jews were not acceptable. The National City Bank of New York—100,000 of whose 400,000 depositors are Jews—employs only six Jews. Of the 4,200 employees in the New York home office of the Equitable Life Insurance Company, 1 per cent are Jewish.

Similar conditions are to be found in the teaching profession. A recent survey of 179 American universities revealed that 36 employed no Jews on their faculties, 62 schools had faculties which were 1·8 per cent Jewish, and 87 more schools had staffs averaging 2·2 per cent Jewish.

If you happen to be of Chinese ancestry, your chances of getting a job carrying a tray in a Chinese restaurant, or ironing shirts in a Chinese laundry, or selling herbs or souvenirs in Chinatown, are relatively good. On the other hand, not even a Ph.D. college degree or Phi Beta Kappa scholarship key will serve to lower the barriers against you in many other occupations and professions.

Back in 1920, according to the U.S. Census, more than 50 per cent of the working Chinese in the U.S.A. were employed in laundries and restaurants; and this situation has not changed much since. In a typical pre-World War II year the Oriental Division (sic) of the U.S. Employment Service in San Francisco reported that 90 per cent of its job placements were for service workers, mostly in the culinary trades.

Mining was a chief occupation of the first Chinese to come to America, there being 34,933 thus engaged in California in 1860. But the squeeze was applied and within ten years half of the Chinese miners were separated from their jobs. By 1920 there were but 151 Chinese still engaged in mining throughout the U.S.A.

Even in the beginning Chinese miners were forced to work the "played-out diggings" which had already been abandoned by other miners. Despite this, they paid more than 5,000,000 dollars in taxes to California counties, under a levy assessed against Chinese miners only.

Similarly, back in 1870 there were 30,000 Chinese farm labourers in California, but by 1920 this number had been reduced to 3,617. Now 80 per cent of all Chinese-Americans are city-dwellers.

There were 10,000 Chinese engaged in railroad work in 1870; less than 500 are thus employed today.

In 1870 there were 2,000 Chinese engaged in manufacturing, but by 1920 their number had already been reduced to 100.

Only by extreme brilliance and diligence can you hope to achieve success in many professions in the U.S.A. if you are of Chinese ancestry. Dr. Chien-Shiung Wo is one example, having become one of the leading physicists in America while still in her twenties. Two others are Professors Tsung Dao Lee and Chen Ning Yang, who won a 1957 Nobel Prize for their refutation of the "parity law" in nuclear physics.

The prevailing assumption that Chinese as well as other nonwhites are best fitted to serve whites has long been reflected in the policies of the U.S. Navy.

Up until World War I the Navy sometimes assigned some foreign-born whites, such as the Irish, as stewards and messboys; but after that this branch of service was reserved exclusively for Chinese, Filipinos, Koreans, Japanese, and Negroes. Your duties in this capacity would include preparing and serving meals, cleaning staterooms, washing laundry, shining shoes, and otherwise attending to the needs of white naval officers. After many years of service you might be awarded the *pay* of a chief petty officer, but without the actual *rank*; general courts martial have held that such persons cannot exercise the prerogatives enjoyed by white chief petty officers.

The special handicaps you are under as a Chinese-American are further indicated by the fact that none of your kind has ever served as public officials in California, while groups which arrived after the Chinese, such as the Portuguese, Armenians, and Italians, are well integrated in the economic, political, and social life of the state.

No matter how thoroughly "Americanized" you may become, white America as a whole will not acknowledge you as an American; like all nonwhites, you will be regarded as a "perpetual alien" in the land of your birth.

"There is no likelihood of improvement for generations to come", gloomily concludes Leong Gor Yun in *Chinatown Inside Out*.

"Perhaps in the future our American-born Chinese will have to look to China for their life work", says Ng Poon Chew, a leader of the Chinese community in California.

"To the young Chinese, a China in revolution, where almost anything may happen, offers excitement, opportunity, and possibilities for leadership", adds Albert W. Palmer in *Our Racial and National Minorities*.

Last Hired, First Fired

If you are a Negro seeking a job in the U.S.A., you hardly need to be reminded that Negroes are generally the "last hired and first fired".

And if—like 11 million of America's Negroes—you live below the Mason-Dixon Line, you will know there is much truth in the saying that "A Negro has just two chances in the South—slim, and none at all".

In short, you know what it means to be "naturally born black in a white man's country".

The figures on all this do not lie.

During the depression of the early 1920s, 40 per cent of the Negro labour force was unemployed. In the "good" year 1940, 17 per cent of the Negro labour force remained unemployed, as compared to 7 per cent of the white force. Even in the "boom" year of 1947, 6 per cent of the Negro labour force was unable to find jobs, as compared to 2 per cent of the white force. The depression of 1958 found 16 per cent of Negro workers without jobs by February of that year, as compared to 7 per cent of the whites.

In time of depression, if you are nonwhite you may encounter such movements as the Blackshirts, which in the 1930s paraded the streets of Atlanta carrying placards reading "No Nigger on a Job Until Every White Man Has a Job!" Even Negro bootblacks were forcibly driven from their jobs by the Blackshirts.

If you are not white, not even a world war is likely to long improve your job opportunities. During World War II, many American industries imported white workers from other cities, rather than give jobs to the Negroes living in their immediate vicinity. The textile industry—in which the manpower shortage resulted in a shortage of canvas which held up America's Pacific campaign—steadfastly refused to take on Negro workers, though the number available was huge. Bus companies in Washington, D.C., advertised 200 miles away for white drivers and even hired white Government clerks on a part-time basis, rather than hire any Negroes (it was argued that Negro drivers might make "passes" at white female passengers).

Altogether, the War Manpower Commission estimated that at

H

least a million Negro men and women remained unemployed because of prejudice. Neither the War Manpower Commission nor the U.S. Employment Service took effective action to remedy this situation, however.

In war as in peace, the U.S. Employment Service actually catered to discrimination in private employment. Prior to the war, it referred 60 per cent of its nonwhite applicants to servant jobs. During the war, this figure remained at 30 per cent, with only 3 per cent of Negro workers being referred to war industries. Immediately after the war the figure rose again with 45 per cent of Negro applicants being referred to jobs as menials, and continued to increase after control of the Employment Service was handed back to the individual states at the behest of Southern Congressmen intent upon making the agency even more discriminatory.

The record of the War Manpower Commission was scarcely better; some of its Southern branches collaborated with military draft boards and private employers to "freeze" Negroes on underpaid jobs. In one instance the Governor of Florida wired the War Manpower Commissioner, demanding the return of 438 Negro farm workers whom the U.S.E.S. had recruited during the Florida citrus off-season to pick tomatoes for the armed forces at Camden, New Jersey. In a similar case, Georgia police were prevailed upon to stop a train and forcibly remove a group of Florida Negroes who had been offered jobs in the North.

The *New York Post* even published a report that the U.S. Attorney-General had sent a confidential memorandum to the President, urging that steps be taken to prevent Negroes from emigrating from the South to take jobs in Detroit and other industrial centres; but the Attorney-General denied the charge.

The State Department article "No Segregation in the Economy" ventures to suggest that "there does not exist any reason" why "in some years" the "progress being made" should not bring about equality of opportunity.

In reality, while there has been progress in some spheres, there has been retrogression in others. In many respects it may be said that you, as a nonwhite worker, were born half a century too late. For in 1910 your chances of finding employment in such occupations as manufacturing, trade, transportation, mining, barbering, and white-collar work were better than they are today.

Through the years certain occupations came to be regarded as more or less exclusively white jobs, while other (less desirable) jobs came to be regarded as Negro work. Something of this specialization of labour along racial lines is revealed by the U.S. Census. While the proportion of Negroes in the population is 10 per cent, the proportion of Negro employees in the following occupations is:

WHITE JOBS

Aircraft	0·1%
Petroleum and gas . . .	0·5
Wool and worsted . . .	0·6
Electrical machinery . . .	0·6
Footwear	0·7
Knit goods	0·9
Silk and rayon	1·1
Radio and television . . .	1·5
Printing and publishing . .	1·7

NEGRO JOBS

Servants	45·8
Sawmills	26·3
Forestry	22·0
Hotel and lodging . . .	20·2
Brickyards	16·6
Farm labour	15·5

Those tabulations should give you some idea where your opportunities as a nonwhite jobseeker lie.

Official figures emphasize that Negro *per capita* earnings have risen considerably since World War II. This is true—not only of the American Negro, but of many peoples around the world. But the fact remains that you would be considerably better off white than black in the U.S.A.

To begin with, *per capita* figures do not mean much in such a highly stratified society, since they fail to indicate the mass of poverty on the bottom which supports high incomes for a few on top.

Progress *is* being made, due in large measure to the militancy of the Negro; but discrimination remains.

The *per capita* income of the Negro American is still only half that of the white American.

Something like 15 per cent of all Negro families fall in the lowest income bracket, compared to 7 per cent of all white families.

Only about 1 out of every 15 Negro workers has a white-collar job, compared to 6 out of every 15 whites. Among women, only 6 per cent of the Negro workers are in white-collar jobs, compared to 32·6 per cent of the white women workers.

Nine per cent of all Negro workers, and 21 per cent of all white workers, are employed as skilled labourers; and the same proportions apply among technicians and professionals.

If you are a Negro you will find it exceptionally difficult to obtain vocational training in the U.S.A., as well as in putting such training to use should you manage to acquire it. According to the President's Advisory Committee on Education, your chances of getting a vocational education in the 17 Southern states and nation's capital would be two-thirds greater if your skin were white.

Lost: 40 Acres and a Mule

If you are a person who likes to live on the land and till it, it is only fair to warn you that if you are not white and do not have a lot of money, your chances of making good as a farmer—which have never been of the best—have been rapidly worsening for the past two decades.

Ever since Emancipation, coloured folks have had an especially difficult time getting hold of good farm land. The Civil War promise to give every Freedman "40 acres and a mule" was never kept. Moreover, the big white planters, though rendered bankrupt by the war, often refused to sell adequate plots to Negroes.

White farmers, while having plenty of troubles of their own, managed on the average to get hold of more land than Negroes. By the beginning of World War II, the number of acres being farmed by Southerners compared on the average as follows:

	White	Negro
Farm-owners	140	60
Tenants	120	40
Share-croppers	45	20

Even those figures give an oversized impression, because many giant plantations are included in working out the average.

Getting land to farm is only part of the problem; the next question is tools. If you are an average nonwhite farmer, you will find that your white competitor has on the average four times more valuable tools and equipment than you.

The coming of mechanization to agriculture, far from being a boon to small farmers, has been the bane of many. With tractors, cultivators, and harvesters concentrated in the hands of big plantation owners and giant corporative farming enterprises, many a farm family has been literally tractored off the land as "uneconomic".

Those machines may be colour-blind, but Negro farm families, having a generally more precarious tenure than the whites, have been hardest hit by them. During the two decades from 1935 to 1954, the number of Negro farm operators in the South dropped 42 per cent, as compared to a 29 per cent drop among white operators.

Tenant farmers and share-croppers were, of course, the first to go. At first many of these were precipitated into the dismal ranks of farm "hired hands". But in time mechanization drove many of these off the land altogether, a 31 per cent drop in the number of farm labourers having taken place in the South from 1942 to 1957.

Sad, but that's how it is. . . .

The average age of Southern farm operators being over 50, you can readily imagine the difficulties such folk encounter in searching for jobs in the towns and cities.

The South's Negroes have especially been on the move, and not alone for economic reasons. This will give you some idea as to the trend: at the beginning of the century, 85 per cent of all American Negroes were still in the South, and three-fourths of these lived in rural areas. Now only 63 per cent live in the South, and only half of these are rural residents. Of the six million living outside the South, one-half were born in the South.

But don't think that simply moving out of the South means leaving all job discrimination behind. For in the South, the proportion of Negro workers who get to be managers, officials, proprietors, crafts-men, and foremen is 8·5 per cent; in the North, 10 per cent.

Be Your Own Boss, but——

Official manuals like to harp upon individual Horatio Alger success stories of American Negroes who have "made good". Such people do exist, but their existence does not attest any lack of discrimination, but only that some few have managed to prosper in spite of it. The figures, which the official manuals do not harp upon, reveal that only 0·1 per cent of all nonwhites have annual incomes of more than 10,000 dollars, as compared to 2·2 per cent of all whites (farmers excluded).

Certain fields have traditionally sought to exclude Negroes, such as architecture, chemistry, metallurgy, engineering, publishing, law, and social work. Even the fields of dentistry, medicine, and education have presented special barriers to nonwhites.

Should you be able to obtain professional training despite the fact that such training is not available to Negroes in many areas, you will still find yourself hemmed in by race prejudice.

As a Negro professional or businessman, you will generally find that, due to prejudice, your clientele will be limited to the Negro community.

If you are a Negro and wish to be a lawyer, you must face the fact that many Negro clients prefer to hire white lawyers, who by virtue of their colour are able to obtain a greater degree of justice from the white judges and juries. (It is interesting to recall that the supreme court of Maryland once held constitutional a state law barring Negroes from the legal profession, basing its decision on a previous U.S. Supreme Court ruling that laws barring women as barristers were constitutional.)

If you are a Negro and aspire to be a doctor, surgeon, or nurse, you must face the fact that a great many hospitals will not permit you to treat patients in them.

Throughout the segregated territory and in certain other areas besides, local and state chapters of the American Medical Association will not admit you to membership if you are a Negro doctor.

If you are a Negro nurse practising in Louisiana, Georgia, Alabama, Texas, Arkansas, South Carolina, or Virginia, the state and local units of the American Nurses' Association will not admit you to membership.

If you are a Negro and plan to become a barber, you must face the fact that, although Negro barber shops catering to white patrons were once commonplace, they have virtually disappeared since short hair became stylish for women. Some Southern states have laws prohibiting Negro barbers from cutting the hair of white women.

If you are a Negro and aspire to public office in the segregated territory—and in some other places besides—you may also become a candidate for lynching (see "Who may Vote Where").

For example, Larkin Marshall had no sooner announced his candidacy for Congressman from Georgia in 1948 than the Ku

Klux Klan sent him warnings and burned a fiery cross in front of his home.

The number of elected Negro office-holders in the South can be counted on the fingers of one hand. There is also widespread discrimination against the hiring of Negroes on municipal and state payrolls. The City of Richmond, Virginia, long boasted that it employed no Negroes in any capacity, skilled or unskilled.

City licensing and zoning boards may refuse to license you to practise certain trades if you are not a white Gentile. For example, San Francisco once sought to drive Chinese-Americans out of the laundry business by refusing to license them; Chicago adopted a law against taxicab solicitation and sought to enforce it against Negroes only; Houston refused to license Negroes as electricians; and a Jacksonville, Florida, zoning board refused to permit a Syrian to establish a business in South Jacksonville.

Although the U.S. Supreme Court has declared that, "The right to work for a living in the common occupations of the community is the essence of the personal freedom and opportunity that it was the purpose of the 14th Amendment to secure", the truth is that if you are not a native-born white Gentile you will find your work opportunities in the U.S.A. are limited in a great many ways. The case of one out of many counties where Negroes are not permitted to work or live has been cited in the earlier chapter, "Who may Live Where".

Similarly, when Mrs. Kate Robbins opened up a small dry-goods store in Redbank, Tennessee, the Ku Klux Klan tied a bundle of switches to her door and left a note reading: "No Jews Wanted In Redbank". The note was turned over to the F.B.I., but it took no action. Then the K.K.K. burned a cross in front of Mrs. Robbins' store one afternoon, marched in in full regalia and told her, "We mean business—get out!" She got out.

You Can't Work Together

In most of the segregated territory, state and/or local laws require that industrial workers be separated according to race. A typical South Carolina statute reads as follows:

"It shall be unlawful for any person, firm, or corporation engaged in the business of cotton textile manufacturing in this state to allow or permit operatives, help and labor of the different races to labor and work together within the same room, or to use the same doors of entrance and exit at the same time, or to use and occupy the same pay ticket windows or doors for paying off its operatives and laborers at the same time, or to use the same stairway and windows at the same time, or to use at any time the same lavatories, toilets, drinking-water buckets, pails, cups, dippers, or glasses."

This South Carolina law provides a noteworthy exception, however, as follows:

"This section shall not apply to employment of firemen as subordinates in boiler rooms, or to floor scrubbers and those persons employed in keeping in proper condition lavatories and toilets, and carpenters, mechanics, and others engaged in the repair or erection of buildings."

The law empowers any citizen of the county to institute suit against an offending company for 100 dollars, the money to be turned over to the public school fund. In addition, the company may be fined 100 dollars for each offence and/or its responsible officials sentenced to 30 days "at hard labor".

In North Carolina, a state law requires all manufacturing plants located in cities of 1,000 or more population to provide separate toilets for white and nonwhite workers (separate toilets are mandatory throughout the segregated territory).

You can readily see how the laws prohibiting the races from working together tend to preclude the employment of nonwhites. Because of such laws, relatively few industrial plants in the segregated territory have gone to the trouble and expense of setting up dual production facilities. Several plants have worked whites on the day shift, nonwhites at night.

Both in and out of the segregated territory there is a more or less stringent taboo which prevents the hiring of Negro supervisors over white workers. In one Kentucky case, the Axton Fisher Tobacco Company was awarded damages from the *Evening Post*, it being held libellous *per se* to allege that a company employs Negro males as supervisors over white females.

Uncle Sam as Bossman

Don't think if you are nonwhite that the way to avoid job discrimination is to seek employment with the U.S. Government or in the national capital or colonial possessions of the U.S.A.

In the jobs he hands out and in the territory he administers directly Uncle Sam has discriminated as much as or more than almost anybody else in the country.

If you are in a position to choose in your search for employment, you may prefer to choose one of the states and/or cities which do have laws against job discrimination, even though those laws are but feebly enforced; for the Federal Government has no *law* on the subject, either concerning its own employees, or the employees of firms receiving taxpayers' money through Government contracts, or concerns enjoying public subsidization in the form of tax-exemption.

After Roosevelt's Fair Employment Practices Commission was killed in 1945, the only agency to which Government workers could complain of racial or religious discrimination was a fair employment board of the Civil Service Commission. This board limits its interest to individual complaints; collective complaints will not be heard. To give you an idea as to what may be expected of it: A survey made by the National Committee on Segregation in Washington (1948) compared two groups of 40 white and 40 Negro Governmental employees, who were equal in terms of sex, age, education, experience, length of service, efficiency rating, etc. It was found that the whites had averaged one promotion for every two years of service, while the Negroes had averaged only one promotion every 14 years.

In other words, all else being equal, your white co-worker can expect seven promotions from Uncle Sam to your one.

You can expect to find even worse conditions in private employment with firms holding contracts with the Government. The self-evident principle that tax-money, being collected without racial discrimination, ought to be expended without racial discrimination, is rendered little more than lip-service in the U.S.A.

To be sure, as a result of Roosevelt's initiative, all Government contracts with private industry now contain a clause obligating the industry not to practise racial or religious discrimination. However, a Presidential commission investigating the efficacy of such clauses reported in 1953 that "both industry and Government agencies have largely ignored existing non-discrimination clauses in Government contracts". This has not changed.

As a poor substitute for Roosevelt's F.E.P.C. the Eisenhower Administration has maintained a President's Committee on Government Contracts. But if you have been discriminated against by a firm holding a Government contract you would probably be wasting your time if you appealed to the President's Committee. For the essential truth is that the U.S. Government has never cancelled a contract because an industry practised discrimination, though discrimination is common among very many industries holding Government contracts throughout the country (in the South, there is *no* industry which does not discriminate).

The notion that private enterprises which enjoy public subsidization in the form of tax-exemption are also under special obligation not to discriminate has scarcely scratched the surface of America's consciousness.

From one extremity of responsibility to the other, the factor of discrimination continues operative under the wings of the American eagle. Dr. Ralph Bunche, Negro, was not looking for a job as elevator boy with the tax-exempt fraternal order of Eagles; winner of the Nobel Peace Prize for his work as a United Nations mediator, he was offered the post of Assistant U.S. Secretary of State, but he felt obliged to refuse because he did not want to subject his children to the intense racial discrimination practised in the nation's capital.

Perhaps you read in the newspapers that the Civil Rights Act of 1957 established a Civil Rights Commission. So it did; but a year later the Commission still did not even have a chairman. This did not matter much, since the Commission's life was limited to two years and its powers limited to recommending civil rights legislation, which Congress will probably not adopt, anyway.

The U.S. Information Agency is wont to point out that back in 1928 no Negroes were employed by the Federal Government except as janitors and other menials, but by 1954 they constituted 23 per cent of all Government employees. This is due not so much to any Governmental enlightenment as it is to Negro militancy and the pressures of world opinion. Furthermore, it so happens that 35 per cent of the population of Washington, D.C., is Negro.

Some Governmental agencies have a record of discriminating more than others. The N.A.A.C.P. has charged that the Department of Justice, Interstate Commerce Commission, Federal Trade Commission, and Bureau of Printing and Engraving have been among the worst offenders.

Even the Veterans Administration, in its Southern offices, segregates its few Negro employees.

Of the Federal Bureau of Investigation, the N.A.A.C.P. has said in a letter to F.B.I. Director John Edgar Hoover: "It is increasingly difficult for thousands upon thousands of American citizens to believe that an agency of Government whose personnel recruiting record is so badly tainted with racial bias, will, when it comes to protecting the rights of minority racial groups, give them a square deal."

The capital itself, though administered by a Congressional committee, employs relatively few Negroes except in menial capacities. This has been especially true of the tax-collector's office, purchasing office, and vehicles and traffic department. Both the police and fire departments are segregated; in 1952 Congress intervened to prevent the latter from integrating 16 Negro firemen into white fire-fighting brigades.

All progress reports aside, you will still find that in Washington, D.C., six out of every eight Negro job-holders (public and private) are labourers, domestic servants, or service workers, while only one of every eight white workers falls in this category.

It so happens that America's colonies, or "territories and insular possessions" as they are called, contain a great many persons of different ethnic origin than the Nordic white majority of the U.S. mainland.

Puerto Rico, the Panama Canal Zone, Hawaii, the Virgin Islands, Pacific islands—all these are directly under the jurisdiction of the U.S. Government. You might think that, under the circumstances, discrimination in employment would be less rife in these places. Not so, however.

The situation in the Panama Canal Zone, which is officially described as a "U.S. Government reservation", is fairly typical. The Canal Zone has a civilian population of more than 50,000, some of whom are whites from the U.S. proper, but most of whom are an admixture of Negro, Indian and Hispanic strains. The U.S.A. whites, according to U.S. Government usage in the Canal Zone, are designated "Gold" while the remainder are called "Silver".

The racial differential in hourly wage scales as paid by the U.S. Government in the Zone gives "Silver" workers only one-fourth to one-third as much as "Gold" workers.

Moreover, if you are Silver you will not be paid any bonus for over-time work; if you are Gold you will get premium pay for overtime.

If Silver, you get exactly half as much food-money while doing a job away from your official station as a Gold worker is given each day.

Similar racial wage differentials are commonly in force wherever the American flag flies over nonwhites overseas.

Jim Crow in Uniform

If you are toying with the notion of a career in the U.S. armed forces, or are subject to induction therein, there are certain things you ought to know.

For instance, did you know—

§ That 4,000 Negroes fought in the armies of George Washington in the American Revolutionary War for Independence?

§ That 250,000 Negroes fought in the armies of Abraham Lincoln for the liberation of their people and the restoration of the United States?

§ That 500,000 Negroes fought in the armies of Woodrow Wilson in World War I to help "make the world safe for democracy"?

§ That 1,150,000 Negroes fought in the armies of Franklin D. Roosevelt in World War II to help deny the Axis "Supermen" their "Thousand Years" of world dominion?

§ That Dwight D. Eisenhower as supreme commander of the armed forces said in 1942, "My policy for handling colored troops will be absolute equalitative treatment, but there will be segregation where facilities are afforded"?

§ That President Harry S. Truman, rejecting appeals that as Commander-in-Chief he issue an order abolishing racial segregation and discrimination in the armed forces, issued instead in 1946 an "instructive" which "called upon" the Services to eliminate segregation and discrimination "as rapidly as possible"?

§ That Eisenhower in testimony before the Senate Armed Forces Committee in 1948 said that the armed forces are not concerned with "social reform", and added that "a certain amount of segregation is necessary in the Army"?

§ That when in the same year the *New York Star* asked the Army about continued segregation under the new draft law, the Army replied: "Our policy must continue to be the employment of Negro troop units of appropriate size and conformation in the best interests of over-all efficiency"?

§ That in spite of Truman's 1946 instructive, by 1949 there were still no Negro officers in the Navy, in the Marines and Air Force only 0·6 per cent of the officers were Negro, and in the Army 1·8 per cent?

§ That Negro discontent with the slow motion of Truman's "rapidly as possible" programme led this same year to threats to picket a testimonial dinner to Defence Secretary Louis Johnson, with the result that the dinner was cancelled?

§ That a Presidential investigating committee reported the following year (1950) that Negro servicemen were still largely consigned to labour detail; that the Negro's chance of obtaining an officer's commission in the Army was 1 in 70, compared to 1 in 7 for whites; that in 490 specialized fields of training in the Army, only 190 were open to Negroes; that cadet training schools were still closed to Negroes, et cetera?

§ That in 1957 the U.S. Information Agency had the nerve to point with pride to figures indicating that by 1954 Negroes constituted 3 per cent of the Army's officers, 1·1 per cent of the Marines' and Air Force's, and 0·1 per cent of the Navy's? (Don't forget that Negroes comprise 10 per cent of the population and an even higher proportion of the armed forces. Don't forget too that these official figures do not reveal the extent to which such Negro officers as do exist are concentrated in the lowest categories.)

Nor should you think, if you are in line for compulsory military service, that you can get out of it by claiming induction would subject you to racial discrimination.

Winifred Lynn tried it during World War II, to no avail. To be sure, the Fourteenth Amendment of the Constitution does say that all citizens shall be entitled to equal protection of the law. Taking note of this, Lynn instituted *habeas corpus* proceedings charging that the Selective Service Act would subject him to racial discrimination; but his plea was thrown out by the U.S. Circuit Court of Appeals in New York.

Needless to say, Lynn was not just imagining things.

Suffice it to cite just two of the infinitude of cases in point:

When, during World War II, Colonel William T. Colman, white, specified that he wanted a white chauffeur, and got Private William McRae, Negro, instead, he promptly shot him. A court martial reduced the charge of "assault with intent to do bodily harm" to "careless use of firearms", and Colonel Colman was reduced to a captaincy.

When German prisoners-of-war, assigned to work in the kitchen of an Army hospital at MacDill Field, Florida, refused to work because Negro patients were permitted to eat in the same mess-hall with white patients (albeit on separate sides), U.S. Army officials obligingly ordered the Negroes to another hall, whereupon the Nazis went back to work.

During World War II the armed services of the U.S.A. not only introduced the spectacle of segregated units to foreign lands, but in many instances sought to establish a measure of racial segregation in the civil life of European and Pacific countries.

For example, when Colonel James E. Manley set up U.S. Army headquarters in a Naples, Italy, hotel, he promptly ordered a "No Negroes" sign to be hung in front.

In Britain, the resentment of some white American troops against the equal treatment afforded by the English to Negro American troops reached such violent proportions that the authorities had to grant leave to the two groups on alternate nights.

In the Philippines, white troops pressured some restaurant owners into erecting "Whites Only" signs—introducing a concept previously unknown on the islands.

From Australia, the Associated Press reported the following: "Newest and swankiest of three service clubs for American Negro troops has been opened. From the deep-cushioned leather chairs of its attractive lounge to the streamlined polished metal of its modern kitchen, the Dr. Carver Club is exclusive, 'out of bounds' to all white troops save those fortunate enough to receive special invitations. As one Army officer put it, 'Those boys have been doing their country a great service. The clubs are just a token of our appreciation.' "

In some places, the exported "Made in U.S.A." segregation put down tenacious roots. The proprietor of the Thousand and One Nights Bar in Frankfurt, Germany, charged in 1949 with "conduct hostile or disrespectful to the Allied forces" for having refused to serve two American Negro corporals, replied in his own defence that he had taken his cue from white U.S. Army units which he had seen refuse to serve Negro troopers for five years.

On the home front, the treatment accorded Negro veterans was in strict conformity with the principles of white supremacy. Relatively little recognition was accorded them, even in the Press. Unique among the papers of the segregated territory in that it applauded Negro veterans at all, the Wilson, North Carolina, *Daily Times* in a special edition carrying photographs of all local service men who had been killed in action, grouped the Negroes together, added "Col." (Coloured) after each of their names, and omitted titles of respect in listing their surviving relatives.

Similarly, in the first Armistice Day parade in Birmingham, Alabama, following the end of World War II, the Negro troop units were required to bring up the rear, after the Fire Department, Boy Scouts, schoolboy patrol, and other such outfits had passed in review.

The services have likewise discriminated against Negro veterans.

Shortly after World War II the U.S. Army Air Corps excluded Negro patients from its hospital at Plattsburg Barracks, Washington, D.C. In an official explanation later, the War Department said that Negro patients there had been "unhappy" because of the "severe Winter climate".

In view of such as this, it is not surprising that thousands of American Negro troopers discharged overseas chose to remain there, finding in Europe a far greater measure of freedom than that obtaining in their native land.

One Negro veteran, enrolled in a European medical school, upon being asked whether he planned to return to the U.S.A. to practise, replied: "Do you think I'm crazy?"

Another, singing in a Parisian night club, upon receiving an offer from an impresario to make him great if he would return to the U.S.A., replied: "Thanks, but I don't want to be great; I just want to be happy."

Despite the continuing prospect of racial discrimination in the armed forces, Negroes continued to enlist at a greater rate than their white compatriots—partly because discrimination on the job made discrimination in service seem a lesser evil, and partly in the hope of getting a taste of equality by being assigned to overseas duty.

The Army, for some reason, deemed it necessary to discourage Negro enlistment, and to this end a quota system was adopted, limiting the proportion of Negroes in service to the proportion of Negroes in the population. For a time when the Negro quota had been filled the Army turned away all further Negro applicants; but then it hit upon the scheme of requiring Negroes to score 39 on a test in which all other applicants were required to score but 15.

By way of explanation, the War Department said: "In order to maintain the necessary controls relative to the numbers involved, the minimum acceptable grade on the pre-enlistment examination was raised in the case of Negro applicants."

The entry of the U.S.A. into the Korean fighting in 1950 focused world attention as never before on the status of Negroes in the armed forces.

To begin with, segregation-as-usual appeared to be the policy of draft officials in raising an army for the Korean fighting. Southern Congressmen almost succeeded in writing into the extension of the draft law a provision that any white draftees who objected to fighting side by side with Negroes would be given the privilege of being assigned to all-white units. This was rejected by Congress, however, but evidently on the assumption that segregation would be continued.

John LeFlore, Executive Secretary of the Mobile, Alabama, branch of the National Association for the Advancement of Colored People, wired a protest to General Lewis B. Hershey, head of the Selective Service System, protesting at the segregation of Negro draftees on buses on their way to induction, and also at the fact that "Negro draft registrants called here for pre-induction examinations are forced to eat in the hot kitchen of a private restaurant while white youths called for the same purpose eat in the main dining-room".

The indiscriminate application of the contemptuous word "Gook" by many white American troops to southern Koreans, northern Koreans, Chinese and Japanese alike, gave rise to such resentment that the military authorities were eventually obliged to frown officially upon its use, albeit with little effect.

As living evidence that the various Executive Orders calling for an end of segregation in the armed forces had not been carried out, the all-Negro 24th Infantry Regiment was thrown into the forefront of the Korean fighting at the outset. As Ollie Harrington, creator of the "Dark Laughter" cartoon in the *Pittsburgh Courier*, put it from the mouths of "Tan Yanks" up front, the perils of the war front were as nothing compared to the perils of a Negro sitting "up front" on the home front.

When General Walter Lee Weible in Tokyo ordered four portable swimming pools sent to the hard-pressed American forces in Korea, he specified that Negro troops were to have access to only one of the pools.

Casualties in the 24th were extremely heavy, and replacements and supplies, including shoes, were slow in coming. The white Press made much ado about the spectacle of coloured G.Is. fighting coloured Koreans; but the pages of the Negro Press began to fill with stories of atrocities committed, not by Koreans, but by white American officers against the Negro troops they were leading.

Then came the incident of the 24th being bombed by mistake by the American Air Force, with serious casualties being inflicted.

On August 6, 1951, the 24th's newly appointed commanding officer, Colonel Arthur S. Champeney, white, saw fit to address his troops, telling them he was going to change their reputation from "the frightened 24th to the fighting 24th".

The case of Lieutenant Leon A. Gilbert, who was sentenced to death by a court martial, attracted special attention. A wounded veteran of World War II with a record of ten years' service in the Army, Lieutenant Gilbert, while suffering from shock and fatigue due to prolonged heavy fighting, refused to obey the command of a white superior officer to return with twelve of his men to a position which Lieutenant Gilbert felt sure meant "certain death". Following a storm of public protest, President Truman commuted Gilbert to 20 years' imprisonment at hard labour, dishonourable discharge, and forfeiture of all pay and pension allowances. His wife has three children.

Following the court-martialling of Lieutenant Gilbert, mass court-martialling of whole units of the 24th Regiment ensued, with no comparable action being taken against white units which fell back in haste under heavy pressure.

"The letters we have received from convicted soldiers and the talks we have had with war correspondents strongly indicate that many of these men have been victimized by racial discrimination," said Thurgood Marshall, general counsel of the N.A.A.C.P. "It seems apparent that some of them are being made scapegoats for the failures of higher personnel."

Time and the military marched on, until today the U.S. Information Agency boasts that there are no more all-Negro units in the services, and that segregation has been done away with in service training programmes, base facilities, et cetera. This sounds great, as indeed it is. But don't forget that segregation just happens to be the most *conspicuous* form of discrimination. What has happened is that the American armed forces which were long segregated in form and discriminatory in content are now integrated in form and discriminatory in content. Half a loaf is better than no bread, but there is no mistaking it for the whole.

When in 1958 Lieutenant William B. Morton of Texas, stationed in Stuttgart, Germany, refused to shake the hand of a Negro fellow-officer, Army headquarters in Washington ordered that the charge of

I

"conduct unbecoming an officer" be dropped, with the result that only a modest fine was levied against him.

An American Negro novelist living in Paris proposed to tour U.S. military bases in Europe and make a *sub rosa* survey of the *sub rosa* discrimination still being practised, but even America's Negro newspapers declined to sponsor the project as "too hot to handle".

CHAPTER 9

WHO ARE SUBJECT TO FORCED LABOUR

A DARK skin is just enough to deprive you of a job—and then get you punished for being jobless.

Although there is nothing whatever in the U.S. Constitution guaranteeing the right to work, all of the 48 states have so-called vagrancy laws making it a criminal offence to be without work. This, in spite of the fact that there is what the business community politely refers to as a "normal float" of from three to five million unemployed —a job shortage which increases periodically to as much as fifteen million.

In practice, however, this seeming anomaly does not work a double hardship on the great majority of fair-skinned Americans, inasmuch as the vagrancy laws are enforced mainly against dark-skinned Americans —Negroes, Mexican-Americans, American Indians, gipsies, and others.

Part-time employment is not always regarded as a good excuse—in some places you can be convicted of vagrancy unless you work more than half of the time.

Of course if you can establish the fact that you have funds you may loaf all you wish, as persons of means are specifically exempted by the vagrancy laws.

In short, it is against the law to be unemployed and broke if you are able-bodied and without means of support.

True, when the states of California and Florida during the depression of the 1930s closed their borders to indigents, the Supreme Court overruled them, saying: "The mere state of being without funds is a Constitutional irrelevancy." This judicial observation has not been brought to bear on vagrancy laws, however, which have indeed been held Constitutional.

On their face, the laws of course say nothing about race. Moreover, one must be on the lookout for police action undertaken without regard to any law. In a great many places in the U.S.A.—especially expensive resort and residential areas—the police operate what is popularly known as the "Hobo Express". Should you find yourself broke and unemployed in such a place, and look it, you may be picked up by the police and given a free ride to the city limits or county line, where you will be deposited and warned not to return.

Negroes have composed a folksong about the omnipresent prospect of being charged with vagrancy, which goes like this:

> Standin' on the corner,
>   Waitin' for my brown;
> First thing I knowed
>   I was jailhouse bound.
>
> I asked Mr. Police
>   "Won't you turn me loose?"
> I said, "I got no money,
>   But a good excuse."
>
> And then I heard
>   Judge Pickett say,
> "Forty-five dollars—
>   Or take him away!"
>
> Wish that mean old
>   Judge was dead,
> And green grass growin'
>   All over his head!

Pursuits not Recognized

The crime of vagrancy is regarded as a continuing one, which means you can be sent to jail over and over again on the same charge, just as long as you remain broke and unemployed.

At the same time, the vagrancy laws list a variety of occupations and avocations as being as bad or worse than unemployment.

Of course, if you are a person of wealth you may engage in any or all of these pursuits, and be as idle as you wish, without fear of prosecution for vagrancy.

In most states the penalty for persons convicted of vagrancy is a fine ranging from 50 to 100 dollars, and/or a 30-day sentence, usually on a public work gang. In Arkansas the law specifies that vagrancy fines shall be worked out at the archaic rate of a dollar a day.

Throughout the South, vagrancy laws have taken the place of the

Black Codes enlarged by the white planters shortly after the Civil War with a view to keeping Negroes in a state of semi-slavery.

These Black Codes imposed an annual head-tax which the white planters frequently paid for delinquent Negroes, who were then required to work it out.

Special laws rigidly bound Negro apprentices to their white "employers", and still other laws made the slightest deviation from a labour contract—on the part of a Negro labourer, share-cropper, or tenant farmer—*prima facie* evidence of fraud.

Federal anti-peonage laws enacted in 1875 to free the Indians of New Mexico from peonage had the added effect of nullifying much of the Black Codes.

Twenty Varieties of Vagrants

It was then that many Southern states resorted to vagrancy laws, which they copied almost verbatim from New England states.

Unless you happen to be a very poor white share-cropper or migratory farm-worker, you may well rejoice that most (not all) *white* Americans have been emancipated from involuntary servitude. It was not always thus. The historian J. B. McMaster has written of the white European *émigrés* who became indentured servants to pay for their passage to America: "They became in the eyes of the law a slave and in both the civil and criminal code were classed with the Negro slave and the Indian . . . and might be flogged as often as the master or mistress thought necessary." Contemporary observers of that period opined that slavery was the natural condition of "proletarian whites from Germany and Ireland". Nor were native-born whites entirely exempt. A writer of 1793 recorded how some white parents in Pennsylvania were obliged to "sell and trade away their children like so many head of cattle".

Nowadays, the vagrancy laws remain as a heritage from that bygone era.

The Florida law is typically comprehensive, listing the following varieties of vagrants (quote):

1. Rogues and vagabonds.
2. Idle or dissolute persons who go about begging.
3. Common gamblers.
4. Persons who use juggling, or unlawful games or plays.
5. Common pipers and fiddlers.
6. Common drunkards.

7. Common night-walkers.
8. Thieves.
9. Pilferers.
10. Traders in stolen property.
11. Lewd, wanton, and lascivious persons.
12. Keepers of gambling places.
13. Common railers and brawlers.
14. Persons who neglect their calling or employment, or are without reasonably continuous employment or regular income and who have not sufficient property to sustain them and misspend what they earn without providing for themselves or the support of their families.
15. Persons wandering or strolling about from place to place without any lawful purpose or object.
16. Habitual loafers.
17. Idle and disorderly persons.
18. Persons neglecting all lawful business and habitually spending their time by frequenting houses of ill fame, gaming houses, or tippling shops.
19. Persons able to work but habitually living upon the earnings of their wives or minor children.
20. All able-bodied, male persons over the age of 18 years who are without means of support and remain in idleness.

If you fall into one or more of the above categories—and particularly if in addition you are nonwhite—you might be charged with vagrancy almost anywhere in the U.S.A. as the laws of the various states are very similar.

In a few states, however, there are variations worthy of note.

In South Carolina, the following categories are added to the more common forms of vagrancy:

1. All suspicious persons going about the country, swapping and bartering horses (without producing a certificate of his or their good character signed by a magistrate of the county from which said person last came).

2. All persons who, occupying or being in possession of some piece of land, shall not cultivate such a quantity thereof as shall be deemed by the magistrate to be necessary for the maintenance of himself and his family.

3. All persons representing publicly for gain or reward, without

being fully licensed, any play, comedy, tragedy, interlude or farce, or other entertainment of the stage, or any part thereof.

4. All sturdy beggars.

In Virginia, the vagrancy law is also aimed at:

1. All persons who shall unlawfully return into any county or corporation whence they have been legally removed.

2. All persons who shall come from any place without this Commonwealth to any place within it and shall be found loitering and residing therein, and shall follow no labor, trade, occupation, or business, and have no visible means of subsistence, and can give no reasonable account of themselves or their business in such place.

Are you sure you can give a reasonable account of yourself?

Debt Slavery

"Neither slavery nor involuntary servitude, except as a punishment for crime whereof the party shall have been duly convicted, shall exist within the United States, or any place subject to their jurisdiction", says the Thirteenth Amendment to the U.S. Constitution.

Sounds good, but look out!

"Peonage or debt slavery has by no means disappeared from our land", the Georgia Baptist Convention warned more than half a century later. "There are more white people involved in this diabolical practice than there were slaveholders. There are more Negroes held by these debt-slavers than were actually owned as slaves before the war between the states. The method is the only thing that has changed."

The modern method consists on the one hand of the company-owned commissary—a common feature of the turpentine and lumber camps of the South and the cotton plantations of the South and South-west. In these establishments, commonly referred to as "robbersaries", the "employees" are obliged to obtain their food and other basic necessities of life at exorbitant prices which keep them perpetually in debt and preclude their receiving cash wages for their work. At the same time, this private enterprise system has the support of law-enforcement agencies, who bring to bear the vagrancy and so-called fraud laws, so that the only escape for the debt slave is into a prison camp or convict work gang.

True, the Thirteenth Amendment and the Federal anti-peonage law have been in existence more than three-quarters of a century. Also true, the Supreme Court has ruled that "The state must respect the Constitutional and statutory command that it may not make a failure to labor in discharge of a debt any part of a crime. It may not directly or indirectly command involuntary servitude, even if it was voluntarily contracted for."

But, like many another basic law and court ruling, these have been rendered virtual dead letters through the reluctance of U.S. law enforcement agencies to institute criminal prosecutions under them. Only once or twice in each decade, when some spectacular case finds its way into the public eye, does the Justice Department stir itself in this field. Even then the effect is limited to the individual case concerned, leaving the system itself unaffected.

In 1951 the United Nations established an *Ad Hoc* Committee on Forced Labour, consisting of three members. Such a Committee was proposed by America, the U.N. rejecting a Soviet counter-proposal for a broad committee representative of the organized labour movement of the world. The three-man Committee proceeded to hold hearings, taking volumes of testimony relative to conditions in communist countries.

In reply to a Committee questionnaire, the U.S. State Department declared: "The United States Constitution and laws contain effective safeguards against the existence of such forced labor. The United States, therefore, has no penal or administrative laws, regulations, or administrative rules or practices pertinent to the Committee's inquiries."

The Committee accepted this assertion at face value, together with similar representations received from certain other countries having colonial possessions in Africa, Asia, and South America. A hearing was held, however, in New York for the announced purpose of taking testimony relative to conditions in the Western Hemisphere. When it was further announced that the hearing was about to be adjourned for lack of any evidence, the author of this present work felt moved to send the Committee an offer of evidence. The offer was publicly made, and accepted.

Although the author had lived all his life in a region where forced labour camps abound, he set out with a magnetoband recorder to penetrate the camps and bring out fresh evidence.

Getting into the camps was not easy; it was necessary to tell the bosses that the purpose of the expedition was to record folksongs. But when the songs had been recorded and the bosses had gone away, the real business began. Upon being told the purpose of the interviews, the debt slaves spoke freely into the microphone.

"They can't do no more than kill us," a turpentine worker at Fruit Cove, Florida, said. "I have heard a few of the old men say the only way out is to die out, but I have also heard it said that the truth shall make you free!"

The sordid tales unfolded hour after hour on to the toneband— lynching, flogging, rape, the castor-oil treatment. There was scarcely a man or woman who had not personally felt the bosses' lash.

With such horrors associated with life in the slave labour camps, one may wonder how it is that people are forced into them. The principal factor is starvation. The fact that Negroes are "last hired and first fired" serves to drive many unemployed workers into selling themselves and their families into slavery. Inflation in the slave market has led to cash advances as high as 500 dollars being offered to some skilled workers. Ordinarily, however, 25 dollars or less will do the trick.

The professional "labor recruiter" is in many respects a twentieth-century counterpart of the slave-traders of old. Turpentine camp operators, for example, pay recruiters something like 5 dollars per head for every single man, and 10 dollars for each family brought in.

Joe Hall, who operates a fleet of seven trucks in which he transports hundreds of Negro men, women, and children back and forth between Florida and Pennsylvania as the harvest demands, is a typical labour recruiter. In this traffic he has the active co-operation of the U.S. Employment Service. He tells this agency that he charges no transportation fees—and then proceeds to assess each worker 10 dollars. Obtaining recruits by painting rosy word pictures of the wages to be earned, he generally pays only half of the promised rate, works them under a gun, houses them in a barn, and feeds them on beans after assessing them 5 dollars per week for board. When his workers seek to escape, as they did at Ulysses, Pennsylvania, K.K.K. fiery crosses are burned. When this fails to work, Hall has the escapees arrested.

"Don't you know they can't make you work against your will in satisfaction of a debt?" the author asked a group of forced labourers at Mandarin, Florida.

"They do do it," was their bitter reply.

The alternative to working out a debt with the company or planter is to work it out with the county prison—to "chain-gang it". From the workers' point of view, there is not much choice. Though the chain-gang sentence at "hard labor" may be at the rate of as little as one day for each 50 cents he is said to owe, at least the worker knows there will eventually be an end of it, whereas the private "employer" may conspire to keep him perpetually in bondage.

Corner-stone of the forced labour system is the company commissary. There are some 4,200 members of the National Industrial Stores Association, and their commissaries do a 1,000,000,000 dollar business every year. Symbolic of the compulsion to buy and the compulsion to pay is the toe of a lynched Negro, kept as a "souvenir" on a commissary counter near Hendersonville, North Carolina. Asked whether he would personally take part in the lynching of a Negro, the manager replied slowly, "No, no. I wouldn't—not unless he owed me money."

The fare afforded by the commissary is extremely limited, consisting of a few canned goods, meal, flour, dried beans, and salted or smoked pork fat. Fresh vegetables, meat, fruit, eggs, milk and butter are virtually unheard of. One Negro turpentine worker at Kansas City, Florida, when asked how often fresh meat was available in his camp, replied, "Neither weekly nor yearly." Another, relatively lucky, said that his camp at Moniak, Georgia, offered the workers a choice each weekend of "pig ears, pig tails, or pig feet". Needless to say, such a diet gives rise to all kinds of dietary diseases, such as rickets and pellagra.

Medical attention is almost never available in the camps, the workers being forced to rely upon home remedies and self-medication.

In many camps the bosses will not tolerate any degree of illness as an excuse for not working. At the lumber mill camp operated by McDuffie Stallworth at Pineapple, Alabama, any worker who complains of illness is forcibly given two bottles of castor oil—and made to work, anyway. Childbearing almost never takes place in a hospital and only rarely is there a doctor in attendance—the woman is lucky if she can obtain the services of a midwife. The death-rate among both mothers and infants at childbirth is many times higher among these workers than with the American population generally.

Home life in the slave labour camps is a living hell. The company-owned shacks almost always have leaky roofs; if there are any windows at all, they are protected neither by screens nor glass. Sometimes the cracks in the walls are so large that, as one worker described it, "You can see almost as much of the outside from inside the house as you could if you went out the door." Migratory farm workers frequently are forced to live in even worse "housing", constructed of pieces of tin and cardboard cartons. Flies and vermin of all sorts spread diseases, which take a heavy toll.

In the slave labour camps the mandatory work day lasts from "can to can't"—from "can see to can't see", or in other words, from before dawn until dark. It is one of the woman's duties to wake her husband, feed him, and have him ready to go to work at the appointed hour. If she fails in this, the penalties are often severe. For example, it is the custom of Murray Holloway, the woods-rider for the Cordele Turpentine Company at Cordele, Georgia, to ride through the Negro quarters about 4.30 every morning, shouting for the workers to clamber upon his truck to be driven into the woods. If a man is not ready when called, Holloway may beat the man, and his wife too. For instance, he beat Cleo Odom for not having given her husband breakfast soon enough, and when her husband Joe protested, Holloway knocked him unconscious with a club.

The work, too, is often hazardous. In the turpentine industry, for example, the American operators finally adopted a technique developed by the Soviet Union for increasing the flow of sap by spraying the tree gashes with sulphuric acid. But in the U.S.A., no protection from the acid is provided for the workers who apply it.

In St. John's County, Florida, the author came across a worker who is called "Red Eye" because the acid has nearly destroyed his eyesight.

"We even have to buy our own soda to put on our acid burns," he declared.

It is often the woman's lot to be left with her children as "hostages", since virtually the only real route to escape from the bondage of debt-slavery is for the husband to run away under cover of darkness, leaving his family and possessions behind as "security" to be held until such time as he may be able to procure a *bona-fide* job which will enable him to save enough money to pay off whatever amount the planter asserts the family owes him.

Sometimes the bosses call upon the sheriff or police to bring back runaway slave labourers. At Cross City, Florida, the author heard a boss telephone the sheriff and order him to post guards on all the roads leading out of the area to block the escape of a Negro who had left camp allegedly owing 15 dollars.

At this same camp, a worker told how the boss had killed workers for owing as little as 5 dollars, "and you would have to die, because he would kill you and make the other hands bury you out in the woods."

Most often, the bosses strap pistols on their belts and go after runaways themselves. The authorities not only do not interfere in this procedure, but obligingly grant the bosses permits to carry pistols. When this sort of "free enterprise" fails to "get its man", the bosses call on the hooded Ku Klux Klan for assistance in recapturing the runaways and terrorizing the rest of the workers.

There is nothing at all subtle about the handling of runaways. For instance, when James Wiggins and his wife ran away from the plantation of J. S. Decker at Clarksdale, Mississippi, where they had been forced to work in the fields under a gun, they were brought back in chains and offered for sale for 175 dollars. Similarly, a lumber-mill operator of Lauderdale County, Mississippi, kept one of his Negro workers shackled to his bunk with a log-chain around his neck each night, to prevent him from running out on an alleged 20-dollar debt.

Here are just a few of the typical cases brought to light by the author.

Charles Andrews clubbed with a pine-knot while another boss pointed a pistol at him. His offence: trying to escape from a labour camp near Bunnell, Florida.

Roy Jackson given a "pistol whipping" by the boss of a turpentine camp at Cordele, Georgia. His offence: picking up a shirt which he thought had been discarded.

Robert Graves, sawmill worker of Pineapple, Alabama, tied over a barrel and the "blood knocked out" with a piece of sawmill belt. His offence: leaving work to report, as ordered, to a military draft board.

James Day, worker who escaped from the turpentine camp of William Belote at Moniak, Georgia. Day was forced to leave behind his four small children as hostages for a 200-dollar debt he was falsely said to owe. He appealed to the U.S. District Attorney and the F.B.I. in Macon, to no avail. When he finally went into court to claim possession of his kidnapped children, he was thrown into jail on a charge of having abandoned them! The sheriff, accompanied by boss Belote, offered to release Day and forget about the alleged debt if Day would agree to go back to work at the turpentine camp.

James Alford, who left his wife and two children as hostages for an alleged 30-dollar debt at the camp of Colonel Dorsey at Cordele, Georgia. Colonel Dorsey jailed Alford's wife for refusing to tell where her husband had gone. Alford, who had found a job in Florida with a view to paying the 30 dollars and reclaiming his wife and children, heard of the arrest and so returned to Cordele. Upon arrival he was jailed on a charge of vagrancy, even though he had proof of employment. In court he was sentenced to pay a fine of 150 dollars or serve 12 months at hard labour on the chain-gang.

"You will just have to shoot me or electrocute me or do what you will," Alford told the judge, "but I can't serve 12 months because I have a wife and two children to take care of."

Colonel Dorsey and another white boss were in court, bidding for the privilege of paying Alford's fine in order to secure a slave labourer. The other man carried a paper bag full of money, but the judge awarded Alford to Colonel Dorsey, with orders to work out the full amount of 180 dollars on Dorsey's plantation.

George Messenger and his wife Katherine, elderly white share-croppers of Pensacola, Florida, were sentenced to seven years at hard labour in the Florida State Penitentiary for non-payment of an alleged $232.76 grocery debt contracted by their son-in-law. Their three young daughters were taken from them, placed in orphanages, and offered for adoption.

Not content with the total exploitation of their slave labourers economically, many planters seek also to exploit their women slaves sexually. One of the most notorious cases was that in which a 30-man K.K.K. firing squad executed two Negro war veterans, George Dorsey and Roger Malcolm and their wives, because one of the women had refused to sleep with the white planter for whom they were forced to share-crop.

Many women are also held as domestic servants. Dora Jones, a 57-year-old Negro woman, testified that she had been forced to serve as maid to a white couple for 29 years without pay. In another case, Zenovia Selles, a 23-year-old Puerto Rican girl, was found crying on the streets of New York. She told of being brought in from Puerto Rico to work for an American family as a maid, and after three months had not been given any payment for her labour. In still another case, Albert S. Johnson, owner of a 2,000-acre cotton plantation at Helena, Arkansas, was charged by his common-law wife Dosha Moon with forcing her and her three daughters to work for him under penalty of beating and death. And when Essie Lee Wright, a Negro girl, sought to escape from Johnson's plantation in a truck, Johnson shot the tyres off the truck, explaining to the authorities that she was "obligated to work for him".

Such was the picture of domestic forced labour as the author found and recorded it. He was forced to conclude that at least one and a half million native-born Americans, exclusive of their families, were currently being held in forced labour. It was also discovered that ever since the outbreak of World War II, the U.S. Government, at the behest of American planters, has permitted the importation of millions of farm-workers from nearby colonial and semi-colonial areas. The bulk of these are the so-called Mexican "wetbacks", so named because they swim across the Rio Grande River to enter the U.S.A. illegally, while U.S. border police look the other way. The President's Commission on Migratory Labour, in its Report issued in 1951, conceded that the great majority of these Mexican nationals are peonized on American plantations, with the connivance of governmental agencies.

"Wetbacks who are without funds to pay the smuggler for bringing them in or to pay the trucker-contractor who furnishes transportation from the boundary to the farm are frequently sold from one exploiter to the next", this Report confesses. "For example, the smuggler will offer to bring a specified number of wetbacks across the river for such an amount as ten or fifteen dollars per man. The smuggler with his party in tow will be met by the trucker, who will then buy the wetback party by paying off the smuggler. The trucker, in turn, will have a deal to deliver the workers to farm employers at an agreed-upon price per head.

"Once on the U.S. side of the border and on the farm numerous devices are employed to keep the wetback on the job. His pay, or some portion thereof, is frequently held back. The wetback is a hungry human being. He is a fugitive, and it is as a fugitive that he lives. Under the constant threat of apprehension and deportation, he cannot protest, no matter how unjustly he is treated."

The next largest group of imported forced labourers consists of Negroes from the British West Indies. During the period from 1943 to 1950, a total of 93,178 of these were brought in with the sanction of the U.S. Government. Besides these, there were about 10,000 Puerto Ricans who are working on U.S. farms under contracts sanctioned by the U.S. Government; and many more have been imported and peonized while the Government turned its back.

Just as the planters must generally pay out so much per head to acquire wetbacks, they must also post surety bonds with the U.S. Immigration Service in importing contract labour. The bond required is 100 dollars for each Jamaican, 50 dollars for each Bahaman, and 25 dollars for each Mexican. At least a third of the Mexicans who have been brought in under contract have escaped from the plantations to which they were assigned, and in such cases the planters must forfeit the bonds, which therefore are tantamount to being the purchase price of the workers.

To the planters, labour is labour—they are interested only in getting the work done as cheaply as possible. As the Manager of the California Beet-growers' Association told the President's Commission: "We have used great numbers of the so-called stoop labor class of labor throughout the years. We have gone through the whole gamut. We have used Chinamen, Japs, Hindus, Filipinos, Mexican nationals, Mexican wetbacks if you please, American Indians, Negroes, Bahamans, prisoners of war, and what-have-you. We have always been willing to take any kind of labor that we could get when we needed them."

And a big cotton-planter of Arkansas told the Commission: "Cotton is a slave crop, and nobody is going to pick it that does not have to. Now the Texas-Mexicans have found out they can get other kinds of work, and so the Mexican wetback is about the only reservoir of labor that we know of."

(In 1957, California planters prevailed upon the U.S. Government to import Japanese farm-labourers under three-year contracts. One of these, Keizo Koshigeta, reported in a letter to the Tokyo *Asahi Shimbun* in 1958: "I have been in California for one year now as a farm-labourer, and there has been trouble which we never anticipated at the time we left Japan. The trouble has been over income tax, transfers to other farms, and individual activities . . . we are among the lowest-paid workers in the United States . . . our net pay comes to less than 40 cents an hour. Even when we want to transfer to another farm which pays a gross rate of $1.10 instead of 75 cents per hour, we cannot do so of our own free will. We would like the authorities concerned to give adequate consideration to these points in preparation for the short-term farm labourers who are scheduled to come to the U.S.A. this Spring." In his letter Koshigeta added that every time the Japanese Consul-General in San Francisco visited the labour camp he said, "The difference in political and economic power between Japan and the United States is the reason why everything cannot be done just as you want it to be, but we would like you to endure them if you come up against some hardships.")

Another major group caught in the toils of forced labour are the migratory farm-workers who make their way across the face of the American continent each year in their efforts to eke out a living from seasonal employment. Physical as well as legalistic and psychological coercion is employed to force many migratory workers to "stay put" or "move on" at the dictate of the planters, aided and abetted in many instances by governmental authorities. Just as the substitution of wage slavery for chattel slavery relieved the former slave-owning class of responsibility for the upkeep of their labourers, so has the substitution of migratory labour for resident farm labour served the same end.

The living conditions of these workers are so bad as to defy description. The dismal scenes portrayed of the great Oklahoma "Dust Bowl" migrations to California during the 1930s in John Steinbeck's *The Grapes of Wrath* have not disappeared in the least. On the contrary, a probe by the Colorado State Commission in 1950, and subsequent investigations by the Federal Government, have found that in many respects conditions have worsened.

At the bottom of their plight is the land hunger which especially afflicts the segregated territory. Throughout the Black Belt of the South, where Negroes are in the majority, 73 per cent of all families own no land. In the Red River Bottoms the proportion rises to 80 per cent, and in the Delta Region 90 per cent of all families are landless.

The United Nations, after extensive surveys, has listed the southern region of the U.S.A. as one of the "backward and underfed" areas of the world. Even during the relatively prosperous wartime boom year of 1943, thirty million of the South's people were underfed, according to a survey of the National Research Council. Anaemia due to iron deficiency in the diet, and generally aggravated by intestinal worm infestations, is extremely common. Hookworm infestation reaches 100 per cent of the population of some rural Florida counties. In Tennessee 50 per cent of the entire farm population suffers from vitamin A deficiency.

Returning to his home, the author set about transcribing the recorded interviews and compiling his other data into a Memorandum, which was delivered to the U.N. Committee on September 15, 1952. At the same time, he asked that he be permitted to testify before the final hearings scheduled to be held in Geneva, Switzerland, and to bring some American forced labourers with him. The Committee agreed to hear him, but said it was "not keen about interviewing forced labourers in person, but preferred to hear experts".

The author was given ten days to get to Geneva, at his own expense (all previous witnesses had had their expenses paid, including a liberal *per diem* allowance). Before testifying, the author was questioned privately by the Committee's Secretary, Manfred Simon, who re-marked: "Of course, the U.S. Government does all it can to eliminate forced labour."

The line of questioning pursued by the Committee Chairman, Sir Ramaswami Mudaliar of India, further revealed the group's orientation.

"How can you say that Mexicans are held in forced labour in the U.S.A., when they sign their work contracts voluntarily?" he de-manded.

"Since time immemorial," the author replied, "men have been forced by economic pressures to sell themselves and their families into slavery, and in my estimation this only makes the slavery the more despicable!"

Not finding such replies to his liking, Sir Ramaswami soon in-structed the author to make his prepared statement.

"Forced laborers in the U.S.A. are not prisoners of war or persons convicted of some crime against the state, but rather are 'guilty' only of belonging to some vulnerable racial, economic, national, or occupa-tional group," the author pointed out. "Moreover, their labor is not dedicated to the public welfare, but is exploited purely for private profit.

"However, the Government's having given a free hand to the private exploiters of forced labor does not in any wise mitigate the fact that the system could not function without the overt collaboration and covert sanction of Government at all levels—local, state, and national. If the U.N. Committee is to do justice, it must recognize that in the U.S.A. those laws which constitute the legalistic framework for the forced labor system are cleverly cloaked in other guises. Besides the compulsory military service act, immigration laws, and fraud laws, there are the vagrancy laws, labor recruiting laws, and laws dealing with contracts. In the absence of such 'enabling legislation', the exploiters of forced labor would be obliged to rely entirely, rather than partly as at present, upon such extra-legal instruments of coercion as the club, lash, and pistol.

"The Federal Government as represented by its legislative, judicial, and law enforcement branches—Congress, Supreme Court, and Department of Justice—is charged under the Constitution and Federal law with the responsibility of stamping out forced labor. But the Government makes a practice of not practising the enforcement of these laws, and consequently what the State Department claims are 'effective safeguards' are rendered dead letters and mere scraps of paper.

"Painful though my role may be, I consider it my patriotic duty to do what I can to bring the healing heat of world opinion to bear upon the cancerous growth of forced labor that afflicts my homeland. I do not see how the United States can enjoy either self-respect or the respect of the community of nations if such things are kept hidden.

"For the benefit of any who take stock in such things, let me say that two of my forebears—William Williams and Arthur Middleton —signed the American Declaration of Independence. In the exercise of much the same right to disavow tyranny, I here and now declare my independence from those powers in American life who have usurped the democratic prerogatives of the people and who are responsible for such evils as forced labor in our land. In so doing I am confident that I speak for the great bulk of the American people who believe in liberty and justice for all.

"In conclusion, I wish only to ask, on behalf of all the forced laborers in the U.S.A., that the Committee remove the gag which has kept them in silence, by transmitting their pleas to the General Assembly of the United Nations so that the world may hear and judge."

With that, the author was summarily dismissed by Sir Ramaswami. In its official Press release issued later that day, the Committee suppressed the author's statement. In marked contrast, the Committee had issued voluminous accounts of charges levelled by previous witnesses, against certain other countries. It was not too surprising, therefore, that when the Committee issued its 621-page Report, a mere handful of pages were devoted to charges against the U.S.A. The documentary evidence contained in the author's Memorandum and statement had all been consigned to the waste-paper basket!

"All of Mr. Kennedy's allegations are general charges and do not appear to be supported by any proof", the State Department sanctimoniously concluded the Committee's Report.

In 1956 the Soviet Union announced the liquidation of its labour camps, and by 1957, when the International Labour Organization, in association with the United Nations, drafted an agreement against forced labour, an indictment of debt slavery was prominently included, and the United States felt obliged to sign on the dotted line.

CHAPTER 10

WHO MAY VOTE WHERE

As a native-born or naturalized American citizen, you may think you are free to vote.

Not so, however, if you are a Negro American and live in the South.

So far as black folk are concerned, there has not been a free election held in that region since Federal troops were withdrawn from it after the election of 1876.

To be sure, the Fifteenth Amendment to the Constitution's Bill of Rights, adopted in 1870, asserts that "The right of citizens of the United States to vote shall not be denied or abridged by the United States or by any state on account of race, color, or previous condition of servitude".

But if you wrap yourself in that and start to the polls down in Dixieland, you might find it a mighty poor shield if your colour isn't right (white).

For the fact is that this particular provision of the Bill of Rights was only good for one more-or-less-free national election (that of 1872), and ever since then has been more or less a dead letter in the states where the majority of America's Negro citizens live.

This autonomy enjoyed by the régime of white supremacy which holds sway over the Southern states has been made possible partly by the apathy of the Federal Government and partly because the Constitution allows each state to fix the qualifications of voters within it. Southern officialdom has taken great pains to enact non-discriminatory requirements which can be administered in a discriminatory manner.

Before looking into the prevailing situation, it might be well to glance briefly back into history, to the brief period after the Civil War when free elections were first established and then subverted.

Our Big Lie

That decade of so-called "Reconstruction" is undoubtedly the "best-lied-about" period in American history. Violence was so rife at the polls in the election of 1876 that the outcome, both in the Presidential and gubernatorial contests, was not in doubt. Behind closed doors, the notorious "Deal of '76" was made, whereby the Southern political powers conceded the Presidential election to the Republican Presidential candidate, Hayes, in return for which the North conceded Southern governorships to the anti-Negro candidates of the Democratic Party, and, moreover, agreed to withdraw Federal troops from the region. In such manner a large measure of ideological victory was wrested by the Southern racists from the military defeat they had suffered from the armies of Lincoln.

Having thus betrayed the war aims for which the nation had bled so much, it was deemed necessary to salve the nation's conscience by concocting Our Big Lie as to what had taken place. First given full-length formulation in the book, *The Clansman*, by Thomas Dixon, it subsequently found expression in the film, *Birth of a Nation*, and an entire literature, including such popular contemporary novels as *Gone with the Wind*.

Consequently, wherever you look today, North or South, in periodicals, history books, and official manuals, you will find the Big Lie presented as absolute truth, actually believed by writer and reader alike. The phraseology varies but little. *Life* magazine (1957) puts it thus:

"In a relative instant the Negroes were transformed [by Emancipation] from a frightened confused rabble into a great force to be reckoned with. But no quick change could give them education or organization, and they fell prey to two varieties of troublemaker: carpetbaggers and scalawags. The former were Northerners who hastened South to seek their fortunes in chaos, presumably carrying their possessions in satchels made of rug fabric. Scalawags were renegade Southerners of the same opportunistic breed. Between them they soon organized the Negroes to serve their own purposes. Against this background arose the Ku Klux Klan, composed of whites who tried, by threats and beatings, to drive the Negroes, carpetbaggers, and scalawags from power. Many of the Klan's early leaders were men of dignity, ex-Confederate officers."

The U.S. Government, party to the original Deal of '76, is also an accessory after the fact in helping to disseminate the Big Lie. Here is how the State Department's U.S. Information Service puts it in its bulletin, *The American Negroes*:

"Devoid—understandably—of all political experience, the Negroes

were easily exploited by the politicians and adventurers of the North
(the famous Carpetbaggers) who built fortunes on the ruins of
the South. . . . It was in this epoch that the over-famous Ku
Klux Klan, with its ceremonies calculated to provoke terror, with its
imagery of power, arose. An organization of self-protection created
by the whites of the South, the K.K.K. was originally as much
against the Northern 'profiteers' as against the excesses of the freed
Negroes."

But do not be misled just because contemporary politicos have
affixed the Great Seal of the United States of America to this betrayal
of all those who fought under Lincoln in order that the nation might
have a "new birth of freedom".

It has been said that all societies thus far have had their "necessary
fictions". Certain it is that this fiction, seeking to hide the fact that the
Negro was consigned to second-class citizenship by the Deal of 1876,
has been indispensable to the reign of white supremacy that has held
sway over the South ever since.

For us, the living, the truth about the Reconstruction period is hard
to find, having been virtually buried alive. There does exist, however,
in the Library of Congress and in the Schomburg Collection of the
New York Public Library, two remaining sets of thirteen volumes of
testimony taken during the Reconstruction period by a "Joint Congressional Committee on the Condition of Affairs in the Late In-
surrectionary States". Going into the South when the Klan terror was
at its height, the Committee took testimony from victims of the terror
who were still able to speak—Negroes, and the so-called Scalawags
and Carpetbaggers. The picture which emerges is one of heroic plain
people, white and Negro, joined in the task of building a true democracy in the South to replace the oppressive old order. Duly-elected
white and Negro office-holders worked side by side in the state legislatures and municipal councils, and Negroes elected to the U.S.
Congress and Senate in Washington served ably and well. The
governments created by those poor folks' democracy were, if anything, more honest, conscientious and progressive than either their
predecessors or successors. Among other things, they laid the foundations for public education in the South.

The Ku Klux Klan was not, as the apologia would have it, a
necessary protection against excesses, but a deliberately conceived
terrorist plot, organized and officered by the old landed gentry, to
overthrow the popular democracy, restore plutocracy, and reduce the

Negro once more to a condition of helpless servitude. All this, thanks to national lassitude, it accomplished. (Had it failed, this book would never have had to be written. . . .)

And so, with the overthrow of Reconstruction democracy, the cornerstone of the political tyranny in the Southern states became the dictate: "Voting is white folk's business!"

Populism into Poll Tax

When at the turn of the century under the liberalizing impetus of the Populist movement Negroes began to reappear at the polls, the states in the segregated territory devoted two decades—from 1890 to 1910—to building constitutional and statutory barriers which again rendered Negro Americans politically impotent. In Louisiana, for example, there were 130,334 Negro voters in 1896, but only 1,342 by 1904.

Typical of the techniques employed was the following "Call to Arms" issued on election eve in North Carolina:

"You are Anglo-Saxons. You are armed and prepared and you will do your duty. Go to the polls tomorrow and if you find the Negro voting tell him to leave the polls and if he refuses, kill him, shoot him down in his tracks. We shall win tomorrow if we have to do it with guns."

Requirement of payment of an annual poll-tax as a prerequisite to voting was another means of disfranchisement. White people were somehow led to believe that the tax would operate against Negroes, but not against them, while in reality the tax disfranchised even more whites than Negroes.

The late Senator Carter Glass, as a delegate to the Virginia constitutional convention which adopted the poll-tax, said frankly, "We came here to make distinctions. We expect to make distinctions. We will make distinctions."

Today you must still pay a poll-tax in order to vote if you are a resident of Alabama, Arkansas, Mississippi, Texas, or Virginia. In most of these states the tax ranges from $1.00 to $2.00, but in three states it is cumulative, the maximum in Virginia being $5.08, Mississippi $6.00, and Alabama $30.00.

The Gallup Poll has estimated that "the total number of persons not voting in 11 Southern states because of the poll-tax and other local reasons" in 1948 was 7,700,000; and the situation has not changed much since.

One noteworthy effect of the poll-tax has been the control over Congress it has given to Representatives and Senators from the Southern states. The tax has worked wonders in cutting down the electorate; in one poll-tax state only 13 per cent of the potential voters vote. With so few constituents, the office-holders, with their political machines, are able to buy blocs of votes by paying people's poll-taxes. Returned to office term after term, through seniority Southerners have garnered three times their proportionate share of dominant positions on House committees and twice their share on Senate committees. In this way they have practically dictated America's foreign and domestic policies for many decades.

Repeal of the poll-tax has long been a plank in both the Democratic and Republican platforms, but the anti-poll-tax bills introduced in every session of Congress have always been bottled up by "gentlemen's agreements" between Southern Democrats and certain Northern Republicans.

Nor does there seem to be much hope that the remaining poll-tax states can be persuaded to abolish the tax themselves any time soon.

When the liberal Governor Ellis Arnall abolished Georgia's tax in 1947, gubernatorial candidate Eugene Talmadge reconciled himself by declaring: "I done decided the best way to keep the niggers from voting is to let all the white folks vote, and then pass the word around that Mister Nigger is not wanted at the polls."

Burdensome though the poll-tax undoubtedly is, if you are a Negro living in segregated territory you will find that the tax is the least of the obstacles between you and the ballot box.

Just as it did during the overthrow of Reconstruction, the price-tag on the ballot in many areas still reads, "One vote, one life".

Of course you will not *necessarily* lose your life for voting, but thousands of Negroes *have* died in the struggle for the abolition of political slavery. At present only a token few are actually killed each election year, but the number is increasing. Not since the anti-Reconstruction terror has the road to the polls been so beset with mortal peril.

Death is just one of the possible penalties you might incur. You may simply be beaten, knifed, or otherwise damaged physically. Then, again, you may be deprived of your livelihood instead of your life. You may be:

Fired from your job.
Evicted from your farm.
Driven from your home.
Denied credit.
Terrorized.
Ostracized.

The notion that "voting is white folk's business" is constantly brought to public attention by public officials and such quasi-official organizations as the White Citizens' Councils and the Ku Klux Klan.

In a treatise, *Negro Suffrage—Its False Theory*, the Imperial Wizard of the K.K.K. has attacked the Fifteenth Amendment to the Constitution as a "war spite measure", and predicted that it cannot "much longer endure". After describing the U.S.A. as a "white man's country", the Wizard calls for "clear and frank recognition that racial discrimination is an American national policy". Elsewhere, an authoritative Klan journal declares: "It is better for the negro to be a political eunuch in the house of friends, than a voter rampant in the halls of enemies."

The halls of Congress have for generations resounded with these same sentiments.

"I believe in white supremacy, and as long as I am in the Senate I expect to fight for white supremacy," Senator Allen J. Ellender of Louisiana oft declaimed.

When in 1944 the Supreme Court was prevailed upon to rule against the white primary elections which long constituted the real elections in the one-party (Democratic) South, Senator Burnet R. Maybank of South Carolina said: "Regardless of the Supreme Court decision and any laws that may be passed by Congress, we in South Carolina are going to do whatever we can to protect our white primaries."

John D. Long, a legislator from the same state, was more explicit. "As for the Negro voting in my primary," he said, "we'll fight him at the precinct meeting, we'll fight him at the county convention, we'll fight him at the enrollment books, and, by God, we'll fight him at the polls if I have to bite the dust as did my ancestors!"

"Political equality is a question it were as well for the Negro race to forget in the South," said the Waterboro, South Carolina, *Press and Standard*.

"Our Southern duty is to get around the decision in more ways than one," added the widely syndicated Southern columnist, John Temple Graves.

In the face of physical, economic, and psychological warfare, the South's Negroes have intensified their struggle to get at the ballot boxes. Still, by 1958, when a Conference on Voting Restrictions in Southern States was held in Washington, D.C., not more than one-fourth of the South's 6,000,000 Negroes of voting age were registered to vote. This Conference, sponsored by the Southern Conference Educational Fund (a private group uniting Southern whites and Negroes against discrimination), presented the Department of Justice and Civil Rights Commission with state-by-state reports on violations of the Negro's right to vote. Here are just a few of the highlights the Conference threw upon democracy's low points down South:

Mississippi: Negroes free to vote in only six of the state's 82 counties.

Alabama: Negroes constitute 30 per cent of the population, 6 per cent of the voters.

Georgia: 160,000 of the state's 650,000 potential Negro voters are registered to vote.

Virginia: 60,000 of the state's 750,000 Negroes are registered to vote.

Florida: 148,000 of the state's 370,000 potential Negro voters are registered.

Louisiana: Negroes constitute 30 per cent of the population, 16 per cent of the voters.

If you live in a city your chances of voting are better than if you live in a small town or in the country. But even if you happen to be one of the lucky ones, you can't expect to have much voice, if any, in the conduct of your city's public affairs. Most municipalities in the segregated territory have been gerrymandered by the white office-holders so that the Negro neighbourhood is carved up like the centre of a pie, thus assuring white majorities in each ward-slice.

Something new in gerrymandering has been conceived by the officials of Altamonte Springs, Florida. Alarmed by increased Negro voting which had reduced the white majority to eight votes, they proceeded in 1952 to vote the Negro section out of town.

Atlanta in the same year took a slightly different course. Instead of voting Negroes out of town, it voted more whites in by incorporating outlying districts into a "Greater Atlanta".

In 1957 the voters of Alabama (most of whom are white) in a special referendum authorized the state legislature to liquidate Macon County as a political entity by carving it up and apportioning the pieces to adjoining counties. The reason: a majority of the citizens of Macon County are Negroes.

The same year, the Alabama legislature liquidated the town of Tuskegee as a municipality, simply because 70 per cent of its residents happen to be Negroes. In protest against being thus robbed of the right to self-government, Tuskegee's 4,600 Negroes launched a boycott of white-owned stores.

How Many Windows in the White House?

Your first problem if you aspire to vote but your colour isn't white and you live in the South, is how to get your name on the registration books as qualified to vote and to keep it there.

Originally registration was designed merely as a means of preventing unscrupulous persons from casting more than one ballot, but Negro Emancipation prompted Southern officials to seize upon registration requirements as a means of barring Negroes from the polls.

To begin with, many Southern states open their books for new registrants for a very limited time only—generally at a time far removed from an election, so that public interest would be at a low ebb. Indeed, the opening of the books is often something of a state secret, as there is no desire on the part of the incumbents to increase the number of white voters either. Even if you manage to find out about the opening of the books, you may also find—as reported by the *Birmingham World*—that the registrar has chosen the registration period in which to go fishing.

Or you may discover that the registrar is a white woman who operates in the parlour of her home—where a Negro dare not intrude. The woman may even be fortified by a ferocious dog, specially trained to go after dark meat. Complaints as to this have been most common in Virginia and North Carolina.

In Florida in 1958 the registrar was telling Negro applicants: "Go ahead and register if you can take what comes afterward!" As a result of this sort of thing, in five north Florida counties where there were 16,533 potential Negro voters, only 110 had dared to put their names down.

If you do go to your county courthouse to register, in segregated territory you will doubtless find two lines—one for whites, one for Negroes. If you are a Negro, it might be well to take along a box lunch of some sort, as it is not unheard of for Negro applicants to be kept standing in line for one or more days.

In 1950 Professor Alvin Jones of New Orleans, Louisiana, a militant champion of civil rights for Negroes, was savagely clubbed in the sheriff's office at Opeluses for leading a group of Negro citizens to register to vote. Professor Jones filed a complaint with the F.B.I., but was told that it "couldn't handle" the case. He died a few months later from a blood clot on the brain, a result of the injuries he had suffered.

When your turn does come to register, the registrar will probably insist that you perform to the letter every literacy and educational test prescribed by law. Of course, if your skin were white this would likely be accepted as *prima facie* evidence of literacy and educational fitness.

Your session with the registrar may be something of an ordeal. Most of the segregated states now empower their registrars to require applicants to read or write, *and* understand *and* explain the Constitution. Alternatively in some states the registrar may simply qualify certain applicants as being "of good character and understanding the duties of citizenship". This latter criterion, however, you will generally find reserved for white folks.

This machinery thus enables the registrar to refuse to register you if you are a Negro and he so chooses, even though you may possess one or more college degrees; and at the same time to qualify even the most illiterate whites.

Of course, you are free to appeal against a registrar's decision in the courts, but by the time a ruling can be had, the election will undoubtedly be over.

It is altogether impossible to anticipate what questions a registrar may ask you, except in the State of Georgia, where you are required by law to answer correctly at least 10 from a list of 30 questions adopted by the legislature (as originally drawn, this law would have required 30 correct replies, but it was modified when newsmen discovered that the legislators themselves did not know all the answers).

Elsewhere, the registrar is free to extract his questions from thin air. For instance, according to *Collier's* magazine, Florida registrars in a recent election were asking Negro applicants, "How many windows in the White House?"

The current trend is for the states to vest more and more discretionary power in the registrars so that the actual discrimination can be left to them, without appearing in statutory form.

Alabama pioneered in this field with the Boswell Amendment to her state constitution in 1946; when the Supreme Court voided the measure the state promptly submitted a virtually identical measure, "the little Boswell Amendment", for referendum in 1952.

The same technique has been clearly enunciated in Georgia by the Talmadge legislative leader, Roy Harris, who said that the state would change its election law "by a comma or two" after each adverse court ruling, and "continue to hold Democratic primaries as white as the palm of your hand".

Herman Talmadge, while Governor (he is now Senator) was only a little less optimistic. "If we can't have all-white primaries in Georgia, we want them as white as we can get them," he said.

Two states—Louisiana and Alabama—require applicants for registration to be accompanied by "vouchers"—a registered voter to vouch for your integrity, etc. In some Alabama counties you will find that the registrars insist that Negroes find white vouchers. Others who do accept Negroes as vouchers for Negroes generally limit the number an individual Negro may vouch for from two to four registrants per month.

Don't think, if you put on the uniform of the United States in time of war to defend democracy, that this will in any wise improve your chances of voting in the South when the war is over if your skin colour isn't white. On the contrary, special efforts have been made to deter Negro war veterans from voting. For instance, when Negro vets. marched to the courthouse in Birmingham, Alabama, to register, a local paper called for the K.K.K. to "cope with the problem", and fiery crosses promptly flared from mountain-tops overlooking the city.

If in spite of adverse colour you do finally succeed in registering, you will probably be asked to state your party affiliation. As has already been pointed out, the Democratic Party primary provides the actual contest for public office in most of the South. In the hope of deterring Negroes from registering as Democrats, the party in South Carolina made a "loyalty oath" of allegiance to white supremacy and racial segregation a requisite for participation in the primary.

When Federal courts finally ruled out such mandatory oaths, Florida in 1952 led a move to incorporate the same sentiments in party platforms.

If you live in Alabama and for any reason want to vote Democratic you will have to do so on a ballot bearing the emblem of a crowing rooster and the slogan "White Supremacy—for the Right!"

"Bad Characters" Get Purged

Should you succeed in getting your name on the list of qualified voters, your troubles may have only begun.

For one thing, your name may be purged from the list before you get a chance to vote. Georgia has led the field in conducting mass purges of Negro registrants, the National Association for the Advancement of Coloured People putting the total number purged in a recent election year at 20,000. In some counties the vast majority of Negro registrants were stricken from the lists. Appeals to the U.S. Department of Justice were in vain.

The purge procedure as evolved by Georgia is simplicity itself. You receive a legal summons to appear before the county board of registrars at a specified time (invariably during working hours) to "show cause" why your name should not be dropped because of "bad character, criminal record", etc.

If you fail to appear, your name is automatically stricken; if you do appear, it is usually stricken just the same.

Any white person, it would appear, can challenge any number of Negroes on all sorts of grounds. For instance, G. R. Fossett, who purged 180 Negroes from the voting list of Spaulding County, Georgia, admitted that he did so solely on the basis of their handwriting.

Herman Talmadge, while Governor of Georgia, prevailed upon his legislators in 1949 to purge the state's entire voting list containing 1,200,000 names, and to start all over again with hand-picked registrars and tightened requirements. The Speaker of the Georgia legislature, Fred Hand, told newsmen that this master-purge would keep 80 per cent of Georgia's Negroes from the polls. After one year, less than 15 per cent of the original total (white and Negro) had re-registered.

Florida followed Georgia's example in 1950, but did not go so far as to wipe out the existing lists. Instead, if you are a resident of that state, you are supposed to be sent a postcard which you must sign and return if your name is not to be stricken. Failure to receive such a card (a likely prospect if you are a Negro) is no excuse.

In addition to Georgia and Florida, there are five other states in which you must re-register periodically in order to vote.

When in 1958 H. D. Darby, Negro, filed suit against officials of Jackson, Mississippi, for depriving him of the right to register to vote, the N.A.A.C.P. commented: "Darby is also one of the 1,300 Mississippi Negroes whose names were stricken from the voters lists without reason just before the 1956 election."

One Vote, One Life

If you are a Negro and your name is on a voters' list somewhere in segregated territory, as election day draws nigh you may decide that those whose names are merely purged are the lucky ones.

While the hand of every white man may not be turned against you, you may get the impression that it is. Candidates, office-holders, law-enforcement officers, and Klansmen may severally or collectively resort to intimidation and violence to dissuade you from actually going to the polls.

You may recall that the late Senator Theodore Bilbo, in a statewide election-eve broadcast from Jackson on June 23, 1945, urged "every red-blooded Mississippian to use every means at their command" to keep Negroes from the polls.

Or, if you were living in Georgia that year you may have heard gubernatorial candidate Eugene Talmadge in a statewide broadcast on July 11 predict, "Wise Negroes will stay away from white folks' ballot boxes." Charging that U.S. District Attorneys who had issued statements upholding the right of Negroes to vote were "intimidating white people", Talmadge went on to say: "Maybe it would not be inappropriate to warn some of those fellows to be careful. Neither the U.S. Attorneys or Jimmy Carmichael [his opponent] will have a corporal's guard to back them up. We are the true friends of the Negroes, always have been, and always will be, so long as they stay in the definite place we have provided for them."

In the light of such public utterances, you will not be surprised to learn that when Imperial Wizard Sam Roper of the K.K.K. asked Talmadge how Negroes could be kept from voting, Ole Gene silently scrawled on a scrap of paper the one word, "Pistols".

If you have been living almost anywhere in segregated territory you will be familiar with the K.K.K.'s masked election-eve spectacles, featuring cross-burnings on the court-house lawn.

Sometimes there are innovations, as at Miami, Florida, where the Klansmen strung up effigies bearing placards, "This Nigger Voted", and distributed "calling cards" reading:

Respectable Negro Citizens Not Voting Tomorrow;
Niggers Stay Away from the Polls!

Or the K.K.K. may tack notices to your church door reading, "The first nigger who votes will be a dead nigger", as it did at Fitzgerald, Georgia.

Or the day before election you may receive through the U.S. mails a note on a scorched bit of paper reading, "U better stay home to-morro—K.K.K.", as some folks did at Chattanooga, Tennessee.

Or Klansmen in aeroplanes may fly over your home dropping warnings to stay away from the polls, as they did at Smithfield, Virginia, Columbus, Georgia, and elsewhere.

Or you may awaken on election day to find a miniature coffin on your doorstep, as people did at Statesboro, Georgia.

If, despite such as this, you persist in going to the polls, be careful not to take with you any sort of memorandum—even one you prepared yourself—because election officials are in the habit of arresting Negroes early in the day on charges of carrying "dummy ballots", so that the publicity in the afternoon papers will deter other Negroes from voting.

Upon arriving at the polling place, you may find whites there brandishing firearms at would-be Negro voters, as a state Senator with a shotgun did in a recent election at Manchester, Georgia.

Or you may not be attacked until you emerge from the polling booth, as was the Rev. Archie Ware, 66, at Calhoun Falls, South Carolina. The Rev. Ware was stabbed several times while police looked on, and though he complained to the U.S. Attorney-General, no action was taken.

Or you may not be attacked until somewhat later, as was Isaiah Nixon of Montgomery County, Georgia. Nixon was advised by election officials that while he had a legal right to vote he had better not exercise it. Nixon voted, anyway, and that night the election officials shot him to death in his home in the presence of his wife and children. No one was convicted.

Of course you might not be killed until several weeks after the election, as was Robert Mallard, at Lyons, Georgia. Mallard was ambushed and shot to death by a band of masked Klansmen while driving his wife and daughter home from church. No one was arrested, except Mrs. Mallard.

Smoke-filled Rooms

It has been said that most of the public affairs of the American republic (among others) are settled not in legislative halls in which the people have some voice, but rather in small smoke-filled rooms where special interests have their way.

Be that as it may, certain it is that the small smoke-filled room plays a far more important role in determining the policies of the two dominant political parties than do party conventions or primaries. Though the U.S.A. is not supposed to be a one-party state, in reality the Democratic and Republican Parties have long exercised a bipartisan monopoly over the political life of the nation, their domestic and foreign policies generally differing only as to emphasis, and this more with a view to partisan advantage than to national welfare.

In any case, if you are an ordinary person you will encounter extreme difficulty in penetrating the smoke-filled rooms where the high command of these parties hold sway; and if your colour isn't right and you live in the South you will encounter *extra*ordinary difficulty in entering the door.

You may of course choose freely which party door you will *try* to enter. In more than half of the Southern states where the Democratic Party is all-powerful, no Negroes at all hold party posts, no matter how petty. Even among Republican ranks in these states it is common for a lily-white faction to organize, get on the ballot, and vie with the "regular" Republican slate for seats at the Party's national nominating convention.

And so the choice confronting the nonwhite Southerner is a difficult one. On the one hand, the Democratic Party more or less requires its supporters to endorse white supremacy; and on the other, as has been said with reason, "The Republican Party does not discriminate; it simply doesn't care about people".

Before you start getting ideas about starting a people's party or something of that sort you ought to acquaint yourself with the difficulties involved.

Many states have insured perpetuation of the *status quo* by enacting legal requirements that, in order to get its candidates' names on the official ballot, a party must have received a substantial vote in the previous election. It doesn't take long to figure out how long it would take a *new* party to get on the ballot at that rate.

Other states, more liberal, permit new parties to get on the ballot if they can round up a well-nigh impossible number of signatures to a petition.

The problems of breaking the bipartisan monopoly are not only mechanical. When South Carolina Negroes felt obliged to launch a new party, the Progressive Democrats, they were subjected to all manner of persecution, and voters asking for Progressive Democratic ballot forms were handed Democratic Party ballots instead.

To be a Negro and have a voice in party affairs is one problem; a far graver one is how to be a Negro and a candidate for public office in the South. Only a handful have attempted it in the twentieth century, and not all of them have survived the experience.

G. L. C. Glymph, a Negro grocer of Gaffney, South Carolina, tried for the city council in 1952. Soon he was in receipt of a letter from the Ku Klux Klan, as follows: "It is not customary, as you know, for the colored race of South Carolina to hold public office. Now is the time you should realize your defeat and let withdrawal be your protection for now and hereafter." He withdrew.

This brings us to one sphere in which equality has long since been established down South: any white candidate who stands up for Negro rights is as apt to be knocked down as a Negro candidate. Those Southern whites who, during the Reconstruction and Populist periods, dared uphold certain basic rights for Negroes often paid with their lives.

It was not until the very middle of the twentieth century that the banner of "total equality" was raised by a candidate for public office in the South for the first time. That was done by Stetson Kennedy, white, who announced himself as a "color-blind" candidate for the U.S. Senate from Florida in the election of 1950. A delegation of Klansmen attended his meetings, and the Grand Dragon passed the word around that Kennedy's "head would be blown off" if he continued to speak. The Klan did set fire to Kennedy's property, and on election day he was arrested and threatened with lynching.

You can get yourself killed simply by endorsing such a candidate. Harry Moore, President of the Progressive Voters' League of Florida (a Negro organization), did endorse Kennedy's candidacy, and subsequently he and his wife were dynamited to death as they slept in their home at Mims.

L

If you're lucky, you might escape with nothing more serious than an economic lynching. This happened to a Negro preacher-farmer in Virginia in 1958 when he announced his candidacy for the County Board of Supervisors. On the following day his creditors started foreclosure proceedings after demanding immediate payment in full of an 8,000-dollar mortgage on his farm and home. Only by withdrawing from the political contest was he able to save them.

Most of the few nonwhite candidates to campaign for public office in the South in modern times have done so as "Independents", without endorsement by any existing party organization, this being possible in some contests. Some states also permit candidates to campaign for write-in votes, even though their names do not appear on the printed ballot. Your chances of getting into public office by this route still depend upon your having a white skin and white prejudices, however, since the vote-counters are all white. Write-in votes cast for nonwhites, or for white persons without race prejudice, get thrown out for alleged "misspelling". All but a handful of the votes cast for Stetson Kennedy, for example, were thrown out.

On the other hand, champions of white supremacy have found write-in campaigns an effective means of getting into office. Strom Thurmond got himself elected to the U.S. Senate from South Carolina by this means, defeating the somewhat less racist Democratic Party nominee. Inspired no doubt by Thurmond's example, in 1958 James "Catfish" Cole, Wizard of the K.K.K., announced his write-in candidacy for the governorship of South Carolina on a platform of "Negro schools for Negroes, and white schools for whites".

That will give you an idea what is meant when you hear folks speak of "white man's government" as well as "white man's country".

To sum up, it continues rather difficult for a black man to be a political man down South.

If, like one out of three Southerners, you are a *Negro* Southerner, you will find yourself without representation as such in either municipal, district, state, or national elective bodies of government.

Don't think that by establishing residence in one of the 150 or more Southern counties where Negroes are still in the majority you can find more self-government; the more Negroes there are in any given political entity down South, the less the political expression permitted them.

If you happened to be visiting in Great Britain while the U.S. State Department had on display there its exhibit "Souvenirs of American

Elections", complete with facsimile of the Declaration of Independence, you shouldn't think you could go back to the American South in this century and raise the standard of the American Revolution, "No Taxation without Representation!", with impunity. Nor would the latter-day Tories of the American South be likely to tolerate any refusal on the part of Negro Southerners to pay taxes on this basis.

No doubt about it—much progress has been made, by reaction. Whereas in the early 1870s Southern Negroes played a role in Southern legislatures commensurate with their proportion in the population, and sent seven Negro Congressmen and one Negro Senator to Washington, today no Negro sits in a Southern legislature and no Southern Negro sits in either house of Congress. The last time a Southern Negro was elected to Congress was in 1899.

Act of 1957

Don't let the highly advertised Civil Rights Act of 1957 lull you into a false sense of security. According to the publicity, this law—the first civil rights measure to be adopted by Congress in 82 years—is supposed to strengthen the arm of the U.S. Government in protecting the right to vote. Actually, in its amended form as finally adopted, the law represents one step forward and two steps backward, with the result that Negroes may now be disfranchised with even more impunity than before.

Originally, as passed by the House, the law had some teeth, but these were pulled by the Senate. Senator Richard Russell of Georgia acted as chief surgeon.

"If the Congress votes this law in its present form, it will result in indescribable confusion, wrath, and spilling of blood in a large sector of our common country," he orated. "The concentration camps might as well be prepared, because there will not be prisons enough to lock up the inhabitants of the South. . . ."

The law, he charged, would destroy "the system of separation of the races on which is founded the social order of the Southern states". (The Senator was speaking three years after the Supreme Court decision holding segregation in public education unconstitutional.)

In an effort to appease the Southern Senators, the Senate agreed with rare unanimity to wipe from the statute books the Civil Rights Act of 1875, which had been a dead letter, anyway, ever since the Supreme Court invalidated most of it in 1908. Unappeased, the Southerners insisted that the new law be restricted to the right to vote; and the

Senate agreed. Unappeased, the Southerners insisted that the new law be changed so that all cases arising under it would be tried by jury rather than by Federal judge (the latter having long been customary); and to this retrogressive step the Senate also agreed.

At last the Southerners had what they wanted; traditionally, whenever they have been unable to kill civil rights measures altogether, they have fought to put *administration* of the new laws into their own hands. In the South, where most juries are lily-white, it is not easy to find a jury willing to return a verdict of guilty in any civil rights case in which the complainant is black and the defendant white.

CHAPTER II

LOOK OUT FOR THE LAW

WRIT large in rock over the Supreme Court of the United States, and many another court throughout the land, you can see the inscription, "Equal Justice Under Law".

However, if you happen to be a person of colour you may experience extreme difficulty in obtaining it. As some folks say, before the bar of justice as elsewhere, "Some are more equal than others".

America did not get that way overnight. As the old Negro woman said to the white judge who cautioned her that coloured folks could not expect equal justice all in a minute: "God knows it's been a long minute!"

The legal disability of the Negro in America has roots which go deep into the history of the country. As a chattel slave, there was little or nothing the Negro was permitted to say in court. Prior to emancipation, "free persons of color" also had their legal rights severely delimited by the Black Codes.

In laying claim to the legal rights which the victory of Lincoln's armies brought them, the Negro freedmen encountered bitter opposition at every turn. The Klan gave special attention to the liquidation of all Negroes who dared enter the sphere of law enforcement, even at the lowest level of justice of the peace or bailiff. When the Klan terror had run its course, Negroes were effectively precluded from serving as judges, jurymen, or law officers anywhere in the South; and there were also strict limits, terroristically speaking, to the Negro's ability to institute civil or criminal action against a white person, or to testify against one with impunity in court.

The law operated stringently against the Negro, but seldom for him.

"Is there a law for kinkyheads?" a Florida Negro Freedman bitterly asked the white man who had just defrauded him of his farm.

"Yes, there is," the white man said.

"Then I will go and find it, if I have to go all the way to Tallahassee," the Negro replied.

In those ox-cart days, Tallahassee was a long way off. In reality, then as now, it did little good for Negroes to appeal to state supreme courts in the Southern state capitals. And the cost of travelling all the way to the U.S. Supreme Court in Washington has always been so high as to be prohibitive for most people.

"Do you agree that the Negro has no rights which the white man is bound to respect?" the original Klan asked its initiates—and this has continued to sum up the legal status of the Negro in the South until this very day.

"It's always open season on Negroes," Southern white folks say, by which they mean they are free to kill Negroes with impunity.

The Southern Negro, under constraint not to protest too openly, is obliged to put it in song:

> When a white man kills a Negro,
> They hardly carries it to court;
> When a Negro kills a white man,
> They hangs him like a goat!

Another hazard incumbent upon being naturally-born dark in such a "White man's country" is that of being caught in a police dragnet. Very often when a crime is committed in the U.S.A., dark-skinned persons tend to predominate among those rounded up by the police as "suspect". Sometimes such round-ups are not hinged upon any crime, but are designed to drive reluctant workers into the arms of planters and other employers at sub-standard wages.

The dragnet is such a common occurrence wherever coloured peoples congregate that there is scarcely any need to describe the phenomenon here. Suffice it to recall what transpired when terrorists dynamited Mr. and Mrs. Harry Moore, Negroes, to death as they slept on Christmas Eve, 1951, in their home at Mims, Florida.

"We have found some tracks near the scene," police reported some days later.

"Tracks?" snorted a spokesman of the N.A.A.C.P. "There are tracks all over Florida! If a white couple had been dynamited to death, the police would have had a hundred Negroes in jail the next day— *any* hundred!"

Of course, nowhere among the maze of laws aimed at Negroes in the U.S.A. can you find one which comes right out and says, "You are a second-class citizen". America's race laws are not to be compared with those of Nazi Germany, for example; for the Nürnburg Code frankly relegated the Jews of Germany to second-class citizenship, and explicitly enumerated the rights they were denied. Among these were the rights to vote and hold office. They were barred from the civil service, from holding officership in the armed forces, and from law, medicine, publishing, and farming. After July, 1943, they were barred from places of public entertainment, were denied telephones, radios, newspapers. They were allowed to shop but one day per week, and were forbidden to purchase white bread, eggs, or butter. Nor could they marry "Aryans".

The list of taboos imposed upon American Negroes is not more brief, but these taboos are almost never spelled out in laws, even the interdictions against "intermarriage" being posed impartially in the name of maintaining "the integrity of both races". Thus far, the American ideal of equality has materialized. Indeed, it has gone farther, so that legislation designed to deprive Negroes, Indians, women, trade unionists, or other groups of their rights is commonly introduced under the heading of "protective legislation".

You may encounter printed matter published by the Ku Klux Klan and kindred groups, calling for "clear and frank recognition that racial discrimination is American national policy"; but official national policy continues to be to render at least lip-service to the principle of equality, and, occasionally, under prodding by democratic elements, to take a few hesitant steps to translate the principle into reality.

In short, you will find much more equality on paper than in reality in the U.S.A. The basis of second-class citizenship is not only legislative, but even more administrative. You may be the equal of any man *under the law*, but not *in society, on the street*, or *before the bar* of justice.

Most of the prevailing institutions of white supremacy had their origin in hastily-enacted state and local legislation following the overthrow of Reconstruction which followed the Civil War. In time some of this legislation was, after costly court battles, voided as discriminatory—but in its wake came new laws, more discreet, but none the less effective.

"We have gone to great pains to draft legislation which concedes the equality of the Negro on its face, but which is susceptible to denying it in practice; and we shall continue to do so!" a U.S. Senator from Georgia has said in a moment of rare candour.

The die was cast for a colour-caste society in America when the U.S. Supreme Court, ruling on the case of *Plessy* v. *Ferguson* in 1896, held that the South's new race segregation laws could be enforced, provided only that they render lip-service to the U.S. Constitution by stipulating that the facilities provided be "separate but equal". The vote was 7 to 1, with Justice Harlan dissenting and Justice Brewer abstaining.

What the Court said in *Plessy* v. *Ferguson* in 1896 belongs with the Dred Scott decision of 1857 in the Black Book of American history (on the same shelf with the White Book). The earlier decision starkly denied the humanity of the Negro and sought to bar him for ever from American citizenship and the rights guaranteed "all persons" by the Constitution; the subsequent decision, handed down after twenty years during which the nation in a bloody civil war had stricken the shackles of slavery from the Negro and promised him full citizenship status through three amendments to the Constitution, sanctioned the compulsion of law to force the two races to live apart. What the Court said in establishing this *apartheid* principle which was to endure as national policy for the ensuing ninety years might well be included as Exhibit A in every collection of refined torture-chamber equipment. "The object of the [Fourteenth] Amendment was undoubtedly to enforce the absolute equality of the two races before the law, but in the nature of things it could not have been intended to abolish distinctions based upon color, or to enforce social, as distinguished from political, equality, or a comingling of the two races upon terms unsatisfactory to either", the Court began its disquisition.

"Laws permitting and even requiring their separation in places where they are liable to be brought into contact do not necessarily imply the inferiority of either race to the other, and have been generally, if not universally, recognized as within the competency of the state legislatures in the exercise of their police power. . . .

"In determining the question of reasonableness, it [the state] is at liberty to act with reference to the established usages, customs and traditions of the people, and with a view to the promotion of their comfort, and the preservation of the public peace and good order. . . .

"We consider the underlying fallacy of the plaintiff's argument to consist in the assumption that the enforced separation of the two races stamps the colored race with a badge of inferiority. If this be so, it is not by reason of anything found in the act, but solely because the colored race chooses to put that construction upon it. . . .

"The argument also assumed that social prejudices may be overcome by legislation, and that equal rights cannot be secured to the Negro except by an enforced comingling of the two races. We cannot accept this proposition. If the two races are to meet on terms of social equality, it must be the result of natural affinities, a mutual appreciation of each other's merits and a voluntary consent of individuals. . . .

"Legislation is powerless to eradicate racial instincts or to abolish distinctions based upon physical differences, and the attempt to do so can only result in accentuating the difficulties of the present situation."

All this requires but little commentary. The Court's decision was phrased in terminology coined by the former slave-owners, and which is still mouthed by their descendants as immortal truth until this day. Sanctimoniously, the Court turned its back upon the grossly discriminatory intent and effect of the segregation laws; had the Negroes in those communities where they were in the majority actually enjoyed political freedom and had used it to segregate the whites, the Court would unquestionably have looked upon the matter differently.

At the time of the Dred Scott decision, giving judicial sanction to the "peculiar institution" of slavery, the Court was doing no more than had already been done in the Constitution itself; but in the Plessy decision the Court gave force of law to the regional institution of segregation which was no more venerable than the Constitutional Amendment barring racial discrimination by official bodies.

Since the day it was born, race segregation in America had never manifested itself as a vertical line, but always as an invidious horizontal one. In refusing to recognize this, the Court handed over much of the fruit of the American revolution that was the Civil War to the counter-revolution that was the Klan terror.

Thereafter, whenever a Negro American came into a Federal court (including the Supreme Court) and claimed to have been treated unequally under one of these "separate but equal" segregation laws, the court invariably refused to pass judgment on the principle involved, or even upon the particular law involved; nor did it but rarely call upon the discriminating agency to cease and desist. At most, it was content to award damages to the individual concerned, leaving the law and the facility intact to go on discriminating against countless others. This propensity of the American judiciary—of selecting the most minute technical grounds involved in any given case as the grounds for adjudication, while refusing to come to grips with the basic issues involved—has helped mightily to hold the growth of democracy to a snail's pace.

In sum, race discrimination in the U.S.A. has been voted off the books but into office.

Slight though the substance of equality continues to be, there are those in America who are intent upon restricting it still further.

Many a law-maker does not hesitate, in introducing "nondiscriminatory" legislation, to give full voice to its discriminatory intent. Here's just one example: In 1958 Representative James Weems, a retired Methodist minister, introduced into the Mississippi legislature a Bill requiring the sterilization of all unmarried women following birth of a third illegitimate child. Said Representative Weems: "White people of the South are face to face with an inferior race. It is the duty of the superior to fight with all the mental, moral, and legal weapons it can command."

Courtrooms as well as the halls of legislatures resound with such sentiments. Again, but a single example: General Sessions Judge J. Henry Johnson, of Lexington, South Carolina, has declared from the bench: "God Almighty did not integrate the races just as He did not integrate the birds and other animals." (Elsewhere in this Guide you will find similar statements made from the Federal bench.)

Inequality before the bar of justice is more pronounced in the case of certain charges than in others. For instance, thousands of Negroes accused of raping white women have been put to death in the U.S.A., whereas no white man has ever been executed for raping a Negro woman, although the latter crime is commonplace. In the cases of the Martinsville (Virginia) Seven, the Groveland (Florida) Four, Willie McGee (Mississippi), and others, civil liberties organizations have appealed to the Supreme Court that imposition of the death penalty against Negroes only was racial discrimination in violation of the Constitution; but the Court refused to intervene, and let the executions be carried out.

The social pressures being what they are, many an American white woman, having been discovered with a Negro lover, has cried "Rape!" to save her face—and incidentally sent her lover to his doom.

Doom in such circumstances presents itself in a variety of ways. You may be lynched the old-fashioned way by a mob with rope and faggots; or you may be given one of the new-fangled legal lynchings, where the lynch spirit prevails, but the letter of "due process" is observed. Should there be some difficulty in proving the case in a court of law, the law may find some other way to the same end. For instance, in 1958 the Supreme Court of Alabama upheld the death sentence of Jimmy Wilson, Negro, convicted solely of having stolen $1.95 from Estelle Barker, white (he had also been accused of attempting to rape her, but this was never proven).

Should you ever become the target of such an accusation, not even the U.S. Supreme Court may be able to ward off or delay your demise, even should it be so inclined. Two members of the Groveland Four, for example, after being granted a new trial by the Court, were shot down by Sheriff Willis McCall with the explanation that they had tried to escape.

Only recently have psychiatrists begun to delve into the fact, of common notoriety, that rather many American white women have hysterically cried "Rape!" and pointed to a Negro, *without any provocation whatever.*

As you may well imagine, winking, whistling, or even looking in the direction of a white woman is fraught with mortal peril for non-white men (for details, see chapter on "The Dictates of Racist Etiquette"). Mack Ingram, a 44-year-old Negro share-cropper of North Carolina, was sentenced to two years on a chain-gang on a charge of "assault on a female", all because he was said to have "leered" at a white girl, Willie Jean Boswell, while passing her at a distance of 75 feet in his automobile. When Ingram dared to appeal his sentence, he was haled into court and retried on a charge of assault with intent to rape, which could have resulted in the death penalty. Only after the N.A.A.C.P. intervened did Ingram regain his freedom.

So you see, lynching is always lurking just around the corner; even when you can't see it, you know it's there. . . .

Therein lies one of the chief merits of lynching from the point of view of the lynchers—its power as a deterrent.

Don't let yourself be lulled into a false sense of security by the fact that lynchings have been on the decline. In the first place, this was due to the perfection of more discreet forms of liquidation; and, secondly, as this is written, lynchings have been rising rapidly again for some time.

According to the conservative figures kept by Tuskegee Institute—which counts as lynchings only those committed by three or more persons—approximately five thousand have taken place in the U.S.A. since 1882. The starting date of this tabulation is significant, inasmuch as many thousands more were lynched during the reign of terror between the end of the Civil War in 1865 and 1882.

The record reveals that for every white person lynched, three Negroes have been lynched. This means that your chances of being lynched are thirty times greater if you are black than they would be if you are white.

Of the 48 states, only six—Maine, New Hampshire, Vermont,

Connecticut, Massachusetts, and Rhode Island—have never been the scene of lynchings.

The classic American lynching—in which the victim was commonly hung, then shot, and then roasted, with men, women, and children gathering around in festive mood to sever fingers, toes, and penis to be kept in alcohol as souvenirs—has tended to give way to less overt forms, such as fusillades fired from ambuscade, or dynamite hurled at one's home. Legal lynchings—also on the rise—not only take the form of death sentences meted out by "Judge Lynch", but also violent death in prison, which the prison physician writes off as having been due to "natural causes".

Anti-lynching bills have been almost perennially introduced in Congress, but have just as often been voted down.

Besides the possibility of a lynch mob seeking you out personally, there is always the added possibility of becoming involved in a race riot. Mob violence tends to come in waves. In the first year after World War I (1919), 79 Negroes were lynched, and that same year 25 race riots broke out, the one in Chicago claiming 23 Negro and 15 white dead, plus 537 persons injured. In the Detroit riot of June, 1943, 34 persons were killed, 700 wounded, and 1,800 arrested—the great majority of the victims in all three categories being Negro. On that occasion President Franklin D. Roosevelt did not hesitate to send in Federal troops equipped with tanks.

In the anti-Negro riot which took place in Columbia, Tennessee, shortly after World War II, state police armed with machine-guns led the white mob which shot up and devastated the Negro section of the town.

Nor is it at all uncommon for the police to inaugurate a reign of terror. Birmingham, Alabama, is but one chronic example of this in recent years. Again, in 1958 United Press International reported of Dawson, Georgia: "Police recently beat a Negro severely in his front yard and shot another Negro to death in his backyard . . . another Negro was put in jail when she went there to visit her son. The *Washington Post* said there is an atmosphere of fear among the Negroes of Dawson and that they were afraid to talk to a reporter in their homes."

"The legal equality of the Negro, as established by the Fourteenth and Fifteenth Amendments, is a situation which cannot much longer endure", modern Klan literature asserts. "These Amendments were war spite measures, and must be repealed!" As an afterthought, the Klan adds:

"Fortunately they have not been enforced in the region where they would do the most harm."

In case you don't know what the Fourteenth Amendment says, here it is:

"No state shall make or enforce any law which shall abridge the privileges or immunities of United States citizens, nor deprive any citizen of such right without due process of law."

Sounds good; but if your skin is dark for some reason other than exposure to the sun, it is only fair to warn you that law officers all over the U.S.A. tend to look upon such dark skins as *prima facie* evidence of criminality.

Furthermore, once the law lays hands on you, a dark skin is taken as a waiver permitting the imposition of special penalties. True, there is something in the Constitution forbidding "cruel and unusual punishments"; but in practice that does not always apply, especially to coloured folks. The exaction of confessions by beatings and other forms of torture, politely referred to in the U.S.A. as "third-degree" methods, is much more likely to happen to you under arrest if you are a Negro, Puerto Rican, Mexican, or gipsy than if you are an ordinary white American. Some police seem to feel they have a perfect right to beat on dark skins.

Although it is the duty of the F.B.I. to investigate, and the Justice Department to prosecute, all cases of police brutality, such prosecutions are almost as rare as hen's teeth. (Whereas hordes of F.B.I. agents have been sent after "Reds", hardly a handful have been assigned to protect "blacks".)

At a meeting held in the New York office of U.S. District Attorney Myles J. Lane on July 11, 1952, the long-standing tacit consent of the Federal authorities to third-degree police methods was formalized. The agreement was reached between James E. McInerney, Assistant U.S. Attorney-General in charge of protecting civil rights, New York's Deputy Police Commissioner Frank Fritensky, and Chief Inspector Conrad H. Rothengast—the latter two acting for City Police Commissioner George P. Monaghan.

Nineteen days after this secret get-together, McInerney sent the following instructive to A. B. Caldwell, chief of the F.B.I.'s civil rights section:

"It is requested that in the future my attention be called to alleged violations of civil rights involving personnel of law enforcement agencies in large metropolitan areas before any investigation is authorized. This is desired so that appropriate steps may be taken to minimize the possible deleterious effect on the normal relations between representatives of this Department and other Federal law enforcement agencies and such police agencies."

McInerney frankly admitted this deal, Commissioner Monaghan denied it, and Mayor Vincent Impelliteri urged that any investigation of the matter be conducted behind closed doors. Borough President Robert F. Wagner lamented that "Radio Moscow will blare forth that we have legalized lynching right here in New York City!"

The uncovering of this conspiracy came on the crest of a wave of police brutality in New York City. The National Association for the Advancement of Coloured People said it had received more than a hundred complaints of brutality in the city, but in only two cases was it able to secure disciplinary action.

It is not really so surprising that the Federal agencies charged with defending civil rights entered into such an agreement, inasmuch as the U.S. Supreme Court, in a 5 to 4 decision handed down in 1945, freed Sheriff M. Claud Screws and two of his deputies of Newton, Georgia, for having beaten to death a Negro prisoner, Robert Hall. The Court said the prosecution had failed to show that, in beating Hall to death, the police had acted with the wilful intent of depriving him of a constitutional right.

In consequence of such as this, third-degree police methods are taken more or less for granted in the U.S.A., particularly when the accused have dark skins. For instance, when the Governor of Florida sent his special investigator, Jefferson Elliott, to look into complaints by the Groveland Four (Negroes accused of raping a white woman) that they had been beaten by police, Elliott reported: "No doubt about it—those boys had been beaten before breakfast, after breakfast, and at all hours of the day and night." Despite their protestations of innocence, the state imposed the death penalty.

Just to give you an idea of what you could expect if caught in such a situation: there was the typical case of the Jacksonville, Florida, Negro accused of killing a white man. On the witness stand he repudiated his signed confession, displaying bruises all over his body and naming two policemen as having forced the confession from him. Wearily, the judge summoned the two officers.

"Did you beat on this Negro?" the judge asked.

"Of course not, Your Honor; we wouldn't think of doing such a thing!" the officers replied.

Whereupon the trial went on, and the all-white jury did not hesitate a moment in sending the protesting Negro to the electric chair.

Rather often in recent years the U.S. Supreme Court has ordered the re-trial of Negroes who appealed on the ground that Negroes had been systematically barred from the jury which convicted them. But just about as often, the local officials have then merely gone through the motions of summoning a few Negroes as prospective jurors, who are then dismissed arbitrarily or "for cause" (the real cause, of course, being their colour). The formalities having been thus observed, the Supreme Court more often than not lets the second all-white jury send the Negro to his death.

The ancient hard-won Anglo-Saxon right to trial by a jury of one's peers is not necessarily a good one to invoke if you are not white and live in one of the Southern states of the U.S.A. There, a Negro accorded a trial by a "jury of his peers" is almost always confronted by an all-white panel which considers itself not only his peer, but his superior. This explains why Southern Senators made such strenuous efforts in their successful campaign to amend the Civil Rights Act of 1957 so that persons accused under it may be tried by jury rather than by Federal judge.

To make matters worse, you will find the Klan an old hand at packing courtrooms in order to put pressure on judge and jury in civil rights trials.

The U.S. district attorneys, one of whose jobs it is to protect the rights of citizens, are political appointees made via the White House by prearrangement with the *state* machine of the winning political party. This simply means that, with a few rare exceptions, you can't expect much protection from these Southern gentlemen if your colour doesn't coincide with theirs.

Even if innocent, caught in a dragnet and tortured into confessing a crime you never committed, your troubles will have just begun if you get sent to prison and are guilty of not being white. As the saying goes, they will put you under the jail and throw away the key. Once there, all sorts of exciting things can happen to you: you may be beaten, worked to death, starved, kept in the Black Hole or Sweat Box, or simply forgotten.

Your chances of being forgotten are really quite good. In a recent Miami case the police came into court and confessed their inability to find a certain Negro for whose arrest a warrant had been issued. At the sound of the Negro's name, someone in the courtroom happened to remember that a Negro by that name was already reposing in jail, where he had been for some months without any charge having been brought against him. "An oversight," said the jail officials.

None the less, progress is being made. There is no longer much chance that a heavy ball and chain will be forged around your ankle; nowadays a three-foot steel bar welded around an ankle serves the same purpose.

Though the chain-gang has largely disappeared, the Sweat Box has not. The Florida law authorizing the use of Sweat Boxes (adopted in 1942) provides for a seven-by-seven-foot box, which is divided vertically in half during the daytime, leaving the occupant not enough space in which to sit down. The Box, equipped with metal roof, sits in the sun.

One year before adoption of the Florida law, 22 Negroes were locked into one such Box in Georgia for ten hours.

"Let us out. We're dying!" they shouted.

When the Box was finally opened, one was dead and most of the others were unconscious. The warden said he was "awful sorry".

Unless you are sentenced to life imprisonment, the indications are that you cannot look for a great deal of basic change in the treatment of coloured folks behind bars. In 1952 a grand jury of aroused citizens charged four Florida prison officials—Leamon Parrish, Clyde Markham, James Walker, and Albert Bellott—with "excessively long" confinement of prisoners in Sweat Boxes, and with administering floggings and whippings in which the prisoners "had the flesh of their bodies broken, bruised, and lacerated".

Though the procedure is not recommended, in recent years a considerable number of prisoners in Southern camps have chosen to break their own legs or to sever their ankle tendon rather than endure the floggings which accompany working on the roads. In one such case, the Georgia warden put the victims to work making little rocks out of big ones by pounding them with crowbars while sitting, their legs still in plaster casts.

"This is to teach them that the breaking of legs is not the profitable thing to do," he explained to the Press.

What your life is likely to be like if you run foul of the law down South is summed up in the Negro convict work song:

Bed is hard,
   Work is too;
Beans all week,
   Sunday—stew.

Great big bars,
   Cast-iron locks;
If I tries to leave,
   I get the Box.

Tell me how long
   I gotta wait—
Or is I gotta do
   A little hesitate?

CHAPTER 12

WHO MAY TRAVEL HOW

OFFICIAL U.S. manuals boast that the Supreme Court ruled against race segregation on interstate trains in 1944, interstate buses in 1946, dining cars in 1950, and local and intrastate common carriers in 1956.

But don't let that mislead you.

The laws which in fourteen states have required segregation in transportation ever since 1888 may now technically be dead letters, but practically there is just enough life left in them to get you killed.

Consequently, they are included in this Guide under the heading of Vital Information rather than Historical Curiosities. This is not to suggest that you ought to abide by them, but simply to apprise you of the hazards involved in not abiding by them.

The plain truth is that the great majority of conductors, policemen, judges, and white passengers in that part of the country go right on acting as though the Supreme Court has no jurisdiction over them.

Arrests and/or mob violence as punishment for violation of segregation-in-transportation laws continue so common as to scarcely rate Press notice.

In a typical 1958 case, Mrs. Fannye Casanave, a 55-year-old Negro schoolteacher of South Clairborne, South Carolina, was bodily lifted from an autobus by several policemen when she refused to move to the rear, and carted off to jail in a patrol wagon. Actually, she had been sitting in the section reserved for Negroes, but the driver moved the segregation sign to the seat behind her in order to provide more space for white passengers.

"You're in the white section now. You're violating the law; so move, nigger!" he ordered her.

Segregation in transportation was one of the many innovations ushered in by Emancipation. The first "Jim Crow" car for Negroes made its appearance on the end of a train at Jackson, Mississippi, in 1888, and in 1896 the Supreme Court gave its approval to segregation in all things, provided only that the "separate but equal" fiction was invoked to simulate compliance with the Fourteenth Amendment of the Constitution.

In short order, the fourteen states of Alabama, Arkansas, Georgia, Florida, Kentucky, Louisiana, Mississippi, Maryland, North Carolina, South Carolina, Tennessee, Texas, Virginia, and Oklahoma adopted laws requiring all sorts of common carriers to segregate. In parts of Delaware and Missouri, too, segregation was accomplished by local option or company regulation.

These laws are most comprehensive, requiring segregated seating, eating, sleeping, rest-rooms, baggage-rooms, ticket windows, waiting-rooms, and sometimes entrances to terminals.

Needless to say, such duplication costs money. The *Wall Street Journal*, quoting Vance Greenslit, President of South-eastern Greyhound Bus Lines, upon completion of a new segregated bus station at Jacksonville, Florida, in 1958, has him saying: "It frequently costs 50 per cent more to build a terminal with segregated facilities."

(Many people, apparently, are quite willing to pay to pamper their prejudices. The Union of South Africa, that same year, was boasting of having spent 150,000,000 dollars building separate railways for the transportation of Negroes.)

Far from being mitigated by the passage of time, the American laws imposing segregation in transportation have been repeatedly tightened. For instance, when during World War II non-Southern soldiers showed some disposition to ignore segregation laws, Mississippi altered her law to provide for larger segregation signs on buses—two feet wide and extending from seat to ceiling.

Since aeroplanes were not anticipated by the framers of the segregation laws, you are free to sit where you like in a passenger plane flying through Southern skies, but the moment the plane touches the ground you are apt to come up against segregated waiting-rooms, restaurants, and rest-rooms in Southern airports.

The National Airport at Washington, D.C., was no exception. When Mrs. Helen Nash sought to collect damages after being barred from the airport restaurant because of her race, U.S. District Judge Albert Bryan in 1949 rejected her claim and affirmed that such segregation was not in conflict with the Constitution, Interstate Commerce Act, or any other Federal law.

Another problem arose about 1952 when long-distance buses began to come equipped with toilet. Since the segregation laws had not anticipated toilets on buses, it remained for Southern bus-drivers to hit upon a scheme to discourage Negro passengers from making use of the toilet: whenever one enters it, the driver turns the bus off the traffic lane on to the rough road shoulder, thus jostling and terrorizing the toilet occupant until he emerges to see what has happened.

Laws and customs governing segregation in travel vary widely from state to state and locality to locality. If you wish to avoid violence or arrest for transgressing, it is necessary to proceed with extreme caution, keeping a close watch for all segregation signs, and making inquiries from time to time.

At the Station

The Supreme Court has recently ruled against segregated waiting rooms at train and bus terminals, but in the Deep South that ruling still doesn't mean a thing.

If you are nonwhite, and go through a white waiting-room even in an emergency, you may be in for trouble. For example, one nonwhite who dashed through the white waiting-room of Grand Central Station in Memphis, Tennessee, during 1943, in an effort to catch a departing train, was clubbed with a pistol by a plain-clothes railroad inspector, who turned him over to a city policeman, who arrested him.

You may, of course, travel in an unsegregated manner by private automobile, but under the laws of these states you will have to patronize only those restaurants, hotels, rest-rooms, and similar establishments which cater to your particular race. Moreover, should you attempt to drive through the segregated territory in a mixed group, you will be in grave danger of encountering mob violence, unless the group is composed of *white employers* and *nonwhite employees* who are identifiable as such.

If you are nonwhite, you are further advised that throughout the segregated territory the rules of the road will apply to you equally with whites *only at speeds above 25 miles per hour*. While driving at lower speeds you will find many whites inclined, due to the absence of considerations of self-preservation, to deny you right-of-way.

While there are no laws governing segregation on motor-cycles, it would be extremely hazardous to attempt a motor-cycle trip in the segregated territory with anyone of a different race. The American Motor-cycle Association, by the way, limits its membership to whites only.

You are forbidden by Southern state laws to travel in an unsegregated manner by water on any vessel carrying passengers for fare in the inland or coastal waters of those states.

The laws of Maryland are typical. "All steamboat captains plying waters within the jurisdiction of Maryland" (inland waterways and coastal waters up to three miles offshore) are required to segregate white from Negro passengers while sitting, sleeping, and eating, so far as "construction of the boat permits". Virginia law goes further: companies must provide "separate and non-communicating rooms for the white and colored races".

Should you refuse to be thus segregated, the captain is cloaked with authority to put you ashore at the nearest landing, and you are precluded by law from collecting damages. Furthermore, you may be fined from 5 to 50 dollars for refusing to obey the captain's edicts. He may be fined from 25 to 100 dollars if he neglects to segregate you.

If you happen to be a citizen of some foreign country, you are nevertheless subject to segregation laws and customs in the U.S.A. In 1949 six seamen from the British West Indies were jailed at Savannah, Georgia, after they refused to accept segregated drinking fountains which were installed on board their cargo ship for the use of a repair crew. Asked by local police whether they were white or Negro, the seamen replied that they were British subjects to whom American segregation laws did not apply. Whereupon they were jailed for "disorderly conduct".

In some cities there has even been some effort to establish separate bus stops for coaches which largely serve Negro neighbourhoods. This was done during 1944 at Miami, Florida, when Public Safety Director Dan D. Rosenfelder ordered buses 21 and 22—95 per cent of whose passengers are Negroes—to stop across the railroad tracks in the Negro section, instead of on the other side in front of a large hardware store. Benches and shade were available in the old location; none at the new stop. Rosenfelder explained that the move shortened the bus routes by three blocks and hence "aided the war effort".

If you are nonwhite, be advised that in many instances you are expected to stand back before boarding local or interstate buses until all white passengers have been given seats. In time of war, when transportation facilities were overcrowded, interstate bus companies in the segregated territory sometimes set up a quota system, whereby only a few token nonwhites were permitted on each bus, regardless of the numbers holding tickets or the number of days spent waiting for a seat.

Moreover, at such times you may be required to surrender your seat and get off the bus to make way for a white person. This happened to David Davies, a Negro Marine, at Fayetteville, North Carolina.

When he protested, he was severely beaten by white Military Police.

Ignorance is no Excuse

Should you be arrested for violating segregated travel regulations, it will probably do no good to plead ignorance.

When Marshall Johnson, 15, and his sister Edwina, 16, of Newark, New Jersey, were visiting relatives in Montgomery, Alabama, in 1949, they did not know that as Negroes they were required by law to sit in the rear of city buses. When they took a seat near the front, driver S. T. Law drew a pistol, drove them off, and ordered their arrest. Edwina testified that she had been kicked off. The children were held for two days, and Judge Wiley C. Hill, Jr., threatened to send them to the state reform school until they were 21 years of age. He released them on probation, however, because he felt they "realized their mistake".

Even if you are a diplomatic representative of some foreign government, there is no diplomatic immunity from arrest and perhaps mob violence if you violate the segregation laws and customs.

For this reason, the State Department maintains a special office in Miami, Florida, whose chief function it is to meet visiting Latin American dignitaries as they arrive at the International Airport, and whisk them away in private limousines to be entertained until such time as they can be put aboard another plane to carry them north and out of the segregated territory.

An interesting situation arose in 1944 when two French sailors whose ship was docked at Norfolk, Virginia, offered their seats on a local bus to two Negro women. They pretended not to understand a native white man who tried to explain that this was against the law.

One of the very few instances in which you may travel in an unsegregated manner through segregated territory is in the event that you are an invalid, in which case you may travel with a nurse or attendant of another race. The North Carolina law, which is typical in this respect, specifically exempts from segregation "nurses or attendants of children or of the sick or infirm of a different race, while in attendance upon such children or sick or infirm person". Some states, such as Georgia, Mississippi, and South Carolina, drop the legal fiction of equality and specify *white employers* travelling with *nonwhite attendants*.

Again, if you are an officer of the law and have a prisoner or lunatic of another race in custody, you are exempt from the segregation laws.

By the same token, if you are a prisoner travelling in the custody of an officer of another race, exemption is made. Nevertheless, the courts have ruled that a conductor may require a white officer to sit with his Negro prisoner in a Negro coach, and that the officer may not then sue the railroad for damages.

The Arkansas law is typical in this regard, providing as follows: "Officers in charge of prisoners of different races may be assigned with their prisoners to coaches where they will least interfere with the comfort of other passengers."

Good, Substantial Partitions

Many railroads throughout the segregated territory still cling to separate coaches for Negro passengers.

Arkansas law makes the exception that, "On short railroads of less than 30 miles in length, segregation may be accomplished by wooden partition".

In North Carolina, on trains having but one passenger car, the transportation commissioner is authorized by law to "make such rules and regulations for the separation of the races and with regard to toilet facilities" as may be "feasible and reasonable in the circumstances".

Texas law requires that train coaches carrying both whites and nonwhites be divided by a "good and substantial wooden partition with a door therein".

Here are some other legal provisions worthy of note:

Alabama. Motor transport companies are required to have separate waiting-rooms for whites and Negroes, separated by "a partition constructed of metal, wood, strong cloth, or other material so as to obstruct the vision between the sections".

Arkansas. Copies of segregation law must be posted "in a conspicuous place in each coach and waiting-room". Trains which break down are exempt from complying with segregation laws until the train reaches a point where additional cars are available. Railroads which do not segregate are subject to fines from 100 to 500 dollars for each and every unsegregated train run. Fine for passengers who violate law: 10 to 200 dollars. Buses must display sign four inches high indicating white and coloured sections. Upon refusal of any passenger to be segregated, the law says: "The person in charge shall proceed to the nearest town, city, hamlet, or village, and thereupon it shall be the duty of the first available peace officer to remove said passenger and subject him to arrest."

Georgia. Train passengers who refuse to be segregated and officials or employees of the railroad who do not enforce segregation or "fail to assist in ejecting said passenger" are guilty of a misdemeanour. In Atlanta, if you are nonwhite, you may enter the white waiting-room at Union Station to patronize the news-stand. At the Terminal Station, however, you are not allowed to enter the white waiting-room *for any purpose whatever.*

Maryland. Trolley conductors may, when all other seats are filled, permit a Negro to share a seat with a white, but "only with the permission of the occupant". Railroads are required to segregate, with signs in each coach with "appropriate words, in plain letters, in some conspicuous place". Partitions instead of separate coaches are permissible in all counties except Prince George, Charles, St. Mary's, Calvert, and Anne Arundel. Passengers and companies which do not comply with segregation laws are subject to fines of from 300 to 1,000 dollars.

Mississippi. Law does not require that transportation facilities be equal, but only that they be of "same kind". Intercity buses and street-cars must carry segregation signs visible from all parts of the vehicle. Local trolleys must be divided by partition or adjustable screen.

North Carolina. Any passenger subjected to *non*-segregation may recover damages from transportation company at the rate of 100 dollars for each day thus spent. Fines derived from violations of segregation laws are specifically set aside for the state educational fund.

South Carolina. Trolleys transporting whites only or Negroes only must bear illuminated signs reading "White" or "Colored" clearly visible for 300 feet after sunset.

Sole Judges

The segregation laws generally empower the operators of trains, buses and boats to judge your race on the basis of physical appearance, and to segregate you accordingly. The Tennessee statute is representative:

"It is the duty of the conductors in charge of passenger trains to determine the race to which passengers belong and to keep them separated . . . and he must exercise ordinary care in doing so; and if . . . he makes an honest mistake in determining the race of a passenger, the railroad company is not liable to damages for such mistake; but if the conductor, through negligence, makes a mistake in taking a white passenger to be a Negro, the railroad company may be held liable for substantial damages, and in a proper case may be held liable for punitive damages."

The Virginia law is more brief, providing simply: "If the passenger fails to disclose his race, the conductor and managers, acting in good faith, shall be the sole judges of his race."

If you are a Negro who appears to be white, conductors are not likely to insist that you travel white if you express a preference or determination to travel as a Negro.

On the other hand, if you are a white who appears to be a Negro, conductors may forcibly segregate you as a Negro.

On the basis of a number of court rulings, a white person mistakenly forced to travel as a Negro may readily collect damages from the company on the grounds that the facilities were not equal. Negro passengers travelling in the same coach would have extreme difficulty in collecting damages on the same ground.

An example of the police powers enjoyed by the operators of common carriers took place in 1943 at Memphis, Tennessee. Although there were no local or state laws requiring nonwhites to enter or leave buses by the rear door, a bus-driver ordered several Negro soldiers to do so. When they refused, he locked the door and signalled for a policeman, who clubbed the soldiers off the bus.

It must also be pointed out that some operators feel inclined to exercise police powers on the streets as well. For example, in 1946 Walter Lee Johnson, a Negro veteran with three years' overseas service, was walking along an Atlanta street and greeted a buddy he spied on a passing street-car: "Straighten up and fly right!" The white motorman, W. D. Lee, thought the remark was intended as a jibe against him, and so stopped the trolley, stepped out, and shot Johnson, killing him. Charged with "disorderly conduct and shooting another", Lee was released by police court Judge A. W. Calloway, after hearings packed by Ku Klux Klansmen.

Lower 13

Few aspects of segregated travel have been subjected to more litigation and adjudication than the denial of sleeping-car berths to Negroes.

If you are nonwhite and make a reservation for such a berth outside the segregated territory, you may find it safe enough to remain in your berth after the train penetrates segregated territory.

But if you seek to obtain such a reservation while *inside* segregated territory you may still have extreme difficulty or even be refused point-blank.

Some Southern Negroes who can afford to travel by sleeper get results by making their reservation by telephone, and then sending a white friend to pick up the ticket. Or, they pick up the ticket in person, by pretending to be a messenger sent by a white person.

Once they have the reservation in hand, it is more difficult for train officials to deny them the berth without subjecting the company to suits for damages.

The most common solution, however, continues to be the practice of ticket-sellers to assign nonwhite applicants to "Lower 13". This is the designation given by Negroes to the private drawing-room in each sleeping coach, since there are 12 upper and 12 lower berths. In other words, this is one of the few instances in which it pays to be nonwhite, since in such circumstances you can get the private drawing-room for the lesser price of a simple berth.

It is interesting to note in passing that Georgia law, in requiring segregation in sleeping-car coaches, goes on to say: "Provided that nothing in this section shall be construed to compel sleeping-car companies or railroads operating sleeping cars to carry persons of color in sleeping-cars or parlor cars."

Texas, in a "Public Health Act", specifically prohibits Negro sleeping-car porters from using berths or bedding ordinarily used by white passengers.

As in the case of seating arrangements, exception is made in the case of a nurse or servant in attendance upon an employer of another race. The only other statutory exception is in the case of cabooses attached to freight trains, where sleeping quarters are set up for the train's crewmen.

Last Call to Dinner

If you are nonwhite you may encounter almost as much difficulty in eating as in sleeping while in transit by train.

In spite of court rulings against discrimination in this sphere, you may find that, while travelling through segregated territory, only the "last call to dinner" will be addressed to you, after most whites have finished eating.

Traditionally, dining-cars in this territory were equipped with a cloth screen which could be drawn around two tables at one end of the car, thus shielding any nonwhite diners from the view of whites. It was found that some white Southerners actually became nauseated unless the curtain was drawn.

Today such curtains still survive on many a dining-car, especially those attached to local and intrastate trains in the segregated territory.

As in other spheres, the courts have been highly reluctant to assert equality in dining-cars. It was in 1942 that Elmer Henderson, Negro, filed a complaint with the Interstate Commerce Commission charging that he had been denied dining-car service on two occasions while on an interstate trip on the Southern Railroad. Upon entering the diner, he had found whites occupying one of the tables set aside for Negroes, and Negroes occupying the other, with a curtain between them. He was told there were no seats available. The I.C.C. ruled that this was no basis for awarding damages.

Mr. Henderson then appealed to the U.S. District Court in Baltimore, Maryland, which sent the case back to the I.C.C. for reconsideration. Again the I.C.C. ruled that the Southern Railroad was within its rights. Meanwhile, the railroad changed its regulations as follows:

1. One table in each diner to be reserved exclusively for Negroes.
2. A curtain to be drawn around said table.
3. A "Reserved" card to be placed on said table when not in use by Negroes.

In 1948, the Federal court in Baltimore held that racial segregation as enforced against Henderson was not contrary to the Constitution, Interstate Commerce Act, or other Federal law.

In 1950, however—after eight years of litigation—the case was finally ruled upon by the Supreme Court, which ordered the abolition of discriminatory dining-car practices on interstate trains. By way of complying with the Court's order, the Southern Railroad's assistant Vice-President, R. K. McClain, issued the following instructive:

"The Steward shall seat diners so as to promote efficient service with comfort and satisfaction to the diners. When entering singly, women will be seated with women, men with men, young people with young people, elderly persons with elderly persons, white persons with white persons, and colored with colored. In following the above illustrations, stewards will bear in mind (occupied space permitting) white passengers should be seated from the buffet or kitchen end of the dining car, and colored persons from the opposite end."

One month later, the Negro concert artist Muriel Rahn filed suit for 17,000 dollars damages against the Southern Railroad, charging that a dining-car steward had refused to serve her and had humiliated her publicly.

Jim Crow Rides On

And so, as you can see, Jim Crow rides on, despite court rulings telling him to get off. . . .

You should note especially the situation in interstate bus travel, a sphere in which the Supreme Court "outlawed" segregation as far back as 1946.

One year after that decision was handed down, the Committee on Racial Equality and the Fellowship of Reconciliation jointly organized a "Journey of Reconciliation" to test the efficacy of the Court's finding. A group of 16, white and Negro, travelled by interstate bus through Virginia, North Carolina, Tennessee, and Kentucky (they did not penetrate the Deep South), refusing to be segregated. They were arrested 12 times, and fines and sentences were imposed. When the group spent the night at the home of the Rev. Charles Jones, white, at Chapel Hill, North Carolina, a mob stoned the house.

Of the Supreme Court decision it may be said, however, that while it has by no means eliminated segregation on all interstate buses, it has facilitated somewhat the collection of damages by nonwhites who have the financial means to press court action against a bus company which segregates them.

But you will find that even this consolation has its limits.

For instance, shortly after the Court decision, the Rev. William Simmons sued the Greyhound Bus Lines for 20,000 dollars for segregating him. A jury in U.S. District Court at Roanoke, Virginia, while recognizing that the Rev. Simmons had been illegally segregated, refused to award him any damages. However, Judge John Paul refused to accept this verdict, and instructed the jury to reconsider and make a nominal award. Whereupon the jury allotted the Rev. Simmons 25 dollars.

The South's laws requiring segregation in transportation have long been buttressed by supplementary laws investing the operators of trains, trams, boats, and buses with special police powers as "conservators of the peace and public safety" to assign passengers to certain seats. With the segregation laws nominally invalidated, this secondary line of defence has been used to keep segregation going.

Virginia, which happened to lack such a law, hastily adopted one after the Supreme Court acted. The new law made it a misdemeanour to create any unnecessary disturbance in a common carrier by "running through it, climbing through windows or upon seats", or by "failing to move to another seat when lawfully requested to do so by the operator". Mrs. Lottie Taylor was arrested for refusing to be segregated by such means, but the Supreme Court of Virginia held in 1948 that a state law may not be employed to enforce a regulation of a private company which is repugnant to a U.S. Supreme Court decision.

Don't jump to the conclusion that this means that administrative segregation is on the way out. For, a decade later, in 1958, the U.S. Supreme Court refused to review the conviction of two Negroes, Johnny Herndon and Leonard Speed, who had defied a new Florida law which empowers bus drivers to assign seats on the basis of "weight distribution and safety factors".

This loophole, if left open, is just large enough to let Jim Crow ride on indefinitely.

CHAPTER 13

OPEN TO ALL (WHITES)

If you think any law-abiding orderly person can enter any restaurant, hotel, cinema, auditorium, park, playground, golf-course, swimming pool, bathing beach, or other such place of public accommodation in the U.S.A. regardless of race, you've got another think coming. . . .

Not since 1883, when the U.S. Supreme Court invalidated the Civil Rights Act of 1875, has there been any national law against racial discrimination in public places.

During the 12 years of its existence, that law assured all persons in the U.S.A. full and equal access to hotels, common carriers, theatres, and other places of amusement, subject only to such regulations as applied to *everyone alike*.

In those bygone days if you were denied admission because of your race you could file a complaint in Federal court, which would impose a heavy fine and sentence against the proprietor, and award you substantial cash damages.

About that same time the Reconstruction legislatures of five former Confederate states—Louisiana, Florida, South Carolina, Arkansas, and Mississippi—adopted similar civil rights laws (this was, of course, before the poor whites and Negroes were disfranchised by the Klan terror). But with the exception of Louisiana, all these laws were repealed when the democratic white-Negro régimes were overthrown by the oligarchic white planters. The Louisiana law, an Act of 1869, is still on the books; but it has long since been forgotten, and should you seek to claim your rights under it, you should be prepared for fireworks.

Today in more than half of the 48 states of the U.S.A. there are no laws prohibiting racial and religious discrimination in places of public accommodation. Those state civil rights laws which do exist are of varying degrees of comprehensiveness and are inadequately enforced. For instance, on March 1, 1953, Kenneth Brush, a barber of Waterloo, New York, finally consented to give a haircut to Clyde (Butch) Williams, an 8-year-old Negro lad, only after the boy's mother sent a letter to the *Waterloo Observer* complaining that previous refusals by the shop had made it necessary to take her son 40 miles to Syracuse to have his hair cut.

The old English common, or unwritten, law, on which most American jurisprudence is based, has undergone an interesting mutation in the U.S.A. in that in the segregated territory the courts have held that *proprietors* of public places have a common-law right to *exclude* Negroes, while outside this territory some courts have held that *Negroes* have a common-law right to *enter* places of public accommodation.

Delaware and Tennessee have written laws upholding the right of proprietors of public places to practise racial discrimination.

The Delaware law, adopted after the Civil War, empowers proprietors of hotels, restaurants, theatres and similar establishments to refuse accommodation to anyone who may be deemed offensive to the majority of the clientele.

The Tennessee law, adopted in 1875 and patterned after that of Delaware, was somewhat modified in 1885 by a provision that "all well-behaved persons" must be admitted to public places—except that the right of proprietors to segregate their patrons according to race is reserved.

Although not all states in the segregated territory have written laws upholding the right of proprietors of public places to practise racial discrimination, such sanction has often been extended by the courts.

For example, in a North Carolina case the court ruled that the guests of a hotel "cannot be lawfully prevented from going in or be put out . . . unless they be persons of bad or suspicious character, or of vulgar habits, or so objectionable to the patrons of the house, on account of the race to which they belong, that it would injure the business to admit them . . .".

Alabama, it should be mentioned, does have a law which prohibits members of one race from using toilet facilities in a hotel or restaurant that is operated for members of the other race. This is, of course, intended to keep Negro employees of white establishments from using the facilities provided for the white clientele.

For quite some time Massachusetts had a law forbidding white women under 21 years of age to enter a restaurant or hotel operated by a Chinese, it having been contended that Chinese proprietors foster prostitution.

If you are a nonwhite motorist, you are, of course, precluded from stopping at any motel in the segregated territory, except in the very rare ones operated for nonwhites. This is also true of the border areas, and in the vicinity of some Northern urban centres where hotel facilities for nonwhites are available.

It appears that in most of the states having civil rights laws you must be a citizen of the U.S.A. in order to press a claim that you were discriminated against because of your race. A New York court, for example, has ruled that an African-born Negro who was not an American citizen was not entitled to the protection of the civil rights law of that state. The courts of Nebraska have also taken this position.

In California, on the other hand, you do not have to be an American citizen in order to press charges under that state's law against racial discrimination.

Only one of the states which have civil rights laws, Ohio, has ruled that a proprietor of a public place cannot circumvent the law by assigning different hours for white patrons and Negro patrons only.

Maine and New Hampshire have laws forbidding proprietors of public places to advertise in such a manner as to suggest discrimination against any "religious sect, nationality, or class"; but neither of these laws has ever been construed as forbidding *racial* discrimination.

The courts of four states—Pennsylvania, Massachusetts, Oregon, and Utah—have taken the position that a ticket to a public performance is nothing more than a licence which the manager may revoke at his own discretion, so that you, the patron, can only demand a refund of the price of the ticket if refused admission. This the courts have alleged to be a common-law principle.

Only in the state of Washington have the courts held that a ticket is a lease rather than a revokable licence, so that patrons who are discriminated against may sue for damages as well as for the price of the ticket.

In all the segregated territory there seems to be no court case on record of a nonwhite somehow acquiring a ticket to a performance for whites and demanding admission on the basis of it.

Virginia has a *state* law requiring racial segregation in theatres and similar places, and South Carolina has a *state* law requiring separate entrances for whites and nonwhites at circuses and tent shows. But throughout the rest of the segregated territory, such segregation is largely accomplished by municipal ordinance. Typical of these laws is that of the city of Atlanta, as revised in 1945. Entitled "Offences against the Public Order, Peace, and Morale", this law declares:

"It shall be the duty of the proprietor or person in charge of any place of public assembly, where attendance of both races is permitted, to allot different sections or portions of the place of assembly to be occupied by white people and different sections or portions to be occupied by colored people."

A fine of 25 dollars and/or 30 days' imprisonment is provided for any proprietor or patron who violates this law. Adopted while World War II was still in progress, this revision was sponsored by the Ku Klux Klan, and was primarily intended to put a stop to the unsegregated meetings which were then being held by the American Veterans Committee in Atlanta's U.S.O. (United Service Organizations) hall.

The effect of such exclusionist laws and regulations is rough on the nonwhites. As one young Southern nonwhite girl has put it: "I didn't think so much about things I couldn't do till one day I went downtown and stopped by a movie house to look at the picture outside, and I thought I'd like to see it, and I looked for a sign for the colored entrance, but there wasn't any; just a sign for the white, so I knew I couldn't go. I have to go all the way to Greensboro to see the movies, just because I'm colored."

Come and Bring Your Lunch

Both in and out of the segregated territory, the refusal of hotels catering to whites to admit nonwhites costs the proprietors considerable sums in their inability to play host to interracial conventions.

For example, when the National Education Association met in a New Orleans hotel, the management installed a step-ladder at a side window and suggested that Negro delegates use it rather than the main entrance and lobby—whereupon the Negroes refused to attend.

In the same way, on those rare occasions when the Atlanta Biltmore Hotel has permitted an interracial conference to be held in its conference rooms, it has refused to serve meals to the Negro delegates, even in the privacy of the conference room. Consequently, the Negro delegates had to bring their lunches with them, or make the long journey to that section of the city where they could obtain a meal.

Those hotels which refuse to accommodate Negroes generally will not accept whites and Negroes who may be travelling together, as

N

Presidential candidate Henry A. Wallace and the Negro baritone Paul Robeson discovered in Illinois and elsewhere in 1948.

Cornelia Otis Skinner, the noted actress, found it virtually impossible to obtain hotel reservations for herself and her Negro maid during a 1948 tour of the segregated territory. One Southern theatrical agent suggested that accommodation might be more readily available if the maid would wear a nurse's uniform. Only four hotels in the South would finally take in both, and even these insisted that the two sleep in separate rooms, and that the maid use only the service elevator. Attempts by the two to sit together in railroad dining-cars were to no avail. Taxis would accept both, but if Miss Skinner went to her hotel first, the maid would be dumped on the sidewalk and told to call a Negro cab for the remainder of the ride to a Negro hotel.

Such problems may be encountered almost anywhere in the U.S.A., even in those states which have civil rights laws.

For instance, the famous pianist Hazel Scott was refused service in a Pasco, Washington, lunch-stand in 1949, despite the fact that she had been snowbound and had not eaten for many hours.

Appearances are more important in such matters than citizenship status. For example, in Decatur, Illinois, Dr. Bidhan Chandra Roy, personal physician of the late Mohandas Ghandi and former Mayor of Calcutta, and five of his countrymen were refused service in a restaurant while travelling on an official mission for the Government of India. The restaurant operator said later that she had presumed that the party consisted of American Negroes. Because of such incidents, many visiting dignitaries of dark complexion feel obliged to wear some distinguishing article of their native dress, rather than American-style clothes.

Even in the civil rights territory, the laws are quite generally circumvented by a variety of devices and subterfuges. If you are nonwhite, or are travelling in "mixed company", the hotel clerk may insist that he has no vacancies, even though you may hold an advance reservation.

In restaurants, the head waiter may insist that all vacant tables are "reserved", or he may seat you out of sight or near a hot kitchen, or you may be allowed to sit indefinitely without service, or you may be served food too salty to eat, etc.

Eat, Drink, and be Merry, if . . .

There was a time when many liquor bars in the segregated territory catered to both whites and nonwhites, albeit in separate rooms.

Such establishments have now almost disappeared, and in some states, such as Louisiana, they are prohibited by law. These laws forbid the dispensing of alcoholic beverages to whites and nonwhites under the same roof, no matter how substantial or impenetrable the partition between them.

In some places whites and Negroes are prohibited from drinking in the same neighbourhoods, as in New Orleans, where Judge Frank Stick in 1949 forbade the establishment of a night club for Negroes in the city's famous French quarter.

Similarly, the county board of El Paso, Texas, in 1949 put a stop to famous band dances at which white and Negro couples had been separated by a row of chairs. This action was taken at the request of U.S. Major-General John L. Homer.

On at least one occasion, a Federal court has been used by a judge to inveigh against whites and Negroes drinking together. Judge Atwell of Texas, sitting as guest magistrate in Federal court in New York, was lecturing the daughter of a woman who operated a speak-easy which served Negroes as well as whites.

"White folks and colored folks cannot live together," Judge Atwell told her. "You should go somewhere else to live among different people. Get your inspiration from American girls who are what American girls ought to be."

(This same Judge Atwell, commenting years later on the Supreme Court school decision, was to say that mixed schooling was a "civil wrong rather than a civil right".)

If you prefer books to bands, do not be misled by the "Open to All" inscriptions over public libraries in the segregated territory. It is common knowledge that these inscriptions mean "Open to All Whites". If you are fortunate, there may be a branch library for Negroes in your community. Of course, such branches are generally stocked with worthless books, but through the branch you may be able to order volumes from the main library. Or you may know some sympathetic white person who will loan you his library card, or will borrow books for you. If you call for the books yourself, you must let the librarian assume that you are merely serving as a messenger for the white card-owner.

In all the segregated territory, only two states, West Virginia and Texas, have *laws* specifically providing that some sort of library service be made available to Negroes—on a segregated basis, of course.

Where not to Go

Virtually all of the public swimming areas in the segregated territory have been reserved for whites only, including those which have been purchased and operated with tax money.

This means that if you are nonwhite you are precluded from entering the surf at Miami Beach or any of the South's other famous beaches. In a few instances you will find that some remote and relatively inaccessible and undeveloped spot has been made available to nonwhite bathers. However, if you are a female nonwhite, you can enter a white beach if you are accompanied by a white infant who is under your care.

This phenomenon has inspired Harry Golden, publisher of *The Carolina Israelite*, to put forward what he calls the Golden White Baby Plan. Under this Plan, white mothers interested in getting rid of their babies for some hours would pool them at a central location, where Negroes could pick them up and use them as a guarantee of safe passage to all sorts of public places from which Negroes are ordinarily barred, and then return the babies to the pool when no longer needed.

Tax-supported swimming pools are another public facility which have long been reserved for whites only, both in and out of the segregated territory.

In St. Louis, Missouri, young whites beat up Negroes when an attempt was made on June 21, 1949, to open the pool on a non-discriminatory basis.

In York, Pennsylvania, the City Council kept the municipal pool closed for two years rather than admit Negroes, and in 1949 finally sold it to a private operator who would be free to discriminate.

In New York City, extra-legal exclusion is accomplished in public pools on the upper East Side by Italians, who through terrorism force Puerto Ricans as well as Negroes to swim in the polluted East River.

You can't Worship Together

Racial segregation is at its peak throughout the U.S.A. every Sunday at 11 a.m., the hour when millions of Americans congregate to worship the God who "hath made of one blood all nations of men" and the Christ who "is our peace, who hath made both one and hath broken down the middle wall of partition between us".

Before the abolition of Negro chattel slavery in the U.S.A., Negro slaves were sometimes admitted to a "reserved" section or gallery of white churches.

This practice varied with the individual slave-owner, there being a difference of opinion as to whether the teachings of Christianity would promote submissiveness or rebellion.

The National Council of Churches has reported that over 90 per cent of Negro churchgoers are affiliated with all-Negro denominations. Of the 5 per cent who belong to *interracial denominations*, 95 per cent attend racially *separate churches*.

The number of white churches in the segregated territory which will admit Negro worshippers may be counted upon the fingers of one hand.

The exception to this rule comes when the Negro janitor of a white church dies after long years of faithful service, whereupon the funeral service may be conducted in the white church, with white and Negro mourners carefully segregated.

But otherwise the worship of God is conducted on a strictly segregated basis throughout the territory, as Glen Taylor (then Senator of Idaho) discovered when he sought in 1948 to enter a Negro church at Birmingham, Alabama, through a door marked "Negro Entrance", instead of the one marked "White Entrance" which had been set up by police for the occasion of his appearance there. He was charged with disorderly conduct, fined, and sentenced to 39 days in jail. Upon appeal, Federal courts upheld his conviction, and the U.S. Supreme Court refused to review it.

In what is seemingly the first such case on record in the segregated territory, a Negro college professor in 1948 sought to join the white congregation of Atlanta's Unitarian Church, a relatively liberal denomination. His bid was refused, and the pastor was fired for seeking to admit him.

Similarly, when the Rev. Joseph Rabun, an ex-Marine chaplain, came back from World War II to espouse "right supremacy, not white supremacy" from the pulpit of the First Baptist Church of McRae, Georgia, he was fired by the Board of Deacons, which is dominated by the family of Senator Herman Talmadge.

The inauguration in recent years of a nationwide "Brotherhood Week", in which the various religious denominations are expected to invite a guest speaker of some other faith or race, has been attended by a great many birth-pangs in the segregated territory.

For example, on the eve of Brotherhood Sunday in 1949, the board of elders of the Capitol Christian Church at Tallahassee, Florida, cancelled an invitation which their pastor had extended to Dr. James E. Hudson, chaplain of Florida's college for Negroes.

Elsewhere in the region, white pastors who have insisted upon inviting Negro ministers as guest speakers on Brotherhood Sunday, despite threats from the Ku Klux Klan and members of their congregations, have met with variable success. A number of congregations have been split, and pastors fired, over this issue.

When a convention of South Carolina Baptists in 1947 called for enactment of fair employment legislation, telegrams and telephone calls from the deacons back home led them to rescind their action.

The Civil War-wrought breach between the Southern and Northern branches of the Protestant denominations has not been narrowed in recent years, despite all proposals and plans for reunion. Militant declarations by the Northern branches, such as the dedication of the Presbyterians in 1948 to an "unsegregated church in an unsegregated society", have scarcely been published in the South.

That same year the National Council of Churches adopted by a large majority a recommendation that all of its affiliated denominations abolish separate churches for whites and Negroes; but even after a decade this resolution had not had any noticeable effect upon church segregation in the South.

The World Council of Churches, meeting in Chicago in 1950, condemned racial prejudice as anti-Christian, but refrained from going on record against racial segregation inside churches or out.

Outside the South, some progress toward desegregation in worship has been made in a few spots. For instance, when in 1957 the neighbourhood surrounding the Normandie Avenue Methodist Church in Los Angeles had become 60 per cent Negro, the Bishop sent in a Negro pastor, Nelson Higgins, Jr., whereupon the lily-white congregation quit in a body.

"I have no objection to the new minister, except that he's black," said John Henry Seal, a laundryman.

Pastor Higgins stuck to his post, however, and eventually drew a mixed congregation to him.

Generally speaking, you will find that Protestant denominations in the segregated territory make few apologies for practising racial exclusiveness. Many, in fact, are inclined to quote the Scriptures in justification, asserting that all nonwhite races are under a curse visited by God upon the "sons and daughters of Ham".

On This Rock: Two Churches

The Roman Catholic Church, which on the world stage has a relatively less racistic record than many another Christian creed, nevertheless long proved willing to accommodate itself to race prejudice in America. Of the 17 million Negroes in America, less than half a million are Catholic. Only recently has the Church begun to abandon race segregation, and this desegregation has thus far taken place in more Church schools than Church services.

As recently as 1950, for example, white members of St. Mary's Catholic Church at Piscataway, Maryland, barred nonwhite members from entering the front door and threatened to throw them out if they refused to use the side doors and sit in the rear of the church. Father Hannon, an official spokesman at the Chancery of the Archdiocese in Washington, D.C., pointed out that the side door is "practically the same" as the front door and is only a little farther away.

When a group of Catholics of Washington, D.C., planned their Holy Year pilgrimage to the Papal City in 1950, the Very Rev. Monsignor John S. Spence, in charge of the group, announced that the city's nonwhite Catholics were "not being encouraged" to participate. This policy of advising nonwhite Catholics to "forget about the pilgrimage" had the endorsement of the Most Rev. Patrick A. Boyle, Archbishop of Washington, the Associated Negro Press reported.

"The exclusion of Negro Catholics from 'white' Catholic churches is one of the most disturbing aspects of segregation which Latin Americans find in Washington, D.C.", the National Committee on Segregation in the nation's capital reported. "A devout Catholic from Panama entered a Catholic church in Washington. As he knelt at prayer, a priest approached him and handed him a slip of paper. On this paper was the address of a Negro Catholic church. The priest explained that there were special churches for Negro Catholics, and that he would be welcome there."

As a matter of historical record, the Catholic Church in the segregated territory actually went backward—from *segregation within the church* to *segregated parishes within the diocese*.

An authoritative report on this trend, citing a typical case, has been made by the Rev. George Wilson, S.S.J., in the *Reporter* of the Knights of Columbus.

"Up until 1919", he writes, "the west wing of the Immaculate

Conception Church in Jacksonville, Florida, was reserved for the use of the colored people, but because of existing conditions they were not able to participate in the general activities of the parish. A new parish was established and placed under the charge of the Fathers of the Society of Saint Joseph, whose work is exclusively devoted to the Negro cause."

In plain words, the Negro communicants were evicted from the church and put into an all-Negro church.

This sort of thing has happened not only in the South. Currently in New York City, for example, recent Puerto Rican immigrants (some of whom are Negroes and of mixed ethnic backgrounds) are being segregated into basement services by some Catholic churches, while the Irish, Polish, and Italian communicants continue to hold Mass upstairs. This arrangement is clung to long after Puerto Ricans come to constitute a majority of the congregation.

Here is still another account of the Catholic method of handling such matters, as reported by Rosario de Paul in "A Lesson in Race Relations in the Far South", published in *Colored Harvest*, organ of the Society of Saint Joseph.

"The Eighth National Eucharistic Congress held in New Orleans is now a matter of history", he writes. "The problem was how to conduct a truly Catholic Congress in a 'Jim Crow' state. . . Hearing rumblings of wholesale discrimination and segregation, this reporter went to the Congress with the avowed purpose of checking. . . . Following are the findings:

"At every civic and religious function adequate space in choice sections were reserved for the colored. At times some white people attempted to usurp the places reserved for colored, but they were promptly and peremptorily ordered to vacate. The colored Catholics formed a whole section of the parade. Because it was felt that Negroes had special problems, a sectional meeting was held at Xavier University.

"It is conceivable that these arrangements might have been interpreted as efforts to segregate the colored, but such an interpretation would be nothing short of distortion of the facts and an indication of an unwillingness to be fair. They were, rather, marks of special favor and consideration for the colored.

"It was a magnificent public demonstration of what is going on every day where the Catholic Church is in a position to make felt her powerful influence, not by revolutionary violence, but by Christian fortitude."

Interestingly, when the Catholic Church purchased the Ku Klux Klan's Imperial Palace in Atlanta and converted it into the Co-Cathedral of Christ the King, Bishop Gerald P. O'Hara invited the Klan's Imperial Wizard to sit among the honoured guests at the dedication ceremonies. Afterwards, Bishop O'Hara told newsmen "the Church never was anxious to make any issue over the Klan". (In 1950 Bishop O'Hara was expelled from eastern Europe following charges that he had been engaged in espionage activities on behalf of the U.S.)

It was not until November of 1955 that rulings were won from the Supreme Court making it clear that the principle involved in the 1954 ruling against segregation in public education is also applicable to segregation in other tax-supported public facilities, such as parks, playgrounds, swimming pools, golf courses, and beaches.

As in the case of the schools, however, the segregationists are very far from bowing to this judgment. They were quick to note that only tax-supported facilities were covered by the ruling; privately-owned and operated "public" facilities were left free to bar or segregate Negroes. Many communities, like Greensboro, North Carolina, promptly sold their municipal swimming pools to private operators; and the same thing happened to many a municipal golf-course. Ocean Ridge, Florida, and a number of other communities closed their ocean bathing beaches when Negroes penetrated them in 1958 for the first time.

Especially determined to maintain segregation in recreation, entertainment, and social spheres, the terrorists also went to work. When, for example, the Negro jazz artist Nat "King" Cole performed on stage for a white audience in Birmingham, Alabama, in 1956, as he had a legal right to do, he was bodily attacked by a band of white men led by J. E. Mabry, Editor of the journal of the White Citizens' Council (soon afterward Mabry was among the Klansmen convicted for the ritual castration of the Negro J. Aaron).

That same year, school officials at Summerville, Georgia, acting upon a request made by the Ku Klux Klan, padlocked the football field of the local white high school to prevent a scheduled game between two Negro high school teams. The match had been sponsored by the town's Junior Chamber of Commerce to raise funds with which to purchase musical instruments for the white school's band.

Far from putting an end to segregation in these spheres, the Supreme Court decision had the immediate effect of inspiring a spate of new municipal and state laws invoking "police power" to prevent whites and Negroes from playing together under any circumstances, whether on public or private property. Typical of these new laws is that adopted by Montgomery, Alabama, in 1958: "It shall be unlawful for white and colored persons to play together . . . in any game of cards, dice, dominoes, checkers, pool, billiards, softball, basketball, football, golf, track, and at swimming pools or in any athletic contest."

CHAPTER 14

THE DICTATES OF RACIST ETIQUETTE

In many sections of the U.S.A. the ordinary rules of etiquette do not apply when you are dealing with persons of another race.

In such circumstances you are supposed to forget what you have been taught is proper behaviour in human relations—much of it is altogether taboo in interracial relations.

There exists a special interracial etiquette to govern such relations. You will find it well-nigh inviolate in the Southern states, but no matter where you go in the U.S.A. you may encounter groups and individuals who insist upon its observance to one degree or another.

But on the whole, regional variations in interracial etiquette conform more or less to the institutionalized forms of racial segregation in the area. The dictates of the etiquette are therefore most stringent in the territory long segregated by law, diminishing progressively in the border areas and relatively free territory.

Be advised, however, that there is no nook or cranny anywhere in the U.S.A. where whites and Negroes can commingle in the public view without being made aware of the fact that they form an inter-racial group.

Even in those sections of the country where it is possible for whites and Negroes to visit each other in the privacy of their homes, you may find, if nonwhite, that it is advisable not to go calling upon white persons without a definite invitation for a specific time; otherwise you might encounter white guests there who would make you uncomfortable, to say the least.

Southerners, whites and Negroes alike, having been steeped for generations in the atmosphere engendered by the interracial etiquette, usually know precisely—almost instinctively—just what is expected of them in all situations.

But in the border areas—where everything is sort of betwixt and between—no one can know for certain what to expect, and this uncertainty gives rise to a certain added tension in interracial encounters.

The existence of an *interracial* etiquette has also given rise to two separate and distinct *intraracial* etiquettes—one governing relations among whites, the other governing relations among Negroes. Consequently, your race may be judged quite as much by the etiquette you employ as by the physical characteristics you manifest. Indeed, in any apparent contradiction between the two (that is, if you look white, but act black among blacks) the Southern white community considers the etiquette decisive. The obverse (if you look black, but act white), needless to say, only gives rise to homicidal tendencies in the Southern white community.

Since a *faux pas* under the interracial etiquette in this section is popularly regarded as a capital crime, it might be well for you to acquaint yourself as thoroughly as possible with the code. Even if you were born and raised in this section, you couldn't possibly learn, in one lifetime, all there is to know on this subject. It is therefore treated at some length here.

Inside the South you will find few if any opportunities to treat persons of the other race as equals.

If you are nonwhite you may find that in some places with some people you can "take a few liberties" (as white folks put it), while in other places and with other people you will have to "toe the line".

Class counts in interracial etiquette, sometimes. For instance, if you are a professional-class nonwhite, some white workers will not insist that you tip your hat in greeting them, as they invariably would if you were also a worker. But watch out for exceptions—some poor whites like to go out of their way to exact deferential treatment from professional-class nonwhites.

Your chances of achieving anything like mutually respectful relations with a person of the other race are somewhat improved if you both belong to the same class. Any such relation you might establish in segregated territory will have to be indulged in privately, however.

If, despite being nonwhite, you succeed in finding some influential white who will associate with you with some semblance of equality in public, a peculiar phenomenon may ensue: white tradespeople, upon observing such fraternization, may conclude that it is the stylish thing to do, and begin to serve you in a manner to which you have not been accustomed. (This could happen only in non-segregated territory.)

As with other etiquettes, maximum security lies in cultivating the general *attitude* required; if your attitude is right, you *may* be excused if you make a mistake as to form. In fact, with regard to interracial etiquette, if your attitude isn't right you can get into serious trouble even though you meticulously observe the prescribed form.

The essence of the interracial etiquette is that it is *invidious*, reflecting a comparative status-relationship of superior-inferior.

The Black Codes, which before the abolition of chattel slavery in the U.S.A. governed the conduct of "free persons of color", summed up very nicely the relationship which has been enforced by the inter-racial etiquette ever since. The Louisiana Black Code was typical:

"Free persons of color ought never to insult or strike white people, nor pressure to conceive themselves equal to the white; but on the contrary they ought to yield to them in every occasion, and never speak or answer to them but with respect, under the penalty of imprisonment according to the nature of the offense."

Memorializing this continuing relationship, there stands in Louisiana a heroic-size bronze statue of the "Good Negro", hat in hand and head bent, inscribed as follows:

"Erected by the citizens of Natchitoches in grateful recognition of the faithful service of the good darkies of Louisiana."

Needless to say, the "good Negro" in the dominant view of the Southern white community is the one who "knows his place and stays in it". Conversely, the "bad nigger" is one who refuses to treat every white person as his superior. A Negro undertaker, resident in Mississippi, has put it like this:

"In this part of the country a Negro can only go so far. The white folks want you to stay in your place, and if you get out of it too much they are going to put you back in it. The white man is the boss of the South and you got to talk to him like he is boss. It don't make any difference how much money you have or how much education, he won't look at you as his equal, and there is no use in your acting like you're his equal if you want to stay here."

That is what another black man meant when he said more briefly, "When you in Rome, Georgia, you got to act like it."

But *how*, precisely, you will want to know.

This is where the interracial etiquette steps in. Its function is to prescribe correct form for every conceivable sort of contact between whites and Negroes, in such manner as to serve as a constant reminder to the former that they are superior and to the latter that they are inferior.

The interracial etiquette is, in other words, a compulsory ritual denoting first- and second-class citizenship.

It has more than psychological and social significance, serving also the basic economic and political purpose of facilitating the exploitation of nonwhites by whites, collectively and individually.

By dividing workers along racial lines, the etiquette helps keep profits up and wages down.

All this being so, you can understand why enforcement of the etiquette is so rigorous. It does not often find expression nowadays in written law, but does enjoy much the same status as unwritten common-law. Its venerable genealogy goes all the way back to the Black Codes and master-slave relationship, which evolved into the complex of segregation laws and, simultaneously, *mores* buttressed by the authoritarianism of tradition.

You will find the etiquette, therefore, being imposed by legal as well as extra-legal means—that is to say, by police as well as mob action.

If you are nonwhite and offend some white by a breach of etiquette, the usual procedure is for the white to exact an apology, and, if that is not forthcoming, to launch a physical attack upon you. If he fails to derive satisfaction in this manner, or if you seek in any wise to retaliate or defend yourself, he will likely summon a white mob or officer of the law. The officer may join in the attack upon you, and/or arrest you on some such charge as "disorderly conduct" or "assault and battery".

Although the penalties imposed for failure to abide by the etiquette are greater if you are nonwhite than vice versa, whites as well as nonwhites have been lynched for committing *faux pas*.

If you're white, however, the penalty is somewhat more likely to consist of social ostracism and economic sanctions; if nonwhite, even if you are spared a rope lynching you may be given an economic lynching.

Neither the caste system nor the Nazi system, nor any monarch or potentate, has been more imperious in insisting upon gestures of obeisance than the white supremacist in the Southern part of the U.S.A.

In the circumstances, it is not difficult to understand the Southern Negro who said, "It is reason enough to at least pretend you respect white folks when you know they will get you killed for disrespecting them."

Some white folks go so far as to take offence (and action) against nonwhites whom they consider to be "acting uppity" or "putting on airs". There is really no way of anticipating everything that might provoke such a reaction.

Some Negroes, for example, working on a job with whites, upon being promoted from a job such as freight-handler to that of shipping clerk have avoided trouble by refraining from donning the white collar that ordinarily would mark such a metamorphosis.

Others, having built for themselves a fine home, have refrained from painting the exterior, in order not to antagonize whites in the community whose homes are not so fine.

A large automobile can also prove to be a liability in some sections. When Robert Mallard, a Georgia Negro farmer, was ambushed and shot to death by thirty masked Klansmen (1948), the white community said it was because he "drove too large a car".

And so if it's safety you're looking for, you can do no better than to take the advice of the Negro folk song which puts the etiquette in a nutshell:

> Now if you're white,
> You're all right.
> And if you're brown,
> Stick around.
> But if you're black,
> Get back, *get back*, GET BACK!

Social Equality is Out

The avowed reason you are not permitted by interracial etiquette to associate on a basis of equality with the other race is because it is assumed that social intercourse must inevitably lead to sexual intercourse, which—it is further assumed—would be biologically bad.

Insistence upon the validity of this theory of a master race has not abated in the face of testimony to the contrary submitted by the foremost anthropological scientists of the world. The master race theory is the more remarkable in view of the fact that no two races have ever agreed as to which is a master race.

A majority of the white inhabitants of the U.S.A.'s segregated territory say they would "rather die" than associate with nonwhites on a basis of social equality.

As a matter of fact, whites as well as nonwhites have died at the hands of mobs for having indulged in social equality.

There is a general feeling on the part of the Southern white community that any white person who associates with Negroes is "lacking in self-respect" and is "lower than they are".

As is usually the case, nonwhites were punished most severely. It is not surprising, therefore, to find that most nonwhite Southerners tend to avoid social contact with whites. As one dusky domestic has put it, "I feeds white folks with a long spoon."

Thou shalt not Sup Together

One of the most stringent commandments of the interracial etiquette is that you shall not partake of food with a person of the other race.

Should some sort of emergency arise in which it appears necessary to eat with the other race, the etiquette requires that everything possible be done to indicate that it is not being done on a basis of equality. Wherever possible you are supposed to sit at separate tables, preferably with some article of furniture between the tables to further symbolize the segregation. Whites are supposed to be served first.

Here's how one group lived up to the etiquette under difficult circumstances. Four Southern white fishermen, together with a nonwhite man whom they had hired to row their boat, found themselves in the middle of a lake at lunchtime. Before partaking of food they required the nonwhite to sit in the bow of the boat, and laid a fishing pole laterally across the boat to segregate him from them.

There are precious few situations in which the bar against co-racial eating is lowered in the segregated territory.

However, if you are a nonwhite nursemaid and wish to consume an ice-cream cone or soda pop along with the white child in your custody, you are permitted by the etiquette to do so, provided you take the refreshment with you—that is, you cannot sit at a table, use utensils, or have a drink of water (except in a paper cup).

If you are male, you are free under the etiquette to drink intoxicating liquors with males of the other race. In formulating this etiquette, the whites have swallowed their pride in this instance in order to swallow nonwhites' liquor.

However, if a white man should offer you a drink, he will hardly expect you to drink from the bottle after the manner of his white fellow workers, but rather to find a receptacle of some kind. On the other hand, should you offer a white man a drink from your bottle, he may drink from it if there is no receptacle at hand, and rationalize his behaviour by assuming that the alcohol will sterilize the germs which nonwhites are supposed to monopolize.

In either situation, if a new, unopened bottle of liquor is involved, the etiquette recommends that all white men be allowed to drink from it first, before the remains are passed around among nonwhites.

As for smoking, if you are male you may also feel free to indulge with males of the other race.

But if you are female, you are not thus privileged. Under the *mores* of the segregated territory, white women would still regard it as highly presumptuous if a nonwhite woman were to drink or smoke in their presence. However, it is permissible to partake of snuff in the presence of white women.

Warning: If you are a nonwhite male, you are not under any circumstances supposed to offer to light a cigarette for a white female in segregated territory (this is regarded as an intimate gesture reserved for white males only).

Sex can be Dangerous

If you are a white man, good interracial etiquette requires only that you be discreet in having sexual relations with a nonwhite woman.

In segregated territory, it is imperative that the relationship, if more than casual, be no more than concubinage. Such relationships continue quite common, and many are common knowledge in the community. It is often possible to indulge in such a relationship, and yet retain the respect of the white community.

Even so, the white community does not tolerate that such relationships be dignified by any joint public appearance, or public manifestation of affection or love. The general sentiment, as expressed by one Southern gentleman, is: "I'll f—— one, but that don't mean I have to love 'em."

As a case in point consider what took place in 1950, when Leon Turner, Malcolm and Melvin Whitt, three white residents of Kosciusko, Mississippi, shot up the residence of Negro share-cropper Thomas Harris, killing Mary McAfee, Nell Harris, aged 4, and Sonny Man Thurman, aged 13. The three white men had just been released from jail, where they had been lodged on a charge of "criminality" for raping Harris' 17-year-old stepdaughter, Pauline Thurman.

Interracial etiquette's sanction of sexual intercourse between white men and nonwhite women extends also to children born of such intercourse, so that in many Southern communities the white father can contribute more or less openly to their support.

o

On the other hand, sexual intercourse between white women and nonwhite men may not even be discussed in white circles. The mere idea of any degree of mutuality or reciprocity in such relationships is ruled out as unthinkable by the white community. Consequently, whenever such a case comes to light, it is automatically interpreted as rape.

This taboo extends with unabated force to the profession of prostitution. White women are not permitted to cater to nonwhite men in the segregated territory, even in communities where all other forms of prostitution flourish openly and enjoy police protection.

Such interracial prostitution as does exist is carried on by "call girls" who can be reached by telephone only, and arrangements are made to meet at some secluded rendezvous. Transportation is a problem, as many white cab-drivers refuse to deliver white prostitutes to or from nonwhite neighbourhoods.

Nonwhite men have been mobbed for merely driving through white "red light" prostitution districts at night.

If you are a nonwhite woman, the courts of the segregated territory offer you little or no protection against rape by white men. Even when there are confessions, convictions are seldom brought in. For example, three white youths who confessed to a Christmas Eve rape of a 17-year-old Negro girl at Decatur, Georgia, were nevertheless acquitted by the DeKalb County jury.

While ordinary etiquette frowns upon overmuch public display of physical affection, interracial etiquette goes on to rigorously insist that nonwhites refrain from all manner of love-making in public (i.e. within sight of whites).

This taboo is 100 per cent effective; few Southern whites have ever seen Negroes kissing, for example, whereas public kissing by whites is commonplace. Moreover, the taboo enjoys quasi-legal status. For instance, when Hattie Mae Bell, 16, kissed her soldier sweetheart goodbye at the Atlanta, Georgia, train terminal, she was badly beaten by a policeman and arrested on "suspicion of having venereal disease".

How to Avoid White Women

If you are a nonwhite man, your very life may depend upon your ability to keep a safe distance from white women in segregated territory.

Generally speaking, it can be dangerous to get within arm's reach of one.

In fact, the farther you stay away from them, the safer you will be.

This is most true of the segregated territory, but you will find it hazardous to associate with white women anywhere in the U.S.A.

You need not harbour any amorous intentions to get into serious trouble. For instance, Eugene Talmadge (later Governor of Georgia) once publicly flogged a Negro chauffeur for eating candy out of the same paper bag with his Northern white woman employer while driving through Georgia. Others have been lynched for allegedly winking or whistling at white women (hence, you may want to avoid whistling, or blinking in any manner that might be construed as a wink, in the presence of a white woman).

Any unnecessary physical contact may also prove fatal, including accidental bumping. Even if you are employed as a chauffeur you are not supposed to offer physical assistance to a white woman to alight from an automobile, unless she is infirm.

The fact is, you do not even have to come into physical contact—mere proximity to a white woman has signed the death warrant of many a nonwhite man.

It is even dangerous to approach a white man's house to ask for a drink of water; white housewives have been known to scream hysterically at the unexpected sight of a nonwhite man, with dire consequences for the latter.

There are special risks associated with being alone with a white woman. Offers of affection from a white woman are often subject to sudden retraction. Should the relationship be discovered by white persons, the odds are very great that she would accuse you of rape in order to save her own face. The perils of such relationships are so great that many nonwhite men in the segregated territory are inclined to give white women, especially those who wax amorous, the widest possible berth.

Love is no excuse for making love with someone of the other race. In fact, it is the worst possible excuse in the eyes of the white community.

When a nonwhite youth employed in an Atlanta drug-store felt moved to write a love-note to a white waitress, he also felt moved to move to another community. He knew that many like him have been lynched for less.

How to Make an Interracial Introduction

None of the ordinary rules of etiquette apply to interracial introductions made in the segregated territory.

Such introductions are invariably pitched on a highly informal plane.

The interracial etiquette prescribes that nonwhites always be introduced *to* whites, never vice versa. This holds true regardless of relative ages, class, education, or distinction.

Here is a correct sample of interracial introduction:

Addressing oneself *always* to the white person *alone*, one says:

"Mr. Jones, this is Sam, the coloured yardman I was telling you about."

Whereupon the white person says: "How're you, Sam?"

And Sam replies, "Tolerable, sir; just tolerable."

Hand-shaking is Taboo

Under no circumstances does interracial etiquette permit you to shake hands with a person of the other race anywhere in segregated territory.

This taboo is primarily designed to prevent nonwhite men from coming into physical contact with white women; but you will find it applies almost as rigorously to hand-shaking between men.

If you are a nonwhite man and some non-Southern or other white woman offers to shake hands with you in the presence of Southern white men, the consequences might be severe.

The importance attached to this taboo against hand-shaking is illustrated by an event which took place at Columbus, Georgia. Three teen-age Negro boys, Robert Ford, Matthew Brown, and Ernest Chester, were kidnapped at gunpoint on the city's streets by five white men. After being driven to a secluded spot, the boys were asked whether the white speakers who had appeared at the Negro high school during Brotherhood Week had shaken hands with the school's Negro Principal. When the boys insisted they didn't know, they were stripped naked, severely flogged, and forced to run for their lives while the men took pot-shots at their heels.

To Speak or not to Speak?

Ever since the days when the segregated territory was slave territory, the lines of communication between whites and nonwhites have been gradually withdrawn, so that in many areas today the two races literally are not speaking to each other.

As one nonwhite school teacher puts it: "Some white people speak to you on the streets, some grunt, and some ignore you."

This is the direct result of a quasi-official non-fraternization order which was put into effect by the erstwhile Confederate states over three-quarters of a century ago, and which has continued with unabated force until today.

In fact, the social gulf between the two races has constantly widened, so that today whites and nonwhites are farther apart than at any time in American history.

How to Address the Other Race

Compulsory modes of address are another traditional means whereby interracial etiquette seeks to achieve its purpose of maintaining a master-servant relationship between the white and Negro races in the segregated territory.

Reduced to essentials, here's what the etiquette of interracial address requires:

1. If you are white, *never* say "Mr.", "Mrs.", "sir", or "ma'am" to nonwhites, but always call them by their first names.

2. If you are nonwhite, *always* say "Mr.", "Mrs.", "sir," or "ma'am" to whites, and never call them by their first names.

The forms of interracial address carry over to references to third persons. For example, if you are nonwhite, whites will insist that you refer to other whites as "Mr." or "Mrs." Conversely, if in a conversation with whites you refer to other nonwhites, you are expected to do so by their first names, or, at most, by calling them "Brother Smith" or "Sister Jones".

Should you, in a conversation with a white, refer to a nonwhite as "Mr.", the white person is likely to say: "Who? I never heard of him." Should you persist in the same form of address, the white is likely to say eventually, "Oh, you mean that nigger, Sam Smith. Why didn't you say so?"

If you are a nonwhite house-servant, even though you may have suckled, bathed, and fed the children of your white employer since their birth, you will be expected to address them as "Mr. Bob" or "Miss Jean" just as soon as they reach puberty.

When you as a nonwhite have occasion in segregated territory to address a white man whose name is unknown to you, you are expected to call him "Bossman", "Captain", or some other title of respect.

The plural form, to be used in addressing more than one white, is "white-folks".

If you spend any length of time in segregated territory you will undoubtedly learn how it sounds to be addressed as "nigger". The most you can hope for by way of respectful public address from most white persons in this region is to be called by your last name rather than by your first.

Regardless of your age, class, distinction, or education, you are apt to frequently be called "boy" or "girl". However, if your hair is actually grey you are more likely to be called "uncle" or "auntie". If you maintain a professional-class appearance, you are likely to be called "Doctor", "Professor", or "Parson", regardless of your real profession. Such titles are approved by the interracial etiquette as "salutations without prejudice".

The sanctions and taboos governing interracial address apply with full force to telephone conversations, although, of course, there is the difficulty of ascertaining the race of the person to whom you are speaking. The spread of public education with its effect upon dialect is intensifying this problem. It is expected, therefore, if you are employed as a maid in segregated territory, that in answering your employer's telephone you will hasten to say "sir" or "ma'am" so that the caller will know to speak to you as a nonwhite. Should you neglect to do this, you will find that many callers will ask, "Is this the maid?" before proceeding with the conversation.

The interracial etiquette has also evolved a formula whereby whites, in telephoning nonwhites, can avoid saying "Mr." or "Mrs." For example:

"Hello. . . . Is this the residence of James Smith, the coloured doctor? . . . Well, I want to speak to his wife."

If you are nonwhite you may also come up against the etiquette in placing long-distance telephone calls inside the segregated territory; operators have been known to refuse to handle calls for nonwhites if they insist upon identifying themselves as "Mr." or "Mrs."

You are also expected to abide by the etiquette in conducting written correspondence with persons of the other race. If you are white and have occasion to write a nonwhite, etiquette prescribes that you omit "Mr." or "Mrs." in addressing the letter, and refrain from saying "Dear" in the salutation, but simply begin "John" or "Mary".

You will find that newspapers in the segregated territory scrupulously observe the usages of interracial address. For instance, when the celebrated contralto Miss Marian Anderson visited the region, some papers referred to her as "Anderson", while others simply said "Marian".

Those few papers which carry brief sections headed "News of Interest to Colored People" sometimes permit their correspondents to use titles of respect for nonwhites. Some of these, however, insist that nonwhite women be referred to as "Madam" rather than "Mrs."

Even in the border areas, where college faculties sometimes include a few nonwhite professors, newspapers frequently telephone to ascertain whether a certain professor should be referred to as "Mr." or not.

There is a general feeling among whites in the segregated territory that they would lose face among both whites and nonwhites were they to permit the latter to address them familiarly.

And so only rarely will you find the etiquette set aside in this respect. Class is a factor sometimes. If you are a nonwhite working man, you may be able to call some white co-workers by their first names and get away with it. Similarly, if you are a nonwhite professional, some white professionals may tolerate your addressing them thus familiarly.

Whether or not there are witnesses to the act of familiarity is an important consideration. As one nonwhite worker has put it, "If I don't care whether I get what I want or not from one of these old crackers, I might call him anything. Like if I want a cigarette, I may say, 'Hey, buddy. Give me a smoke.' I would just about get it if he was the only one around."

It must be said, however, that if you are nonwhite you simply cannot live in segregated territory unless you employ the approved forms of interracial address. As one nonwhite Southerner of Cleveland, Mississippi, has put it: "If 'Mr. Charlie' has something that I want, there is nothing that I can't do to get it. That is purely because he has something, and if I don't get it from him, where in the world can I get it?"

Compliance has been institutionalized to the extent of being reflected in the Help Wanted advertisements in newspapers of the region, such as the following which appeared in the *Florida Times-Union*:

"Neat colored girl wanted for maid, No Yankee-talker need apply."

While economic sanctions are the most common form of coercion, you may, particularly if you are nonwhite, encounter more violent methods of persuasion, including mob action or arrest.

During World War II two Negro soldiers were murdered at Flora,

Mississippi, for saying "Yes" instead of "Yes, sir" to a group of local white civilians.

Should you ever be called upon to appear in court in any capacity in segregated territory, it is especially necessary to observe the usages of interracial address, if you wish to see any measure of justice done.

If you are represented in court by legal counsel, the same applies to him, regardless of his race.

In a typical Atlanta case, the defendant was summoned by the court clerk as "Clifford Hines, Nigra" (a prevalent compromise pronunciation midway between "Negro" and "nigger"); whereupon Hines's white Northern attorney addressed him as "Mr. Hines"; whereupon the prosecutor, noting the white jury's reaction, referred to the defendant as "this nigger"—and rested his case.

How to Converse with the Other Race

If you keep in mind that you are supposed to act superior or inferior —depending upon whether you are white or nonwhite—you shouldn't have any difficulty conducting a proper conversation with a person of the other race.

An effective technique for nonwhites, as described by one of them, is as follows: "I don't talk to a white man like I do to a colored. I let him do the talking—let him take the lead. That's what he wants, and if he says something to me I don't like, I say, 'Now, Mr. Jones. Don't you think I ought to do so-and-so?' And then most likely he will say, 'Yes.' But you better not go straight at the thing with a white man, or he'll think you're trying to act smart."

A somewhat different attitude, as expressed by another nonwhite Southerner, was: "I can make them think they own the world. It is nothing but a lot of jive that I hand them. If I was a little better off I would get away from around here, and all of the white folks could kiss where the sun don't shine. This place is all right in a way, but a man has to be less than a man to get along most of the time."

You can't Say That

There are a few simple rules nonwhites are supposed to observe in conversing with whites:

1. Never assert or even intimate that a white person may be lying.
2. Never impute dishonourable intentions to a white person.
3. Never suggest that the white is of an inferior class.

4. Never lay claim to, or overtly demonstrate, superior knowledge or intelligence.

5. Never curse a white person.

6. Never laugh derisively at a white person.

7. Never comment upon the physical attractiveness of a white person of the opposite sex.

The penalties for violators of this code are often quite severe.

During 1948 ten white men called at the home of Martin Flowers, a Negro resident of Leake County, Mississippi, and accused him of "a lot of big talk in the community". Forcing him from his home at gunpoint, they began firing at him. When Flowers' cousin fired back, wounding one of the whites, he (the cousin) was jailed and sentenced to seven years for assault with intent to kill.

How to Talk Back and Live

If you are nonwhite there are not many ways whereby you, acting as an individual, can talk back to whites in the segregated territory and live.

A lot of nonwhites have lost their lives trying it.

When 15-year-old Hubert Watt, nonwhite, insisted that he had paid a bill to white storekeeper Johnny Mosiason, Mosiason gave him a beating while police officer Johnny Moon held a gun on Watt's older brother to keep him from coming to the rescue.

The whole principle of reciprocity in human relationships—for example, "If he curses me, I'll curse him"—is ruled out if you are a nonwhite and the other person is white.

If you have a grievance you feel obliged to voice directly to the responsible person, the acceptable method is to do it in the form of a non-belligerent question, such as, "Do you think that's the right way to treat anybody?"

Or, you might prefer to voice your complaint to some disinterested white person who you have reason to believe will relay it to the white who has mistreated you. But be careful not to *suggest* that the complaint be relayed.

In any argument with a white person, it is safest for nonwhites not to say anything contradictory by beginning, "I think that . . ." but to put each point in the form of a question beginning, "Don't you think that . . .?"

The traditional form of protest which nonwhites have found to be

P

acceptable to the whites of the segregated territory is song. Complaints and petitions which would never be tolerated in prose form are not only condoned, but are sometimes laughed at and even given some consideration when put to song.

Here are some samples:

Slave-gang

White man kill muscogee duck;
Give the nigger the bones to suck.
A cold cup of coffee and the meat's mighty fat;
White folks growl if we eats much of that.
White man in the dinin'-room, eatin' cake and cream;
Nigger in the kitchen, eatin' them greasy greens.
A aught's a aught, a figger's a figger—
All for the white man, and none for the nigger.

Chain-gang

Old Cap'n Bill
From Campbell Hill,
Always mean to a nigger
And always will.
If I'd a knowed the Cap'n was bad,
I wouldn't a sold that Special I had.
Cap'n got a shotgun just like mine,
If he beats me to the trigger, I won't mind dyin'.

Work-gang

Some of these days
    (About twelve o'clock)
This old world
    Am gonna reel and rock.
Me and my buddies
    And maybe two-three more
Gonna raise hell
    Around the payhouse door.

Which Door to Enter

When in segregated territory, it is decidedly dangerous to enter a white person's front door if you are nonwhite.

On the other hand, if you are white you will find that a white face is the equivalent of a search-warrant anywhere in the South, enabling you to enter the front door of any nonwhite's dwelling, regardless of the economic and social class to which you and the occupant belong.

As one Southern nonwhite woman puts it: "The only white people who ever come to my house are bill-collectors. They just walk right in and call me 'Freda'."

Of course in segregated territory interracial social calls are regarded as unthinkable. Such casual visiting as takes place is generally done in the yard, on the steps, or, at most, on the porch.

You will find rural and small-town whites of the segregated territory most insistent that you use their back door, even when you are employed by them. As the saying goes, "some will, and some won't" speak to you at their front door. Some are too lazy to go around to the back door. Others will compromise by meeting you at a side door.

In the larger cities—especially among apartment-dwellers who have no rear door—you will have relatively greater opportunities to enter white dwellings through front doors.

If you are both nonwhite and male, there is an added element of danger in approaching a white dwelling. Here's how one Southern nonwhite man copes with this problem:

"When I go to a white man's house I stand in the yard and yell, and wait for him to come to the door. If he tells me to come, then I go up to the door and talk to him, but I don't go in unless he tells me. If he tells me, then I go in; but I don't sit down unless he tells me."

Because of all such uncertainties, many whites and nonwhites transact their interracial business in segregated territory in an office or on the street.

When to Sit and When to Stand

It is regarded as improper for a nonwhite to sit down in the parlour of a white home. This applies just as rigorously if you are employed as a servant in such a home. You are expected to do any essential sitting in the kitchen or in your own quarters, if any.

On the other hand, if you are white the etiquette says you may feel free to sit anywhere in a nonwhite home, without waiting for an invitation.

The taboo against whites and nonwhites sitting together in segregated territory also applies to automobiles. If you are nonwhite, most Southern whites will insist that you sit in the back seat of their car. If the car has but one seat, some will insist that you ride on the bumper or fender, rather than sit beside them. You will find this to be true even of some white truck-drivers with whom you may work—they will insist that you ride in the back of an open truck in the heat, cold, or rain, rather than permit you to sit with them in the cab of the truck.

When not to Wear Your Hat

If you are a nonwhite man in segregated territory you are required to remove your hat while talking with white persons, regardless of their sex. If you fail to remove your hat in talking with a white man, you will be told to do so; if the party to whom you are speaking is a white woman, some white man may knock off your hat.

Refusal to comply with this custom has precipitated as much mob violence as alleged rape of white women by nonwhite men. In fact, you may be arrested for wearing your hat while talking to a white person.

Some nonwhites have, however, evolved certain evasive tactics in connection with this custom:

1. If they see the white person coming soon enough, they can remove the hat before he reaches them, thus avoiding the significance of the gesture.

2. If a white person engages a nonwhite in conversation unexpectedly, the nonwhite can remove his hat and wipe his brow, as though motivated solely by the heat.

3. A nonwhite man can refrain from wearing a hat.

Inside segregated territory there are a number of places where whites may keep their hats on, while nonwhites are expected to remove theirs. This includes hotel lobbies, office buildings, and the like.

Outside segregated territory many elevators now display signs urging men to keep their hats on to save space. Not so in segregated territory, however. The reason for this rigidity in elevator etiquette lies not in the tradition of Southern courtesy, but rather in the conviction that nonwhites must be required to remove their hats in the presence of whites, no matter what the extenuating circumstances.

In the segregated territory the etiquette also approves the wearing of hats by white men inside nonwhite homes. If as a nonwhite you should voice objection to this, you are likely to be told that it is a business call, and therefore no disrespect is intended. Sometimes nonwhites prevail upon whites to remove their hats by refusing to do business with them unless they do.

Racial Etiquette on the Road

There was a time—before many nonwhites owned automobiles of their own—when the rules of the road were applied equally to them, it being assumed that the vehicles they drove were owned by whites.

But as soon as nonwhites began to acquire cars (often at great sacrifice, to escape segregation in public transportation), white motorists began to insist upon a right-of-way based on whiteness.

Of course the rules of the road as set forth in the traffic regulations of the states and communities of the U.S.A. ostensibly apply to all motorists equally, regardless of race. But, in segregated territory especially, you will often find that traffic laws are superceded by interracial etiquette when the motorists involved are of different race.

In short, if you are a nonwhite motorist you are expected to stay in your place as a second-class citizen. The etiquette says, "When on wheels, do as you would on foot."

This means that whenever you see a white face, whether it is rolling or walking, you are expected to act as though you had seen a "Slow" or "Stop" sign.

If the other motorist or pedestrian is white, he may claim right-of-way regardless of any traffic regulations to the contrary; and if you fail to grant him right-of-way, you may have to suffer the consequences.

Put still another way, if you are nonwhite you can *never* be sure of having right-of-way while driving in segregated territory; whereas if you are white you can *always* be sure of having right-of-way if the other motorist is nonwhite, and you wish to assert your racial prerogative.

In other words, if you are nonwhite, the only time you can safely claim right-of-way in segregated territory is when the other motorist is also nonwhite; while if you are white, you can claim not only legitimate right-of-way in encounters with white motorists, but also racial right-of-way over nonwhite motorists.

Like an Army officer employing his rank, or a police officer flashing his badge, as a white motorist you can invoke your whiteness as a badge of authority for taking precedence over nonwhites.

One American motorist found he could get through heavy traffic with far greater speed by painting "Beware—Reckless Driver" on his car in large letters. Nonwhite motorists in segregated territory would do well to look upon *all* white motorists as reckless or drunken drivers, for there is no predicting when they will put race above regulations.

This would seem to be especially true of white women. As one Southern nonwhite motorist relates it, "These white women act like they think these brakes are colored too and can just naturally stop dead still when a white woman comes busting into an open highway."

White drivers are inclined to resent it when a nonwhite motorist displays greater acceleration after stopping at an intersection, or tries to pass them on the highway. This is especially true if the nonwhite is driving the more expensive automobile.

A white woman haled into the 151st Street traffic court of Harlem, New York, offered as an excuse for running through a red stop light that, "A nigger had just pulled up beside me, and I just couldn't let him get ahead of me."

If a white motorist refuses to let you pass—unless you are willing to risk a collision in which you would suffer most of the consequences —you should bide your time until some other white motorist comes along and forces him to make way, whereupon you can more safely follow suit without causing him to lose face.

You are most likely to get into trouble at intersections, while seeking to make a left turn. Although the laws of most states say that you are supposed to signal and then complete the turn after the *first* oncoming car has cleared the intersection, many white motorists will run right over that law, and you too if you fail to wait until *all* oncoming whites have passed. The theory here is that it is intolerable for a nonwhite to deliberately delay a white.

The guiding principle of interracial etiquette, on the road as elsewhere, is "Whites first".

So real is this that nonwhites all over the segregated territory tell the story of the nonwhite driver who, upon being haled into traffic court for driving through a red light, explained to the judge that he had seen white folks going ahead on the green light, and naturally assumed that the red light meant it was time for nonwhites to go.

The truth is that a vast amount of skill is required to be a successful nonwhite driver in segregated territory. For one thing, the police are far more vigilant in halting and prosecuting nonwhite traffic violators. Once accosted, your chances of talking yourself out of a summons or conviction are infinitely less than they are for white motorists.

You may, in fact, be arrested for violating the racial etiquette of the road, and charged with "careless and reckless driving".

If you happen to be a nonwhite physician, you can't expect the police to give you escort or exempt you from parking regulations in an emergency, as they would if you were white.

Apart from the peril of police action, there is the real possibility of physical attack by aggrieved white motorists, assisted by white by-standers, if you resist.

Finally, there is the inescapable fact that in an interracial collision in segregated territory the nonwhite motorist has little or no chance of collecting for damages done to his car or person, no matter how grossly the white motorist may have been violating the law.

A survey of police records of interracial collisions in the segregated territory would reveal that in at least 80 per cent of such cases only the nonwhite motorists are arrested.

One of the best forms of protection for nonwhite motorists in the South is a dilapidated car. White motorists are less likely to impose upon the driver of such a vehicle, it being assumed (1) that the brakes are no good, (2) that the owner will care but little if it is wrecked, and (3) that the owner is financially unable to pay for any damage done the white car.

Keep Moving

On the sidewalk as on the road, interracial etiquette is all-pervasive.

If you are a white pedestrian, the etiquette requires nonwhite motorists waiting at an intersection for a green light to give you all the time you care to take in getting out of the street after the light changes.

But on the other hand, if you are a nonwhite pedestrian, you had better leap for the kerb the instant waiting white motorists get even a yellow caution light indicating that the signal is changing to green. Making nonwhite pedestrians leap for their lives is a favourite sport of many Southern white motorists.

Police are likewise inclined to distinguish between white and nonwhite pedestrians.

In a typical instance, Mrs. Donetta Bell, a nonwhite instructor at Jackson College, Mississippi, was singled out of a group of white jaywalkers who were crossing a street in the middle of the block, and jailed.

In the exercise of their police powers to keep anyone from obstructing the sidewalks, many Southern communities go beyond the law to prevent "loitering" by nonwhites.

Should you insist upon some sort of human or constitutional right to stand pat provided you are not obstructing traffic, you are likely to be arrested for vagrancy or creating a disturbance.

In many Southern towns—especially on Saturday afternoons, when the sidewalks are crowded—some whites will insist that you step off the sidewalk and into the street to let them pass. If you fail to do so, you may be shoved or knocked into the street anyway.

Refusal to make way for white folks is generally referred to as "bumptious conduct"; and it was to such that the *Overseas Sentinel* of Key West, Florida, addressed itself as follows:

> "The subject of 'Race Segregation' comes to the fore when note is taken of too many complaints being registered concerning the unwarranted actions of various colored residents of Key West while shopping or strolling on Duval Street. Members of the colored race are firmly reminded that there are certain limits of convention beyond which 'they shall not pass'. It is highly probable if complaints continue to come in that definite boundary lines will again be established in the city and active control of the situation be enforced."

Where to Shop

If you are nonwhite you will find that many business establishments, both inside and outside the segregated territory, will not welcome you as a customer.

Department, clothing, and millinery stores are especially inclined to cater to white only, or to nonwhites grudgingly if at all.

A prominent Jewish woman residing in New Orleans was mistakenly thought to be a Negro by a clerk in one of the city's large department stores, and so was denied the right to try on a hat. The woman sued and collected substantial damages.

Due to the reluctance of nonwhites to trade where they are not wanted, a thriving business of catering to them in stores in nonwhite neighbourhoods has developed. Some of the whites who operate these stores are wont to save face by explaining, "Their money will spend too, won't it?" These merchants are also inclined to charge exorbitant prices for inferior merchandise.

If you prefer to take your chances in the big uptown stores of the South and border territories, you may:

1. Be ejected.
2. Be insulted.
3. Be served only after all whites have been served.
4. Be intercepted by a shopwalker whose job it is to direct all nonwhites to basement counters.
5. Be denied the privilege of trying on clothes.
6. Be required to try on clothing in the privacy of your own home.
7. Be required to put on a cloth skullcap before trying on millinery.

As an indication of what you may encounter, one national chain store instructs its salespeople in the South to address all professional-looking nonwhite men as "Doctor", but never to accord any title of respect to nonwhite women.

In fact, if you are a nonwhite woman, many stores may refuse to do business with you if you refuse to give your first as well as your last name. Nonwhite women who have sought to use only their initials and last name in an effort to avoid familiarity from white salespeople have been denied the right to make purchases.

If you are contemplating making any purchases on a time-payment plan, you can avoid having white collectors calling at your home by making payments by mail or at the firm's office.

It is extremely risky for a nonwhite to accuse a white of short-changing him; many nonwhites have lost their lives in this way, and lesser injuries are common.

When Army Private Walter Hayward, a Negro, levelled this charge at a bus-driver at Biloxi, Mississippi, the driver struck him in the mouth and slapped his wife to the floor. When Hayward drew a knife to protect his wife and inflicted a superficial wound on the driver, he (Hayward) was jailed for eight years.

A major shopping problem of an interracial nature which plagues some white women in the U.S.A. is a fear that if they purchase certain low-priced frocks, identical ones will also be purchased by nonwhite women, thus causing the former to lose face in the eyes of the white community.

Keep Out of Lines

The time-honoured principle of "first come, first served" is altogether inoperative in a vast number of interracial situations in the segregated territory of the U.S.A.

In this area, if you are nonwhite you will generally be expected to keep out of lines formed by white people. You are supposed to wait until all whites have been served, or, if provision has been made, to form a separate line for nonwhites. The latter is usually customary in such matters as voting, public health services, and similar things.

In some instances, white customers may even resent your taking your chronological place in lines formed for service in grocery stores and such establishments.

In boarding buses and trams in the South, nonwhites are virtually always expected to wait until all whites have entered. This prerogative enjoys quasi-legal status.

When Pauline Garth entered a Birmingham bus ahead of a white woman, she was slapped off by conductor V. V. Porter, arrested, fined 100 dollars, and jailed for six months.

No exception to this rule is made in time of war for nonwhites in uniform.

Nocturnal Activity

Before the Civil War, curfews for Negroes were common throughout the slave-holding states. The signal was usually a bell which was rung at sundown, after which all Negroes were required to remain in their quarters, under penalty of being jailed or flogged. To roam at large after dark, slaves were required to have written permission from their owners, while "free persons of color" had to have written permission from the Mayor or an alderman.

In Key West, Florida, it was the duty of the Provost Marshal, James Filor, to enforce the curfew. When the bell rang and the Negroes ran for their homes, the white townspeople would sing after them:

> Run, nigger, run!
> Filor will get you!
> Wish I was in Filor's place,
> I'd give them niggers a longer race!
>
> Oh, Filor's sly as a mouse—
> Locked the niggers in the market-house;
> Kept them there 'til half-past nine—
> Five dollars was their fine.

While most curfew *laws* have disappeared from the books, the Florida cities of Palm Beach and Miami Beach require all Negroes to be off the streets and out of the city limits by 8 p.m., unless obviously engaged in domestic service, delivering merchandise, or some similar work. If you are a Negro and are not wearing a domestic's uniform, you may be detained by police unless you make your departure from these communities before the deadline. Last-minute buses are crowded, and taxis for Negroes are scarce.

Elsewhere in the country, it is unsafe for nonwhites to be on the streets in many business and residential sections after certain hours at night. This is due to a feeling on the part of many police officers that nonwhites are more criminally-inclined than whites.

There is also the possibility of mob action. A Negro woman who was flogged by a band of white men at Brandon, Mississippi, was informed that their purpose was to "keep niggers off the streets after dark".

Even in New York City's bohemian Greenwich Village, if you are a nonwhite man you will find it dangerous to escort a white woman to the night clubs in the neighbourhood.

If you are of Mexican or other Hispanic ancestry, you will find it hazardous to venture at night into non-Mexican neighbourhoods in Los Angeles and other cities of the West and Southwest.

If you are a Negro, a number of Southern communities will not permit you to remain in their city limits after dark. You may generally enter such towns with impunity during daylight hours to work, shop, or conduct other business, but will be expelled or arrested if you remain after nightfall. Make inquiries, or look for signs like this:

> Nigger, Don't Let the Sun
> Set on You in Orange City

ALARUM AND EXCURSION

IT goes without saying—the author's tongue-in-cheek having more than once slipped and betrayed his indignation—that this has been a mock guide, couched in the jargon of tourism, simply to point out the Way of White Supremacy in all its ugliness. And so wherever it says "you should", of course you should not; for racism is the obverse of morality.

Some may say this book presents a one-sided picture. And so it does.

An entire literature harping upon the other side already exists. To be sure, great progress has been made—but by reaction too. The author confesses to being not so impressed by what has been done as he is oppressed by all that remains to be done. Hence this book.

Some others may say it is a defeatist book, devoting too much space to people who have been knocked down by racists. Actually, these are people who stood up against racism. Millions more are standing than can ever be knocked down; and even among those who go down, those who can, rise again.

Some may say I have been over-critical of America, but it is precisely because I love my country so much that I want her to live up to the best that is in her.

Some may even say I lack faith in America, while in fact the book is a testimonial to the infinite faith of countless Americans (this one included) and their determination to translate that faith into ever more finite forms.

Of course, the Klan says I am "White outside, black inside"; when in truth I am not at all white in their sense of the word. And yet it is as an ostensibly-white Southerner and American that I say racism hurts my people too. Prejudice has ever blighted its subject even more than its object. Egoism, no less than altruism, bids us abjure the doctrine of white supremacy.

The Negro in America is not entitled to equal treatment; he is entitled to more than equal treatment, the very best being poor compensation for the cruel cross he has been made to bear.

This Guide has dealt mainly with the physical hazards incumbent upon being "naturally born black" in a self-styled "white man's country"; many more volumes would be required to touch upon the psychological penalties which compel the millions of innocents who are made to feel "out of place" from the cradle to the grave to look upon the land they love as a veritable torture chamber of lifelong torment which knows no surcease. It is not at all difficult to understand that the first thought of the American Negro soldier, upon being asked what should be done with Hitler should he be captured alive, was: "Paint him black and sentence him to life in Mississippi!"

My people are not congenitally bad people. The racial prejudice which afflicts some of them was made, not born. Left to their own devices they would soon learn to live with their fellow-Southerners as good neighbours should. I would remind them once again of the warning of the Negro educator to our grandfathers: "You cannot keep the Negro in a ditch unless you stay in the ditch with him." I would repeat after the Populist leader who said to our fathers, Southerners all: "You are kept apart in order that you may separately be fleeced of your earnings. Racial prejudice is the keystone of the arch of financial despotism which beggars both." Having got behind the mask of the Klan and penetrated the councils of other professional hate-mongers in our time, and there having seen with my own eyes the fat cheques signed by avaricious employers and demagogic politicos, I know as well as any man whence cometh the bitter crop of race hatred.

To my benighted brethren in whom inculcated prejudice dies hard, I can only say: it will not hurt, the shock will soon pass, and afterwards you will like yourself better than ever before. If this is not enough, then let me add, for your consolation only, that the end of compulsory segregation is not going to usher in an era of compulsory association. Human relations of any consequence will continue to require mutual volition of the individuals concerned.

No doubt about it: we Americans have a rocky road to travel before we can enter into the promised land of liberty and justice for all.

Behind Little Rock there stands a Stone Mountain of prejudice. And yet a faith like ours can move any mountain.

What happened to that republic which our forefathers conceived in liberty and dedicated to the proposition that all men are created equal? What has that new birth of freedom envisioned by Lincoln at Gettysburg been waiting for?

That noble heritage, which ought to be ours by birthright, has been denied us by mean men of little faith but much greediness, who will leave us, if we let them, an America cast in their own image.

It is now evident that if we wish to reclaim our birthright for our-selves, for our children, and our children's children, we have got to fight for it once more.

The time has passed—if indeed it ever existed—for compromising with those who would compromise the American ideal.

In the days, months, and years immediately ahead, the danger of regionwide race rioting against Negroes—of mass massacres of innocent men, women, and children—is real and imminent.

In this situation we must prevail upon our Government to serve notice that the law of the land is going to be inexorably enforced against all transgressors, whether they be high or low, few or many.

If we fail in this, we may not be able to avoid the ultimate national tragedy and disgrace of race war.

Even if we succeed, it is not enough. The order of our day must be: Popular escorts where possible; military escorts where necessary!

The call here is for decent white Southerners to step into the breach and do their manifest duty.

More, the call is for Negro Southerners to seek out those white Southerners who are in the habit of mouthing that word "brother-hood"—churchfolk, trade unionists, Masons, Rotarians, Boy Scouts. Corner them in their cloisters! Shake them by the collar! Shout out, loud enough for all the world to hear, that the hour has struck for them to put up or shut up for evermore!

For unless we Southerners, white and Negro, get together and go arm-in-arm to the schools, polls, parks, buses, and every place else we have an equal right to go, the day will go to those who thirst for our blood in the streets.

As the Negro miner said to his coal-blackened white brothers-in-the-union, "If we're ever going to get anywhere, we've got to get there together!"